The Billion Dollar Mistake

The Billion Dollar Mistake

LEARNING THE ART OF INVESTING THROUGH THE MISSTEPS OF LEGENDARY INVESTORS

Stephen L. Weiss

WILEY

John Wiley & Sons, Inc.

Published by John Wiley & Sons, Inc., Hoboken, New Jersey.
Published simultaneously in Canada.

For general information on our other products and services or for technical support, please contact our Customer Care Department within the United States at (800) 762-2974, outside the United States at (317) 572-3993 or fax (317) 572-4002.

Wiley also publishes its books in a variety of electronic formats. Some content that appears in print may not be available in electronic books. For more information about Wiley products, visit our web site at www.wiley.com.

Library of Congress Cataloging-in-Publication Data:

Weiss, Stephen L., 1955-
    The billion dollar mistake : learning the art of investing through the missteps of legendary investors/Stephen L. Weiss.
        p. cm.
    Includes bibliographical references and index.
    ISBN 978-0-470-48106-6
        1. Investments–United States.   2. Capitalists and financiers–United States.
    I. Title.
HG4910.W368 2010
332.6–dc22

                                                                2009032182

Printed in the United States of America
10 9 8 7 6 5 4 3 2 1

To Lauren, Lindsay, and Shelby
My motivation, my inspiration, my joy

Contents

Acknowledgments   ix

Introduction   1

Chapter 1   **Kirk Kerkorian: Due Diligence Is Due Every Time**   11

Chapter 2   **David Bonderman: Does This Mean I Also Overpaid for the Rolling Stones?**   31

Chapter 3   **Aubrey McClendon: Falling on the Wrong Edge of the Two-Edged Leverage Sword**   51

Chapter 4   **Bill Ackman: Detour from Discipline**   69

Chapter 5   **Nick Maounis: "Trust, but Verify…"**   89

Chapter 6   **Leon Cooperman: The Pirate of Prague Meets the Prince of Princeton—and the Boy from the Bronx Gets Squeezed**   109

Chapter 7   **Richard Pzena: Fashions Change, History Persists—or Does It?**   129

Chapter 8   **Geoff Grant: Style Drift—It's Hot Till It's Not**   149

Chapter 9   **Volkswagen and Porsche: The Hare
               Finally Wins and the Shorts Get Squeezed**   171

Chapter 10   **Chris Davis: It Was Dressed like an
               Insurance Company, but It Didn't
               Quack Like One…**   195

Chapter 11   **Madoff Investors: Hook, Line, and Sunk**   215

Epilogue   **Me Too: Mistakes I've Made and Lessons
               I've Learned**   235

Notes   237

Glossary   241

About the Author   249

Index   251

Acknowledgments

Many were involved in making this book possible, some of whom I will undoubtedly neglect to mention. I apologize to those I have slighted; please understand that this is not intentional but rather the function of a cluttered mind.

To my wife, Lauren, my best friend, confidante, and steadying influence. She has always enthusiastically encouraged me to continue writing, believing in my ability despite struggling through reading the same words over and over and over again. To Lindsay and Shelby for keeping me grounded, keeping me smiling, and, with the rare exception when they didn't call home during their evenings out, allowed me to concentrate on my writing; to my niece, Allie, for her support; to Howard "the Hose" Jurofsky, my closest friend, for momentarily putting aside his addiction to anything having to do with televised sports to provide insightful feedback; to Susanna Margolis, editor extraordinaire, without whose assistance this book would not have been possible; to my agent, Andrew Stuart, who not only secured my first contract but was also instrumental in collaborating on the concept for this book; to my publisher, John Wiley & Sons, and some of the nicest, most effective, and knowledgeable people in publishing: Debby Englander, who gave me this opportunity; Kelly O'Connor, who provided incredibly insightful suggestions through the editing process and whose generous feedback I'll always be thankful for; Adrianna Johnson, for being part of the team; Natasha Andrews-Noel, senior production editor *par excellence*. To Sushma Subramanian and Alex Halperin for providing valuable research assistance. To Allen Meisels, who introduced me to my agent. To Bethany Norvell, Owen Blicksilver, and Linda Gardner. To those who opened their homes, offices, and files to me, willing to discuss painful episodes in their lives and careers in the spirit of helping others avoid similar mistakes. To Norma Hill, one of the most generous and positive individuals whom I have ever met despite suffering the loss of her life savings, and to Burt Ross, who kept me laughing throughout our interview despite still fresh wounds that would have justifiably bred much bitterness in others.

And to my mother, who, upon seeing the artwork for the cover of the book, told me how proud she was, then inquired as to why, if I was able to write an investment book, I wouldn't tell her whether to sell her shares in Verizon or AT&T. To my in-laws, Harriet and Irwin Karassik and Beth Karassik, because my wife said to include them and also because they were truly supportive.

Introduction

Those who cannot remember the past are doomed to repeat it.
—George Santayana, 1905

Like many people, I first became interested in investing out of a desire to become wealthy. My parents were divorced, I was 13 years old, and I lived with my mother and brother in New York City in an apartment in the famed East Sixties. This was at a time when Manhattan rents were much more affordable than they are now—a good thing, since we didn't have much money. The building was populated with what were then called stewardesses—young women who juggled their schedules so their shared apartments wouldn't seem too crowded at any one time—and professional athletes, less well paid back then, who all seemed to work as stockbrokers in the off season for extra money so they could date the stewardesses. For a hormonal teenager who loved sports, living there was utopia.

To me, my athlete neighbors seemed to have it all—certainly, to have everything I could ever want. Billy Mathis lived in the building—a fullback on the Super Bowl Champion New York Jets, a smart fellow preparing for life after football by working for a brokerage house. Then there was the guy who looked old to me—he was probably no more than 30—who drove a brand-new Porsche, had a new knock-out girlfriend every week, and hung out with the athletes. I asked Billy what that guy did for a living, and he told me he worked on Wall Street. That did it. I didn't know how I was going to get there, but I knew Wall Street would be my eventual destination. Wall Street, I was sure, could give me everything these heroes of mine had: the Porsche, the athletic prowess, the beautiful women, the cool apartment of my own, and the pocket money to pay for it all.

Well, I got to Wall Street. There were a few detours along the way—as well as some adjustments when I arrived. But it has been an exciting and fulfilling career that has been enriching in a great many ways. One major way is the lessons I've learned from it, and I learned just about all of them by observing the mistakes of others and making a few myself.

My mistakes started with my very first investment—before I ever worked on the Street. I bought 100 shares of Con Edison, the giant electric utility that serves all of New York City and a bit beyond. It seemed safe, had a nice yield, and was a good way to get my feet wet. I made a couple of points of profit, so I sold the stock—my first trade. It was akin to winning the first horse race you ever bet on. You begin to think that it's easy, that you're smart. In fact, it was a bull market, and any stock I purchased was likely to have gone even higher. But I didn't know that. Instead, I was looking for my next big win, and when someone told me to buy Caesar's World, the casino company, and I made even more money, I thought I was a real genius. I made the classic error of mistaking a bull market for brains. So I sold the stock, booked the profit, then stood on the sidelines feeling like a jerk as Caesar's continued to trade higher and higher.

That was a very basic lesson—a punch-in-the-jaw warning about the seduction of trading versus investing. I would relearn the lesson in many forms over the years.

Money Mistakes

This book catalogs some of the exceedingly costly mistakes made by some of the world's smartest, savviest, most successful investors. Yet if I just lop a bunch of zeros off the number of dollars lost, I can find virtually the same mistakes among my relatives and friends. I'll wager you can too.

One family member got bored with blue-chip stocks and the dull brokerage firm he had been with for years and was dazzled by the reputation of a "boy wonder" stockbroker. After all, the boy wonder drove a Rolls-Royce and catered to elite clients. So this relative switched his account and never made a dime; actually, he lost money. Good public relations, I learned—great car, celebrity clients—is no guarantee of good investment judgment.

Neither is somebody else's recommendation of an investment opportunity, especially if that somebody else is a family member.

My stepfather's son brought him an investment he said was a can't-miss opportunity. Not only that, but they would be investing with one of the son's very good personal friends. My stepfather went almost all in. It turned out to be a fraud; millions of dollars were lost, including my stepfather's fortune and my mother's security. It taught me that something that "can't miss" can miss, that something too good to be true is probably not true, and that it's wise to disregard any personal relationship when it comes to investing.

That works the other way too. When I finally became a bona fide professional investor, I automatically became the family expert on stocks, and the calls started coming thick and fast. When, after many refusals, I yielded to my mother's importuning and suggested a stock for her to buy, of course it sank in value. It would be a year or so before she would ask again. I never offered her another investment suggestion, but I would hear about my poor stock advice almost as often as I was reminded about the Mother's Day gift I didn't buy her the year she told me just to buy a card. The real lesson for me? Do not invest money on behalf of friends or relatives. Do not give them stock tips. Tell them to speak to *another* professional. It will make Thanksgiving a lot more pleasant.

The seductiveness of a thrilling personality . . . the can't-miss opportunity that turns out to be a fraud . . . the stock pick that goes bad for someone you care about: These mistakes aren't exclusive to the Weiss family. You'll read about them in the pages of this book: different names, different amounts, same blunders.

I think what it comes down to is that money is potentially more of a personality changer than psychedelic mushrooms. It does funny things to people—even to smart people, even to very rich smart people, sometimes causing them to make billion-dollar mistakes.

Money Lessons: Scalable Mistakes

That's what this book is about: the big, expensive mistakes made by legendary investors—a.k.a. very rich smart people. Except in one case—that of people who invested with Bernard L. Madoff—the people making the mistakes the book chronicles are all either professional investment managers or billionaire entrepreneurs. Their mistakes were significant and career defining. Some were able to continue managing large asset pools, while others would struggle to rebuild their reputations. One would even commit suicide in order to erase—or perhaps avoid—the experience of failure.

Why explore the mistakes these very, very wealthy investors have made? That's simple: so you can try to avoid them. For the fact is that although these mistakes were committed by extremely success-ful and well-known pros, they are common, garden-variety invest-ment mistakes—the same garden-variety mistakes average, everyday retail investors make. Only the scale is different.

That makes *The Billion Dollar Mistake* an investment book with a unique perspective. It's not a do-what-I-did-and-get-rich kind of book. Rather, it's a don't-do-what-I-did-and-get-rich book.

The distinction is important. The shelves are full of investment guides that describe the habits and practices of successful investors. Well, there's probably no more successful investor than Warren Buffett, and even he doesn't get a hit every time he steps into the investment batter's box. In fact, although it's nearly impossible to measure accurately, conventional wisdom suggests that the best portfolio managers are correct only 60 percent of the time. An indi-vidual investor thus has almost as much chance of making a mistake as of achieving success. It therefore stands to reason that avoiding mistakes is critical to making money in the market. Bottom line? Understand what these guys did wrong, and you improve your chances of not falling into the same trap. And that, in turn, can help you become a better investor. As with the teacher who made learning fun, the bonus within these pages is that you will also be entertained, since each story was selected both for the transferabil-ity of its lessons and for the enjoyment value of its story.

Remember the famous reply by legendary Ohio State football coach Francis Schmidt, when he was asked, back in 1934, how he was going to beat archrival Michigan, titans of the Big Ten? Said Schmidt: "Those fellows put their pants on one leg at a time, the same as everyone else." So do these fellows. The pants may have been designed by Ermenegildo Zegna, but the guys wearing them make the same misjudgments, miscalculations, and missteps you and I are capable of making; they just do so for more money.

Who Am I to Say So?

It's fair to ask what qualifies me to explore these billion-dollar mis-takes and the people who committed them. I've told you how I got to Wall Street; by now, I've spent nearly a quarter of a century there. With some experience in entertainment management coupled with training as a tax attorney—attributes not inapplicable to the task of writing this book—I've spent most of my professional career working for some of the financial industry's signature investment banking firms, including Oppenheimer & Co., Salomon Brothers, and Lehman Brothers. (Granted, Lehman flamed out spectacularly through myriad spectacular missteps, but I can lay no claim to those mistakes.) I've headed research departments and managed equities trading. I've also worked at a hedge fund—SAC Capital, where I was a senior member of the management team—and managed my own small fund. And I admit to being a stock addict and a student of the markets who loves the energy and complexities of trading.

On September 11, 2001, I was working for Lehman Brothers and had been booked to fly to San Francisco on United Flight 93. At virtually the last minute, I decided to postpone that trip and focus on pressing work at the office in Lehman's downtown New York headquarters. You know the rest. Flight 93 crashed into a field in Pennsylvania, while in New York, the falling structure of the World Trade Center across the street sheared off my office walls. Thankfully, I had already evacuated my staff and coworkers; we all got out.

It was a seminal event for me and I wanted to get some distance, take some time with the family, try something else for a time. I left the physical Wall Street and launched a hedge fund in an office a mile from my home. After a while, the distance from the mainstream world of "the Street" seemed too great; I missed the hustle, and like so many of the people I've written about in this book, a passion for the wider world of investing brought me back.

Along the route of this odyssey, I got to know some of the most successful, influential, and colorful investors in the business. I've formed relationships with staff at such celebrated investment firms as Tiger Management, Soros Management, Omega Advisors and Kingdon Capital. I've been in meetings with Warren Buffett, Carl Icahn, and T. Boone Pickens—as well as with scores of investors whose celebrity is limited to the investment industry. I have also spent time with the likes of Bernie Ebbers from WorldCom and with Jeff Skilling and the late Ken Lay from Enron.

I admit that I am in the habit of deferring to the business and investing judgment of billionaire investing legends. My thinking is that if someone has been smart enough to earn such a large sum of money—even if a billion doesn't buy what it used to—then that person is a worthy candidate for my personal admiration society. And the truth is that I have never walked away from a meeting, however brief, with one of these über-wealthy investors and thought: "What a lucky bastard! How did he get to be worth a billion?" On the contrary. Each of them had something special; you could tell in a split second that they were exceptional.

Which of course makes their mistakes even more interesting.

The Soul of a Master Investor

In the pages that follow, you will be introduced to a gallery of personalities who could not be more different from one another: from the so-called Pirate of Prague to a former seminarian who is one of the most upstanding investors on Wall Street; from the son of a poor raisin farmer who became one of the world's richest men to the well-born, well-connected great-nephew of a state governor and U.S. Senator who became another of the world's richest men; from a literature-quoting "boy wonder" of the business to a mature, no-comment investor renowned for his deep and wide-ranging research.

Not all of them spoke on the record for this book, although most did, and they are quoted directly in the chapters devoted to them. Some spoke willingly—on the record and off. Others agreed to talk only after I made it clear that while their cooperation was optional, their inclusion in this book was not. Still others became involved to ensure that the facts surrounding the mistakes were accurate. Almost all were interested in the book's concept and believed it a good thing to put their experience to work so that they could help individual investors improve their results, lessen their investment risks, and avoid the same mistakes the billionaires had made.

I applaud them for their cooperation. After all, no one likes to talk about their blunders, especially if it's a billion-dollar blunder. Given also that investing is the profession these individuals are engaged in, discussing your failures in public—for existing and potential clients to read about—is a pretty bold, pretty brave move.

In a way, both the cooperation and the reluctance are in keeping with what I've observed about billionaire investors over the years. For the most part, they tend to keep their own counsel; they like to soak up as much information as possible, but in the end, they willingly—indeed, willfully—live and die by their own decisions. They are intuitive people, yet they activate their intuition only after they have done their homework. They lack patience with others who are not as prepared as they and have no tolerance for those who do not share the same commitment to effort. Nor are they typically willing to offer a second chance to those who do not seize the initial opportunity to impress them with their drive, intelligence, and judgment. Yet as individuals, they seem—all of them—able to charm a banana from a monkey's grasp when they want to.

Above all, or so it seems to me, they are passionate about what they do—the business of investing—while not emotional about their investments.

A while back, my wife and I vacationed on a Caribbean island with a group of friends, including Rich Pzena, profiled in Chapter 7. Pzena is one of Wall Street's brightest stars and, by universal consensus, one of its nicest guys. He had just taken his firm public a couple of days before the vacation, and the short sellers were after him. As the rumors circulated, shares in his company came under significant pressure, at one point falling almost 20 percent.

We knew none of this. All we could see was that Rich was on the phone from time to time—staying in touch with the office, not unexpected with any high-powered businessman. His voice was measured, largely unemotional, and no doubt comforting to his colleagues. He spoke logically and, as always, intelligently. Once he hung up the phone, there was no visible residue from the business transpiring back in New York. We were there to relax and play, and Rich relaxed and played with the rest of us. It's not that he didn't care about what was happening to the stock price of the company he had started from scratch and built with his own hands; it's that this is how he manages his business—by ascertaining the facts, considering what they mean, and then, and only then, deciding the appropriate course of action. Rich was going to stay the course and do what he had been doing—very successfully—for many years. He was not going to let the emotions of others who were selling shares dictate his response. It seems to be the way the best professional investors operate—that is, they do not assume that the stock price is always indicative of the fundamentals.

But don't get me wrong: There is an intensity to the passion they all feel for the business of investing. The first time I met Lee

Cooperman, whom you will meet in Chapter 6, one of the first things he said to me was that "if we both saw a nickel lying in the street, I'd fight you to see who picked it up first." I believed him, and since his track record indicated he had won most of those skirmishes, there was no way I was going to fight him for the nickel. If there were money to be made, Lee would be the one to make it. He more zealously guards his investors' capital than perhaps anyone I have ever seen.

The classic value investor, as are many of the people in this book, Cooperman also exemplifies the surprising, elusive, often downright mercurial character of these billionaire investors/entrepreneurs—and the difficulty of trying to pin down, much less second-guess, their thinking. Some years ago, Lee was being honored by the United Jewish Appeal as that charity's Man of the Year. The prior year, the honor had gone to Ivan Boesky, the notorious arbitrageur who would later go to prison for insider trading violations. Boesky had pledged $1 million to the charity, an amount that seemed to meet the standard expectation. The day of the dinner to honor Cooperman, a high-stakes office pool got going on the trading floor at Salomon Brothers—an over/under pool on what Cooperman would pledge. My recollection is that, by the end of the day, approximately $10,000 had been bet on either side of $1 million.

I believe Lee donated $400,000, a very generous sum, but obviously no match for Boesky's pledge. Happily for me, I was on the right side of the bet at Salomon, although not because I thought Lee was miserly. Quite the opposite. We live in the same town, where the numerous beneficiaries of Cooperman's charitable largess are evident. What I had bet on, however, was Cooperman's nonconsensus thinking, the ability to disregard sentiment, the lack of a need for ratification of his self-worth via public accolades, the value investor's instinct to step into a situation *after* the excitement, when everyone else is leaving. It's confirmation that these investors do think differently from you and me; they see things in a different way.

Then there's Steve Cohen, my onetime boss, who appears only tangentially in this book. I have never known anyone who could rival his ability to take minute pieces of data and instantly distill them into an investment thesis or profitable trade—which is probably how he grew his firm's assets under management from $60 million to an estimated $15 billion, more than half of which, it is speculated, is his. Yet when we first discussed my going to work for him, he told me that if "this [SAC Capital, his hedge fund] doesn't work, I'll close the firm and run money from my garage." It did work, so he never had to prove what he said, but I do believe that Steve's passion for markets and investing is so great that he would do it from a street corner if that would give him an investment edge.

Interesting people. Intelligent—even brilliant—people. People with inherent instincts for excelling at something they love, something that can be highly rewarding when their instincts are right.

And when they make a mistake, as Fiorello H. LaGuardia said, "It's a beaut."

It's a Mistake, Whether You Blow a Buck or a Billion

Harry Macklowe is not one of the investors profiled in this book, but he could well be. He jeopardized his multibillion-dollar real estate empire when he bought seven New York skyscrapers at the top of the market, overpaying egregiously. Everybody knows that mistake: You're supposed to buy at the bottom of the market and *sell* at the top. But Macklowe simply *had* to own the General Motors building, and in consummating the purchase, he assumed way too much debt.

Is Macklowe's billion-dollar lapse in judgment any different from the prospective homebuyer who *has* to own that newly constructed home on a full acre and overextends himself, assuming too high a mortgage payment? In both cases, isn't this the exact behavior—misbehavior—that sent the global economy into a tailspin in 2008? Macklowe's properties were essentially foreclosed by the firms that underwrote his purchase. The homeowner who had to have the new house was out on the street by 2009, when nationwide foreclosure rates hit an all-time high. The fact patterns are exactly the same; only the scale is different. If Macklowe, a legendary master of New York City real estate, could make such a big misstep, who couldn't?

But here's the real question: What can we learn from Macklowe's error in judgment? What brought him to the decision to contravene investing wisdom—buy low, sell high—and buy the GM building? What was his thinking—and what about it was flawed? Those are the questions this book will deal with. Through actual examples, distilled down to basics, you'll learn what to avoid and what not to do when you invest.

There's a great range of mistakes here. Each of these billionaire investors or entrepreneurs experienced an episode of failure in his own distinctive way. Some made errors of judgment, some of perception. None set out to make a mistake. They all thought they knew what they were doing; their earlier, very substantial success offered good evidence that this was the case. And maybe they did know what they were doing—just not this time. That's how mistakes happen—whether they cost a buck or a billion bucks or several billion bucks, as these did.

Eleanor Roosevelt once said: "Learn from the mistakes of others. You can't possibly make them all yourself." No investment is a sure thing. All investment involves risk. But you can lessen the risk and enhance the likelihood of a profitable outcome if you at least avoid mistakes. The mistakes you will read about here have been made by the smartest, savviest, sharpest, most successful investors around. As best you can, be sure you don't do what they did.

CHAPTER 1

Kirk Kerkorian

DUE DILIGENCE IS DUE EVERY TIME

Like so many of the Armenians who came to the United States in the first great wave of immigration starting in the late 1800s, Ahron and Lily Kerkorian gravitated to California's San Joaquin Valley— specifically, to its raisin industry.

It was a natural. The viticulture industry began, scholars tell us, somewhere around 6000 BCE in what is today Armenia, Azerbaijan, and Georgia, and in that perfect climate for growing and drying grapes, the descendants of those first raisin producers perfected their expertise. Thousands of years later, Armenians fleeing poverty and the oppressions of the Ottoman Empire found California familiar territory for the agriculture to which they were accustomed and fertile ground for their yearnings for freedom and opportunity.

The Kerkorians were able to satisfy both yearnings. When World War I brought raisin production in the Middle East to a virtual standstill, Ahron Kerkorian, savvy if illiterate, rode the raisin boom in the United States to an astonishing height, becoming, on paper at least, a rich man. This wealth did not last, however; Ahron would be caught in the postwar recession of 1921, when the nation suffered the steepest one-year price deflation since the Revolutionary War—a 36.8 percent decline in wholesale prices that swept away jobs and fortunes from coast to coast. Matching the general economic trend, raisins suffered a sharp decline in aggregate demand combined with a sharp increase in aggregate supply. The severe economic contraction that resulted wiped out Ahron's on-paper holdings and plunged the expanding family—a fourth child, Kerkor, called Kirk, had been born in 1917—into hardscrabble urban poverty in what was then the fringes of Los Angeles.

Eighty-eight years later, ironically enough, Ahron's youngest son would evidence a similar failure to foresee an economic downturn. Though the failure would prove costly—to the tune of some $700 million—it would not have the kind of damaging financial consequences that had affected and perhaps had helped mold the four-year-old Kirk. In fact, it would make barely a dent in the Kerkorian fortune, then estimated in the neighborhood of $18 billion, give or take a billion.

Such wealth made Kerkorian at the time the world's forty-first richest individual. And while nearly $10 billion in casino and hotel losses dropped Kerkorian down the list in succeeding years, he remained among the world's top 100 billionaires. Still, even when he stood at number 41, investing $1 billion and ending up with $300 million represents a sizable mistake.

Complacency creates blind spots. And blind spots, in addition to keeping you from seeing what's there to see, prevent you from seeing that you have blind spots. The complacency that cost Kirk Kerkorian $700 million in 2008 may have been inexcusable, but it was almost understandable. Kerkorian had had such a string of hits that it was virtually unthinkable he would flop. That, of course, was the blind spot.

At the age of 91, with no apparent evidence of diminished mental acuity, Kerkorian had every reason to adhere to—and no reason whatsoever to dismiss or disdain—the formula he had employed time and time and time again in achieving a success both unarguable and pretty much unmatched as a trader of companies. Buy an undervalued company, push up the value, be patient while the macroeconomy strengthens, then sell. That was the formula. It had worked brilliantly for decades across a range of industries and in the face of shifting economic conditions. Yet in 2008 it stopped working. Something had changed; there was some sort of shift, some rearrangement in the pattern of facts that had persisted over all his other investments. And Kerkorian didn't see it. He didn't see it because he failed to look for it. Maybe he forgot to look, or maybe he simply figured that with a half century of wildly successful investing under his belt, he really didn't need to look—that he knew what he needed to know without looking. Whatever the cause, the failure to look was a misstep on the part of a man who rarely put a wrong foot forward—at least where money was concerned. And it necessitated a Hail Mary move to stanch the bleeding of other holdings that were propping up the losing investment. All in all, it was an ugly loss for a man who doesn't like to lose and who, in a very long, very colorful, very eccentric life, has rarely lost—again, at least where money is concerned.

Kerkorian's personal life, which often has been fodder for the gossip game, is beyond the purview of this book and extraneous to its purpose—except perhaps to note that the private investment firm through which he does his trading, Tracinda Corporation, is named for his two daughters, Tracy and Linda, by his second wife, Jean Maree Hardy. For more on Kerkorian's colorful life, see the classic biography, *Kerkorian: An American Success Story*, by Dial Torgerson.[1]

Hemingway Meets Horatio Alger

In background and experience, Kerkorian is light-years away from the brilliantly educated, immaculately groomed billionaire investors whose ranks he overarches: rugged wilderness to their manicured golf courses. He himself claims that he first began bringing home some bacon for his impoverished family at the age of nine, and he concedes that doing so instilled in him "a drive that's a little different, maybe a little stronger, than somebody who inherited."[2] Maybe. It is certainly true that Kerkorian's early resume is that of a character out of Hemingway—boxer, bouncer, hero pilot—fitted into a classic Horatio Alger narrative arc.

A tough street kid who learned to box under the tutelage of his older brother, Kerkorian was expelled from one school for fighting and dropped out of another, the school for delinquent boys to which he was subsequently sent, to concentrate on fighting. Eighth grade marked his highest academic achievement, but in boxing, he went on to win the Pacific amateur welterweight crown. Paperboy, golf caddie, steam cleaner, car refurbisher, trail builder for the Civilian Conservation Corps: Kerkorian acquired numerous skills in an aimless succession of jobs until one day, at the age of 24, he accompanied his boss on a flying lesson, got a bird's-eye view of California from the ocean to the Sierra Nevada, and was hooked.

Kerkorian learned to fly at the Happy Bottom Riding Club in the Mojave Desert, hard by what is today Edwards Air Force Base.

It's the place where "the right stuff" was defined and honed, and Kerkorian's teacher was the pioneer aviatrix, Florence "Pancho" Barnes, owner of the club and, in the movie of *The Right Stuff*, the sharp-tongued woman behind the bar. There was a war on; eschewing the infantry, Kerkorian put his piloting expertise to work on behalf of Britain's Royal Air Force, ferrying Canadian-built De Havilland Mosquitoes, famous for their multiple capabilities as combat aircraft, from Ontario to Scotland.

There were two routes across the North Atlantic. One was slower and safer; the other was faster but had a 25 percent failure rate—failure here being tantamount to ditching in the North Atlantic, with serious if not fatal consequences. But the faster, more direct route paid more, and that was the one Kerkorian rode—straight out at jet speed across the west-to-east airflow known as the Iceland Wave. Over two and a half years, Kerkorian delivered 33 "Mossies," broke a crossing record, was given the rank of lieutenant, and managed to save the bulk of his wages—enough to buy a $5,000 Cessna and set up as a general aviation pilot.

He was 28 years old and a bachelor. Like a lot of Angeleños in the immediate postwar era, he had discovered Las Vegas, a city where, at that time, you could still see the night sky. Kerkorian gambled heavily and for high stakes—a habit he would eventually overcome, although he still reputedly enjoys showing up at the tables of one of his casinos now and again. In 1947, however, he needed and was able to borrow money from the Seagram family to pay $60,000 for a small air-charter outfit, the Los Angeles Air Service, which Kerkorian optimistically—some would say bombastically—renamed Trans International Air (TIA). He then scoured the world for war surplus bombers, and although many of them were in poor shape, it didn't matter to Kerkorian because they all had fuel—a commodity in desperately short supply at the time. Kerkorian sold the airplane fuel, paid off his loan, and still had the planes—the basis of TIA's fleet. He operated the airline until 1968, at which time he sold it to Transamerica Corporation, netting $85 million in the deal. It wasn't the last time Kerkorian actively involved himself in the running of a company. But after that, he mostly turned to the business of buying and selling.

Passions Leading to Profit

It is tempting to think we can find in Kerkorian's background the attributes of the business genius he became. He followed his passions, was willing to risk, and had the discipline to scrutinize a situation objectively when it was needed. For example, he loved flying, and aircraft became the cornerstone of his fortune. He loved gambling—at one point excessively—and he turned it into ownership of a large part of one of the world's largest casinos. And perhaps above all, he possessed the eye to see value where others saw none and to read the economy in ways others did not. Of course, he also had the drive—the sheer brazenness—to act on what his eye perceived.

It's tempting indeed to see all this in Kerkorian's tough-kid background, but it's also fatuous at best and dipping into psychobabble at worst. The fact is that in his trading career, Kerkorian followed a tried-and-true, simple, straightforward formula: He bought undervalued companies—occasionally selling off assets to help fund the purchase, added strategic resources to augment and enhance the value of the companies, then sold his stake in the companies at a profit. He exhibited patience in waiting for the value to rise, and he evidenced discipline and agility when it came to knowing when to get in on an investment and when to get out. It is also the case that his choices of undervalued companies were often singular, although eventually, of course, investors would follow where Kerkorian led. But the singularity is notable: Kerkorian would buy planes that could barely move and sell the fuel that made them move; he would buy land in the desert when land in the desert was something people fled from; he would buy a movie studio and turn it into a hotel company. He saw something in each of these circumstances that others did not see. Or he saw the circumstances in unique ways, looking past the obvious to perceive some undeveloped potential that simply eluded others.

That was certainly the case in 1962, when Kerkorian bought 80 acres of desert across the Strip from the Flamingo Hotel in Las Vegas. Since the 80 acres were landlocked by a narrow and useless band of desert owned by someone else, Kerkorian swapped acreage for the narrow band and rented out his parcel to Caesars Palace. He made $4 million in rent money from Caesars and raked in another $5 million when he sold it to the hotel's owners in 1968.

He purchased more land in Las Vegas, fast becoming a boomtown, and in 1969, he built the International, the largest hotel in the world. That year, he also made his first foray into Hollywood. Borrowing $42 million from European banks, Kerkorian paid out $650 million to gain a controlling interest in MGM, then began selling off several of its key assets—backlot acreage, the distribution system, and such memorabilia as Dorothy's ruby slippers from *The*

Wizard of Oz and the chariot Charlton Heston rode in *Ben-Hur*— so that he could turn the company into a casino-resort business.

Show business, hospitality, gambling—Kerkorian saw it all as entertainment. In building Las Vegas resorts in MGM's name, he was simply conflating two epicenters of the genre. Witness the launching of the MGM Grand Hotel in 1973: It offered a spectacle of star performances, a new concept of a Las Vegas resort as a "family" destination, and a celebration of sheer size, for the Grand was the largest hotel in the world for *its* time. Kerkorian sold the place in 1986 for close to $600 million, banking a profit of approximately 500 percent. In 1993, he built a second MGM Grand—again, the largest in the world for its time. Seven years later, in 2000, Kerkorian merged the Grand with Mirage Resorts to form MGM Mirage, a global development company with holdings in "gaming, entertainment, and hospitality" that have continued to earn him a fortune.

Meanwhile, back in Hollywood, Kerkorian was more than matching his Las Vegas trading activity in the movie business—a flurry of buying and selling that captures the essence of the man's financial wizardry. Although in 1979 he had proclaimed MGM mostly a hotel company, he nevertheless paid $380 million in 1981 for United Artists, then sold the MGM/UA conglomerate to Ted Turner in 1986 for $1.5 billion. The sale lasted 74 days—Turner had debt problems—and Kerkorian bought it back for a mere $780 million. In 1990, he again sold the company—this time to multiple investors for $1.3 billion—and in 1996, he again bought it all back. Finally, in 2005, he sold the movie company for the third time—to Sony for $2.9 billion—netting $1.8 billion on the deal.

Clearly, Kerkorian was a master negotiator, extracting prices from the buyers of his assets that were either too high to support the transaction or enticing them into transactions they were unable to afford. He would not have been able to do either had it not been for his vaunted patience—the ability to wait for the market to come to him instead of having to sell into a depressed environment. Kerkorian could exercise such patience because he had the advantage of not being overextended and not being on margin. He had the cushion afforded by a personal balance sheet that can absorb the negative effects from unpredictable and potentially debilitating economic hardship. And this advantage—this cushioning power—remained always available to Kerkorian, despite simultaneous involvement in multiple major investments.

Two other interesting patterns surface in this review of Kerkorian becoming a billionaire. One is his habit of playing with the house's money whenever possible—a lesson he may have learned at Las Vegas casino tables. Wherever he learned it, he applied the lesson to his airline business when he sold the fuel to pay for acquiring the planes, and he applied it again with MGM when he sold off its assets, booked the profits, and had the cream at the top to play with.

The other pattern that emerges is Kerkorian's willingness or perhaps inclination to navigate shifts in the macroeconomy. He was always patient enough to keep pushing up the value of assets he bought without ever being married to the investment. In that sense, he is the quintessential natural-born trader, who enters and exits holdings without any apparent regard to macroeconomic factors. Instead, he relies on his instincts to tell him the value of a holding—whether the value he sees is locked in a company or so mingled with other assets it would require surgery to isolate. It is said, for example, that Kerkorian originally purchased MGM in order to obtain the Leo the Lion trademark, which he intended to use for his hotels. Since that was the value he was buying, it's understandable that he would ultimately break apart the studios and sell the movie library and cinema artifacts. (Again, to Kerkorian, they weren't the point; they weren't the value he was after.)[3]

Of course, playing with house money is a good way to insulate yourself against swings in economic conditions, so the two patterns—patience and navigating macroeconomic shifts—are not unrelated. The seesaw buying and selling Kerkorian indulged in between Hollywood and Las Vegas illustrate the relationship—after starving MGM studios to build the hotels in Vegas, Kerkorian sold MGM in time to avoid the stock market crash and subsequent recession of 1974–75, and he sold holdings in both centers of his investment in 1986, just as the U.S. economy was pulling out of the doldrums and was again on the upswing.

What is clear is that where he could see compelling value in a company, Kerkorian was willing to invest in it even in bad economic times—confident that he could employ strategic initiatives to increase the company's value, then exit the holding as the economy recovered. And what had worked in Las Vegas and Hollywood sure looked like it would work in Detroit as well, as Kerkorian began his on-again, off-again love affair with the auto industry.

Kirk's Cars

Love indeed may have had something to do with it. It is said that Kirk Kerkorian has a sentimental fondness for cars. Not the customized Jaguars or racy Lamborghinis he can easily afford, but rather a Chevy Malibu, a Jeep Cherokee, a Ford Taurus—representatives respectively of what were once known as the Big Three automakers, all of which Kerkorian in his time has tried to buy.

It started in 1990 with Chrysler, the smallest of the Big Three. Kerkorian had struck up a friendship with the company's former chief executive officer (CEO), the legendary Lee Iacocca, who had been credited with turning around the automaker in the late 1970s—assisted, to be sure, by $1 billion of government bailout money. To Kerkorian, perhaps prodded by Iacocca, Chrysler's 1990 stock price—$9 a share—reflected recession fears and poor management rather than the possibilities of recovery. He eventually acquired just under 10 percent of the company—enough to force management to pay attention to him. By the beginning of 1994, the value of his holdings in Chrysler had quintupled to $60 a share. Kerkorian seemed pleased by this growth, and for a while all was quiet.

But "pleased" is not necessarily "satisfied." Sometime in 1995, Kerkorian seems to have concluded that there was more that Chrysler management could do to increase the stock price. With Iacocca again whispering in his ear, and with the stock hitting new highs, Kerkorian determined that the return he had already realized on his investment—a return greater than 500 percent—was insufficient. The company, Kerkorian decided, was still undervalued, and he bid $23 billion to acquire it in its entirety.

He was rebuffed. But Kerkorian is nothing if not a man of conviction where investing is concerned, and he continued to increase his ownership interest in the company. Meanwhile, his bid to buy the company—the threat of a takeover by a single investor—had scared the pants off Chrysler management, directly triggering Daimler-Benz's $36 billion acquisition of Chrysler to create Daimler-Chrysler. Kerkorian tendered all his stock to Daimler-Benz in the merger and, since his initial interest in the company had pushed up the stock price, walked away from the deal with $2.7 billion in profit. That is a 500-plus percent gain—a return in excess of the gross domestic product claimed by virtually all non–oil-producing African countries.

Had Daimler not come along to buy him out, it's likely that Kerkorian in due course would have sold his Chrysler holding in the open market—after all, Kerkorian dates stocks; he doesn't marry them. Probably, given the man's innate sense of timing, he would have ended the affair with Chrysler around the time the market started to become somewhat rocky. Had that happened, it's likely that he would have booked a positive return on the sale, although almost surely nothing like $2.7 billion.

Some years later, in 2007, Kerkorian made a second attempt to control Chrysler; he offered Daimler-Chrysler $4.5 billion for the American subsidiary. He was again rebuffed, and the company was instead bought by Cerberus Capital Management. Cerberus, a private equity firm with a then-stellar track record, acquired 80 percent of the company for $7.5 billion and the assumption of nearly $18 billion in labor costs. In essence, it was a complete write-down for Daimler, since the Cerberus proceeds went into a joint venture between the German auto company and the U.S. investment firm.

Had Kerkorian beaten out Cerberus and actually bought Daimler-Chrysler, it is likely that the financial disaster of 2008 would have wiped out his entire investment. In fact, with Chrysler forced to file for bankruptcy in 2009, that was the outcome for Cerberus. So the Daimler takeover in 1998 didn't just give Kerkorian a huge profit; it also enabled him to dodge a bullet that would soon be on its way. Sometimes it is better to be lucky than smart.

After two bites at the apple with Chrysler, Kerkorian launched his third attempt to control an auto company. He went after General Motors in 2005, acquiring close to a 10 percent stake to become the largest individual shareholder. This time, the guy whispering in his ear was Jerome York, a top executive at the Kerkorian investment company, Tracinda, a former chief financial officer (CFO) at Chrysler, and the man credited with saving IBM. Kerkorian installed Jerry York on the board, and York undertook a number of moves aimed at raising the company's value: operational streamlining, buyouts, other financial restraints, and merger talks with Renault and Nissan. But the GM board nixed the idea of a global alliance, and Kerkorian sold his stock for what was said to be a small profit only—estimated at a mere $112 million derived mostly from dividends.

Thus far, therefore, Kerkorian's record with the auto industry pretty much matched his record with Hollywood movie studios and Las Vegas resorts: one spectacular win, one mildly profitable draw.

His personal history as an investor and gambler's odds both would have told Kerkorian to go for the hat trick.

He did. And he ended up looking like a playground marbles novice in a professional football game.

The Ford Fumble

Maybe Kirk Kerkorian believed in the old saw about third time lucky. Luck, after all, is what attracts people to casinos. Kerkorian had always been on the right side of lucky: He is arguably the single most important figure in the development of the gaming industry. But there are plenty of lucky people in the world—and very few billionaires. So while Kirk Kerkorian may indeed be lucky, his luck is a by-product of incredible drive, vision, and investment brilliance. Nonetheless, even he would have to give a nod to good fortune for having mitigated what could have been much more significant losses with Chrysler and GM than the losses he eventually realized in his Ford experience. Kerkorian should have seen that. He should have been more introspective—and more diligent—in analyzing the Chrysler and GM trades before taking a third run at the motor companies. If he had been, he would have seen how close he came to losing billions from his investments in both those companies. And that might have made him hesitate before taking a third run at the auto industry.

Had Kerkorian done the diligence that was due, his own experience in the auto industry would have offered signals of an industry in trouble. Just consider: When Daimler bought Chrysler out from under Kerkorian in 1998, it was at the peak of the market; the economy as a whole, the auto industry in general, and Chrysler itself had all begun to roar back from a slowdown. It was a merger that appeared logical in terms of the synergies that could be realized in both the operational and marketing sense. Since each company had its niche, the merger would bring expansion without requiring reinvention of the wheel or starting from scratch. The two product lines complemented each other, at least on paper: Scrappy Chrysler had the moderately priced vehicles, from its legendary Jeep brand to subcompacts to trucks, that could round out the venerable German producer's singular focus on luxury—and vice versa. The two companies' marketing experience and capitalization contributions were equally complementary. Moreover, Daimler-Benz had long been the class of the field; these guys were aces at managing auto companies.

Yet not long after the aces took over, the fundamentals began to go south—big time. If a well-run company whose expert managers, steeped in industry knowledge, were unable to stave off precipitous decline in the value of their $36 billion acquisition, what chance did industry outsider Kerkorian stand—even with the assistance of a former auto company CFO? The auto industry is the largest manufacturing industry in the U.S. economy, linked to more other manufacturing and generating more retail sales and more employment than any other single industry. Yet the people running it cannot control the economy as a whole, the costs of basic materials like steel and gas, the price of labor benefits enshrined in collective bargaining agreements, or other fixed expenses. If they can't, it stands to reason that even a financial genius like Kirk Kerkorian can't—even on his luckiest or most brilliant day. And had Kerkorian looked closely at this experience, he would have seen that. Had he seen it, he might have acted differently in the matter of his Ford investment.

In fact, he had precedent staring him in the face. Steve Feinberg, the principal partner of Cerberus, shared a few traits with Kerkorian. Both were self-made billionaires and legendary investors. Both were also publicity shy and, importantly, both were staunch believers in the auto industry. Cerberus's acquisition had already begun to sour before Kerkorian bought his first share of Ford. As two members of the exclusive billionaires' club, and as members of an even more exclusive club—billionaires who own not just cars but car manufacturers—it would have been natural, and it would have behooved them both, to compare notes. If they did not, that was a mistake on Kerkorian's part. As this book confirms time and again, you can learn a lot from mistakes, and it is certainly better to learn from the mistakes of others than from your own.

But if deeper due diligence on Chrysler might have made Kerkorian hesitate, an incisive postmortem on his General Motors experience should have stopped him in his tracks.

Jerry York played a central role in the GM experience. A superb manager and an old auto industry hand, York was invited to join the GM board of directors as Kerkorian's representative—his hands-on auto expertise the perfect complement to Kerkorian's investment savvy. From the vantage of their collective insight and expertise, both men could look down the road—even in 2006—and see a threat of bankruptcy for General Motors. York was on record at the time as having estimated that at the rate the company was burning cash, insolvency could be as close as three years away—a forecast that was to prove eerily prescient. To avoid the threat, York, in his director role, outlined a series of recommendations to his fellow directors and senior management.

He suggested cutting white-collar salaries, which they did; selling such brands as the Hummer, which they did not (Hummer would eventually be sold in GM's 2009 bankruptcy reorganization); reducing union wages and benefits, which was not viable, since such costs were governed by a collective bargaining agreement; and—most significantly—forming that alliance with Renault and Nissan. The idea here was essentially to cede management control of GM to Carlos Ghosn, CEO of both the French and Japanese carmakers. Nicknamed "the Icebreaker" for his ability to cut through anything standing in his way, Ghosn was the most respected manager in the industry at the time and, as the author of both the Nissan revival and the turnaround at Renault, arguably the best.

Not surprisingly, entrenched GM CEO Rick Wagoner did not like this idea, and it was roundly defeated by the board. York immediately resigned from the board, listing his reasons for doing so in a letter to board chairman George Fisher that quickly become public. York cited "the boardroom environmental situation" as a detriment to the change he believed was needed, and he criticized directors for being too deferential to management (i.e., Wagoner), and not sufficiently focused on shareholder value. And thus ended the Kerkorian flirtation with General Motors.

It should have been a warning on three fronts:

1. Added to his Chrysler escapade, this brush with GM offered Kerkorian an insider view, at least by the proxy of Jerry York's astute vision, of the fast deteriorating economic and financial fundamentals of American auto companies.
2. The sclerotic intransigency of the GM board of directors should have been a clue to Kerkorian that the pace of change in this industry—at least any change effected by existing management—was going to be glacial at best. That was significant because at Ford, he would face a board of directors even more entrenched than GM's—members with longer average tenure and a family of heirs tracing their roots in the company back 100 years and with sufficient stock to control every decision and forestall any change.

3. As GM began leading the way that year to clear out inventory by slashing sticker prices—its alternative, so to say, to entering a global alliance—the pressure was on for the other Big Two to do the same. In any industry with a small number of players, the behavior of one tends to influence the behavior of the others, and irrational behavior by one tends to ruin the fundamentals for all of them. Thus the others quickly— and irrationally—replicated the drive to achieve sales at any price. It should have been a tip-off to Kerkorian that all was not well in the industry as a whole.

Yet despite these realities, and despite being privy to information available to only a handful of people, Kerkorian turned his attention to the Ford Motor Company in early 2008. That it was the healthiest of the Big Three at the time was inarguable. Equally inarguable was that being the healthiest of the Big Three automakers in 2008 was like having the best complexion in a leper colony.

Perhaps, when you're a financial magician like Kerkorian, the conviction that you're looking at an undervalued asset comes in a dream or arrives as a physiological sensation—a gut feeling, perhaps, or a shudder of desire. However it manifests itself, Kirk Kerkorian looked at Ford in 2008 and again believed he saw compelling value in the company itself that was not reflected in the stock price. Proclaiming himself bullish on Ford's CEO Alan Mulally and CFO Donat Leclair, Kerkorian in April disclosed that he had acquired 100 million shares of the company and made a tender offer for 20 million more, raising his stake in the company from 4.7 percent to 5.6 percent for a purchase price of $170 million. In June, Kerkorian bought another 20 million shares to bring his stake to 6.5 percent—nearly 141 million shares of Ford stock for a total investment of close to $1 billion.

This was self-deception. With his first Chrysler investment and with his GM investment, Kerkorian had repeatedly maintained that he had no intention of acquiring the companies outright, but the possibility always lurked in the background—and everyone knew it. The possibility so positioned Kerkorian that he could at least acquire a seat on the board as a prelude to effecting change in the way the companies were managed. At Ford, the founder's heirs controlled 40 percent of the voting stock—enough to block any attempts at changes suggested by an outsider, not to mention an unwanted takeover of the company. It's fair to ask, therefore—and Kerkorian should have asked it—what he thought his $1 billion was buying for him.

But the purchase had been made, and if all had gone according to the tried-and-true formula, now was when the fact of Kerkorian's financial resources, the legacy of his experience in investing in the auto industry, and Mulally's management initiatives would start to accelerate the uptick in the company's value. Certainly it was clear that the economy was weak, but the economy had been weak back in 1990 when Kerkorian acquired Chrysler shares and in 1995 when he made his bid for the company. Therefore, it was rational for him to assume that if he were patient, this asset would also recover its value and he would pocket his winnings.

Instead, it all began to unravel. With sales plummeting 35 percent, Ford reported record losses and abandoned its stated goal of realizing a profit in 2009. As its stock price plunged, the value of Kerkorian's $1 billion investment plunged along with it—by two-thirds. Toward the end of October, Tracinda announced in a filing to the Securities and Exchange Commission that Kerkorian had begun to unwind his stake, selling 7.3 million shares at $2.43 a share, nearly 65.8 percent lower than their average $7.10 buy price.

It was widely suggested that Kerkorian pretty much had to sell. Several days before, he had put up another 50 million shares of MGM Mirage—about a third of his total stake in the company—as collateral for his $600 million line of credit at Bank of America. The value of those shares had dive-bombed, forcing Kerkorian to pledge their dividends as collateral as well, while his shares of Delta Petroleum Corporation, also pledged as collateral, were themselves experiencing a multiyear low. Announcing that it saw "unique value in the gaming and hospitality and oil and gas industries," Tracinda asserted it would "focus on those industries." Translation: Stunned by the unforeseen steepness of his loss, Kerkorian may well have needed the cash from his sale of Ford stock to support his MGM Mirage holdings.

What Went Wrong

Here's what Kirk Kerkorian forgot:

He neglected to use his discipline to rein in his passion. While both were essential to Kerkorian's success, these two character

The Ford Fumble: Timeline

After being rebuffed in its attempt to buy Ford's Jaguar and Land Rover operations in 2007, Jerry York, acting for Tracinda, begins meeting with Ford CEO Alan Mullaly and CFO Don Leclair in April 2008.

April 27, 2008: York tells Leclair that Tracinda has acquired 100 million shares of Ford, a 4.7 percent stake in the company.

April 28, 2008: Tracinda makes a tender offer for an additional 20 million shares of Ford at $8.50—for a total purchase price of $170 million—bringing its stake to 5.6 percent.

June 2008: Kerkorian's Tracinda buys another 20 million Ford shares so that by month's end, his stake in Ford totals 140.8 million shares—a holding valued at $995 million. With 6.43 percent of the company, Kerkorian is Ford's largest private shareholder.

October 2008: Ford CFO Leclair resigns October 10; a week later, two key board members step down. Kerkorian lets it be known that he is "concerned." At the same time, Ford's stock price plunges to less than $3.00, demolishing the value of Kerkorian's investment in the company.

October 21, 2008: Tracinda announces it has sold 7.3 million Ford shares for an average price of $2.43 per share. Kerkorian's remaining 133.5 million shares in Ford are valued at $289.7 million—a two-thirds loss in value.

December 29, 2008: Kerkorian liquidates the rest of his Ford stake for a loss estimated at some $700 million—possibly as much as $800 million.

Source: Securities and Exchange Commission filings by Ford Motor Company, Tracinda.

traits eventually breed different results as they become at odds with each other. In the world of investing, emotion is the antithesis of discipline. Nonetheless, Kerkorian's passion for the American auto industry was a determining factor in his investing life; he tried once, twice, thrice, four times to buy into the Big Three. By the end, his batting average had gone from 1.000 to .250, and the reason was the fraying of the discipline he normally possessed. He simply was no longer objective.

Kerkorian succeeded brilliantly with his initial foray into Chrysler. Of course, he had resources and an ability to effect change that very few other investors possess, but that is actually immaterial to this analysis. What counts is the formula that achieved success: Kerkorian bought at the bottom when negativity about the company and the economy was high; he patiently rode out the hard times until the economy and the industry recovered, and he eventually collected a significant premium on his initial investment.

It was a brilliant trade by a legendary investor—a good example of why he is one of the world's most successful businessmen.

Yet in his General Motors experience, Kerkorian was arguably more fortunate than skilled, as he invested in a company whose fundamentals were quickly eroding. What had changed? The competitive landscape, primarily. As everyone knows, U.S. auto manufacturers began to lose major market share to imported cars, which were seen as more attractive and better made. Moreover, legacy union costs affecting the Big Three—but not foreign car manufacturers in the United States—made it tough to price vehicles competitively. And even though the "Kerkorian factor" itself gave a lift to the company's stock, creating the impression of unrealized value, it could be argued that the shares were significantly overvalued during the period of Kerkorian's GM holding—as was indeed borne out by the aftermath.

Furthermore, Kerkorian's primary resource, Jerry York, was a former senior auto executive who was clearly predisposed to invest in the sector. No one will ever know if the changes that Kerkorian and York proposed to the GM board would have saved the company from its ultimate fate of entering bankruptcy proceedings, but given that virtually the entire industry was under significant financial strain, it is unlikely that the company with the worst balance sheet in the industry would have fared much better with York's proposed reforms than it fared without them. In any event, since the reforms were never fully implemented, the point is moot.

Nonetheless, for Kerkorian, the GM experience was a profitable trade—as measured by the share purchase and selling prices plus the dividend distributions. Moreover, he avoided disaster by exiting the trade when he did, and for that he owes thanks to GM's board of directors for turning a deaf ear to his proposals for change.

Kerkorian's second go-round with Chrysler was triggered when Daimler realized it had made a mistake in buying the company and began soliciting offers for its purchase. Kerkorian was willing to pay $4.5 billion for the same company that he had attempted to buy for almost $23 billion in 1995. What was Kerkorian thinking? The very fact that a savvy industry insider, a strategic owner as opposed to a financial one—Daimler—is willing to take a $36 billion hit should be a wake-up call, a hint that excess caution should be employed. And indeed, a year after the transaction closed, Chrysler was all but insolvent, relying on a government bailout to stay in business. Kerkorian's $4.5 billion would have been wiped out.

And so we come to the Ford fumble, and it's as if Kerkorian's genius grows increasingly attenuated as he moves down the list to the last of the onetime Big Three. Why was the steepness of his Ford loss "unforeseen"? Why did everything that had worked for Kerkorian in the past stop working now? What had he missed? What was Kerkorian's billion-dollar mistake? Simple: It was letting his passion override his sense of discipline. His crush turned into a full-blown passion, abetted by significant profits from his first investment in Chrysler. And the passion eventually clouded his judgment.

He knew the economy was weakening; conditions in the gaming, entertainment, and hospitality business, in which Kerkorian had long been a major player, would have provided an early read on consumer trends. But he had seen many economic swoons before and had benefited by being aggressive during those times—his first buy in Chrysler in 1990 being a prime example of that. The difference in 2008 was that it was a different *kind* of economic downturn, just as the downturn that defeated Ahron Kerkorian in 1921 was different in kind from the usual economic downturns everyone could easily recognize. The one in 2008 was caused by an overextended consumer plagued by plunging home values, extremely tight credit—much more severe than in 1990—and the poor competitive positioning of the domestic auto companies. Kerkorian's primary consultant, Jerry York, had not properly calibrated these risks any more than Kerkorian himself had. (It is worth exploring whether York's judgment may have been affected by the terms of his deal with Kerkorian, which enabled him to share only in the upside and not in the risk.) Rather, two very, very bright guys looked at an investment model that was enslaved to prior cycles when economic and business conditions related to one another in different ways. The game had changed, the context had shifted, and they didn't see it. **They didn't see it because they didn't look. At least, they didn't look hard enough. Instead, they relied on what had always worked. That was the failure from which everything else flowed.**

Success can have a funny effect on perception—especially repeated success. Often, succeeding in a first attempt—a winning bet on a horse, a ring toss that falls perfectly over the neck of the bottle, a trade that reaps a superior return—imbues or perhaps infects an individual with a sense of security—almost surely a false sense, but powerful nonetheless. Replicating the success reinforces that false sense of security, lulling the person away from facts and dimming his or her ability to see that times have changed. In men's sports, they call it the winner's effect, when each succeeding victory causes a surge in testosterone that constitutes a performance advantage—until the testosterone level is so high that the athlete begins to misjudge time, distance, impact, risk—and loses.

Kirk Kerkorian orchestrated a brilliant investment in Chrysler in 1990, reaping billions of dollars. He went to the well again and came out okay. These successes were nothing if not a testament to the worth of his investment strategy. There seemed no reason to doubt that the same script—remaining patient through bad company performance to await an improved macroeconomy—would play out again in 2008. It didn't. As in 1921, the macroeconomy suffered a transformational shock, and Kerkorian missed it.

Times change, facts change, and no two investing scenarios are alike. Passion for a company should not be a significant data point of the due diligence process, as it was for Kerkorian, who had loved cars since boyhood. GM, Chrysler, and Ford were like the high school sweethearts who grew up and moved away, but Kerkorian's love for the whole idea of them persisted. Nothing goes on the same forever, nor should your investment approach. That's the one reality an investor should rely on.

Lessons Learned

- *Passion is not an investment strategy.* Don't let passion or initial success drive you to similar investments. There's no such thing as a single template that works forever.
- *Always do your due diligence.* While prior experience with a particular sector, stock, or investment theme is valuable in developing an investment opinion, due diligence must be performed afresh on all aspects of the trade to ascertain the existence and significance of any new factors.

- *There are no return engagements in the investment world.* No two investment fact patterns are the same. The global economy spins on a multitude of moving parts: macroeconomic trends, the competitive landscape, consumer spending. Therefore, hard data must be continuously and diligently updated, and assumptions must be challenged just as continuously and just as diligently. It must be assumed that even the same stock in the same industry always presents a different fact pattern that is likely to demand a different course of action.

- *Question the source of investment advice.* Challenge the basis of the advice, know who's on the other side. Whether you're dealing with a qualified broker, being counseled by a knowledgeable industry insider, or getting a stock tip from your dentist, keep in mind that whatever their reward, they are not likely sharing in the risk. While their advice may be well intentioned, their rationale for the investment, their risk profile, their overall exposure, and so on may be different from yours. Add your own due diligence before acting on any recommendation.

- *Memorialize your experiences.* Compare the investment under consideration to your past experience. If the stock "looks like" or reminds you of a stock you once invested in, recall whether that past investment succeeded or failed. Why? What happened to the stock price after you exited the investment? Were you lucky to get out when you did? Had you been mistaken or correct in your initial analysis of the company's fundamentals? That is, did the stock perform in accordance with the prognostication you derived from your analysis of the fundamentals—or not? If not, how did performance deviate from prognostication—and by how much? Granted, the asking and answering of these questions is not an exact science, but get as precise as you can.

- *Inconsistencies are flags of caution.* Any discrepancies that emerge from your questioning are warning signs; pay attention to them. It is no coincidence that the term "due diligence" was coined in the federal Securities Act of 1933. Practice it.

- *Take advantage of hindsight.* It's 20-20. Don't end up with a 10-10 assessment of the stock. In other words, take care not to squander the one true advantage you have in making the assessment: experience.

2

David Bonderman

DOES THIS MEAN I ALSO OVERPAID FOR THE ROLLING STONES?

In all likelihood, the name David Bonderman won't ring a bell. TPG, the private equity investment firm that he cofounded, has more than $50 billion under management, operates in 120 countries, and employs almost 600,000 people, a headcount equivalent to the population of Boston, Massachusetts. With a net worth estimated by *Forbes* magazine to be comfortably in excess of $3 billion, he is likely wealthier than Donald Trump. But while you generally have to be a millionaire to avail yourself of Trump's product—high-end real estate—there are no practical net worth requirements to experiencing TPG's offerings. In fact, it is likely that at some point in your life, you will have been serviced by at least one of the companies in the TPG portfolio.

For instance, have you ever eaten at Burger King? Or flown on Continental Airlines, America West, or Midwest Airlines? Then you've been served by a TPG company. TPG companies sell you computers from Lenovo and power your cell phone and other electronics with semiconductor chips made by Freescale. They dress you in clothing from Neiman Marcus and the J. Crew Group. Harrah's Entertainment provides you with lodging while you gamble in their casinos, and it's likely that Sabre Holdings booked your travel reservations to get there. You go to the movies produced by the MGM studios of the TPG portfolio—including the latest James Bond entry—and if you speak Spanish, you may listen to and watch its Univision broadcasts around the world. Oxford Health Plans may well insure your medical care; Del Monte feeds you and your family while PETCO feeds your dog. And if you live in Texas, you may be one of the 2 million people buying electricity from TXU Energy.

At one point, TPG owned all or part of each of these companies—and many more. And the firm's influence is just as ubiquitous in Asia, where it has 10 offices, as in the United States and Europe.

So it was not really anything out of the ordinary when, in April 2008, TPG agreed to invest $2 billion in a 120-year-old bank that operated 2,239 retail branches in 15 states and held almost $120 billion in customer mortgages. Nor was it surprising to see other large institutional investors follow TPG into the transaction, putting up an additional $5 billion of capital.[1]

What was a shock was to see the bank collapse that September—the largest bank failure in U.S. history. Among the big losers when the dust had settled was TPG—and of course the money it had infused into the bank simply evaporated.

Different Down to His Socks

David Bonderman was turning 60 and decided to throw himself a party. Laser-focused and serious when negotiating a transaction, he had no problem letting loose during his sparse downtime. To celebrate this milestone, he invited 500 guests to an all-expenses-paid weekend in Las Vegas. Since he didn't yet own Harrah's, he put them up at the Bellagio, in whose ballroom they were wined and dined, and where the entertainment got under way. Possessed of a sharp sense of humor, even if it was at his own expense, Bonderman hired Robin Williams as the emcee for the evening, and Williams did not disappoint. On the contrary: He was at his comic best roasting Bonderman in front of his family and the eclectic crowd of friends, which ran the gamut from a Peace Corps worker Bonderman had met in India 30 years before to fellow billionaires from around the globe. Following the comedy, the guests were bused to the concert hall at the Hard Rock Hotel, where they were serenaded in turn by John Cougar Mellencamp and the Rolling Stones.

As the range of the celebration's attendees attest, Bonderman is a man of contrasts. He was a civil rights attorney in the Justice Department yet built a temporary staircase from the Bellagio's restaurant to the ballroom so his guests wouldn't have to mingle with the hotel crowd. No slave to fashion, seemingly always adorned in rumpled dark suits, his trademark is a pair of brightly colored socks. He eschews limousines as too ostentatious but owns a $45 million jet. A staunch environmentalist donating considerable time and dollars to such organizations as the Grand Canyon Trust, Bonderman's enormous homes and private aircraft produce a Texas-size carbon footprint. He shuns the public media yet deftly handles large groups on the rare occasions when he may address a private equity convention.

Yet "Bondo," as his friends and associates call him, is as far from being a recluse as Paris Hilton. Despite homes in Texas and Colorado, he is just as likely to be found on his Gulfstream jet as in a boardroom, challenging the topography of Papua New Guinea or the landscape of a deal—and feeling equally comfortable in both venues.

How did David Bonderman reach the pinnacle of the business world—with investments and controlling interests in some of the world's most ubiquitous brands? That's one story. And after an unblemished 20-year track record generating average annual returns in excess of 30 percent for his investors and creating his own multibillion-dollar fortune, how did he fall prey to such an expensive and, some would posit, careless billion-dollar mistake—in an episode that from start to finish would take less than six months? That's the story of this chapter.

Sharklike Characteristics

"Natal philopatry" is the term used to describe the habit of some species to return home to give birth. Marine biologists have observed sharks born in a specific area of the ocean return to their birthplace from great distances to breed. David Bonderman was born in Fort Worth, Texas, in 1942 as the "greatest generation" was marching off to war. He returned to the city 41 years later to give birth to a new career working for billionaire Robert M. Bass's far-reaching investment empire. Although Bonderman joined the Robert M. Bass Group, RMBG, as the chief operating officer, he pursued companies to add to Bass's private equity portfolio with sharklike focus, although without the predatory fervor attributed to the famous fish.

Bonderman continues to do such deals, in a friendly sort of way, for his own firm, TPG, today. Instead of ripping apart and ingesting his prey, Bonderman rehabs his acquisitions, providing them with the management expertise—including a replacement management team, if necessary—that will one day allow them to swim off on their own and in the process generate large profits for TPG and its investors.

As befits the definition of philopatric, Bonderman traveled many miles before he returned home to his new beginning in Fort Worth. He was graduated from the University of Washington in Seattle, where he studied Russian and picked up a Phi Beta Kappa key; attended Harvard Law School, where he achieved magna cum laude honors; was an assistant professor at Tulane University School of Law in New Orleans, and then moved to Washington, DC, where he first worked as a Special Assistant to the U.S. Attorney General in the Civil Rights Division before making his mark as a partner in the well-regarded and powerful law firm of Arnold & Porter.

As a practicing attorney, Bonderman specialized in corporate, securities, and antitrust litigation, knowledge that would serve him well in the world of private equity. And while his apparently official residence is in Texas, home is more likely to be in Aspen, Colorado, where his family occupies a 14,000-square-foot mansion situated among 900 acres of a preserve, humorously referred to by colleagues as the Bonderosa.

The homes and a private jet are not the typical accoutrements of someone who is devoutly green, but Bonderman's credentials as a passionate conservationist and protector of the environment are beyond reproach. He has served on the boards of the Wilderness Society and the World Wildlife Fund as well as the Grand Canyon Trust. He has also donated his legal skills to the environmental cause, litigating pro bono for an environmentalist group in California and for landmark preservation groups in both Washington, DC, and New York City—including one case that required him to appear in front of the United States Supreme Court. Whereas most attorneys can only dream of standing in front of the nine most senior members of the judicial branch of government, Bonderman has had multiple occasions to showcase his legal talents in one of the most hallowed courtrooms in the world—and for the record, the jurists have sided with him each time.

He is a man on the move who has never stopped traveling; in fact, he rarely touches down for long. It is said that he logs 2,000 hours a year[2] aboard his private jet, an amount of time that would almost allow for a roundtrip weekday commute from New York to Phoenix. His business travels carry him all over the world to TPG's numerous offices in Asia and Europe as well as all over the United States. Bonderman's personal travel is much more exotic, the better for him to use his command of foreign languages including Arabic, French, and even a working understanding of such relatively obscure dialects as Pidgin and Urdu.[3] The endless voyaging often shows on Bonderman, whose tall, lanky frame can look somewhat disheveled, his thinning hair appearing more raked than combed.

The New Birth

It was as a result of Bonderman's pro bono efforts before the Supreme Court, when he successfully argued to save part of Grand Central Terminal in New York City from destruction, that he met Robert M. Bass. Bass had his own landmark preservation fight going on in downtown Fort Worth, where he was working to save that city's historic buildings from destruction.[4] He sought Bonderman's counsel, and a friendship was born. A business relationship soon followed, as Bass hired Bonderman as the chief operating officer for RMBG, his private investment vehicle. Sid Bass, Robert's older brother, had been front and center with the public, earning acclaim and billions of dollars as he transformed a relatively modest oil and gas inheritance into a multibillion-dollar fortune. Perhaps wanting to stake his own claim in the financial world, Bass established a firm to invest in leveraged buyouts (LBOs—i.e., companies purchased largely through borrowing, the loan secured with the company's assets), and he recruited Bonderman to help make it happen. On the surface, it seemed a strange acquisition of talent: Bonderman had never exhibited any significant interest in the actual act of investing, and investing was a skill that was necessarily embedded in the responsibility for overseeing all of RMBG's investments.

When the New York Yankees purchased Babe Ruth from Boston, in what is arguably one of the greatest talent acquisitions of all time, it ignited something of a rebirth for Ruth, who transitioned

Private Equity Explained

Like hedge funds, private equity firms are investment vehicles funded by such institutional investors as college endowments, pension funds, and wealthy individuals. The managers of these private partnerships are compensated in two ways: a fee of 1 to 2 percent assessed against all the assets under management, and 20 to 30 percent of any profits generated. And while the fee structure is similar to a hedge fund, the lock-up, or term of the investment, is far different. Here's how David Bonderman explained it to a venture capital conference in Hong Kong, complete with sound effects: "Private equity all has long-term lock-ups. So you may like our performance, you may not like our performance, but you're my partner for the next 12 years. (Here Bonderman smacked his lips as if planting a kiss.) At a hedge fund, you're my partner for the next 45 days until you can give me notice and get the hell out." The reason for the more stringent lock-up is simple: It often takes longer for a private equity investment to run its course and thus to yield its return.

The two most popular private equity investments are venture capital, which provides funds to early-stage companies, and leveraged buyouts—the Robert Bass specialty on which Bonderman first cut his investing teeth. TPG concentrates its efforts on the latter, seeking to acquire undervalued, often inefficiently managed businesses. These are usually public companies that TPG takes private or in which it acquires a majority stake. In order to finance the transaction, TPG invests its investors' capital and secures debt financing for the remainder of the acquisition price, using the targeted company's own assets as collateral. Thus the term "leveraged buyout," since the purchase price is met by leveraging—borrowing against—the business being acquired. Ultimately, TPG attempts to sell the company to another entity or takes the company public again through an initial public offering (IPO). In the interim, TPG continues to extract value from the acquired entity through its cash earnings or by selling its assets, including subsidiaries.

To illustrate, imagine that you own a house that sits on two acres, has no mortgage, and desperately needs a paint job. TPG buys it from you, putting up 20 percent of the purchase price in cash, the rest in a mortgage. It spruces up the property and subdivides the land into two parcels. TPG then sells the parcel without the house, recovering the cash of its down payment to you plus a profit, and installs a tenant in the house on the parcel it keeps, using the tenant's rent payments to meet the monthly mortgage payment. But there is still debt, in the form of a mortgage, attached to the property. TPG's hope is that the property will increase in value until it can be sold at a high enough price to pay off the mortgage and retain a profit.

Other people's money: nice work if you can get it.

Quoted in Reuters Blogs, DealZone, Behind the Deals and Deal-Maker, November 17, 2008, posted by Michael Flaherty, http://blogs.reuters.com/reuters-dealzone/ 2008/11/17/bondermans-investor-kiss.

into a full-time, power-hitting outfielder. That was exactly what the Yankees needed to round out their roster. With Ruth as the center-piece, the organization gained worldwide acclaim as baseball's most successful franchise. But at least the Yankees knew Ruth could hit. Robert Bass had no knowledge whatsoever that David Bonderman even knew which side of an investment was up. In other words, there was no track record of Bonderman's investment prowess because he had never been a professional investor. Yet Bass's acquisition of Bonderman was arguably a much greater accomplishment than even the Yankees' acquisition of Ruth. Yes, Bonderman's transition to power hitter was perhaps more difficult than the Bambino's. After all, Ruth had already made his living with a bat, while a spreadsheet and return on investment calculations were new tools for Bondo.

But he went to work eagerly nevertheless. From the outset, Bonderman worked closely with James Coulter, a Stanford MBA 17 years his junior. Together, they built a legacy of success, adding billions to the Bass fortune. Most of their success was due purely to aggressive deal making requiring lots of debt. A case in point was the time they bought the Plaza Hotel in New York City and flipped it to Donald Trump seven months later for a return of almost 60 percent. You could say they trumped Trump: He had allegedly wanted the property long before Bonderman bought it; this way, he had to pay significantly more for it.

Sometimes the private equity partners had help. The government's deregulation of the cable industry offered a big assist, for example, enabling RMBG to realize a huge gain when it sold Wometco Cable TV. And the government lent its assistance to

Bonderman's efforts at Bass one other time, in 1984. Already well regarded within LBO circles, but without the marquee name value of competing financier Henry Kravis, nor caring about it, with this transaction Bonderman and Coulter would cement their reputations as extraordinary deal makers.

It happened because a lot of the nation's savings and loan (S&L) institutions were in trouble. That's not unusual. Financial institutions seem to have no difficulty finding ways to get into trouble. In fact, it's pretty routine. Back in the 1980s, in what sounds like a rehearsal for the troubles of 2008–2009, aggressive lending policies, lax regulatory policy and oversight, and the desire of bank management to grow earnings at virtually any cost drove a number of S&L institutions into insolvency. The government assumed control of these troubled institutions and used federal funds to put them on firmer financial footing. Unlike the problems flowing from the subprime mortgage debacle, the debacle of the 1980s was mostly limited to thrifts, and its magnitude was measured in the tens of billions, not the trillions.

The episode that figures prominently in Bonderman's history concerned the California-based American Savings & Loan. In 1984, when it was seized by the government after a run on its deposits, it was the largest thrift in the country. The bank's board installed new management, but the new team subsequently failed on an ill-advised multibillion-dollar foray into mortgage-backed securities. (Sound familiar?) Seeking new management to take the still-ailing thrift off its hands, the government sought bids for the S&L's purchase. As an inducement to would-be buyers, the government would provide at least $2 billion of federal funds and would take $14 billion of nonperforming loans off the balance sheet, placing them in a "bad" bank. The reconstituted American S&L would be left with a similar amount of performing loans, thus ensuring that there would be a steady flow of earnings into the newly configured financial institution.

The Bass group, its efforts spearheaded by Bonderman and Coulter, won the deal with a bid of $500 million, a small price to pay for such an economically attractive acquisition. In addition to a financially strong institution whose assets would be guaranteed by the government, Bass derived a tax benefit of $300 million and an annual interest payment of $160 million from the "bad" bank. Between the guarantees, the $460 million in earnings, and the tax benefits, it was essentially a riskless transaction.

The financial world looked on with envy as Bonderman and Coulter ascended to the top of their profession courtesy of the largess of the taxpayer. But the story doesn't end there. In fact, it was only beginning. Not quite eight years later, Bonderman would orchestrate a sale of American Savings & Loan to Seattle-based Washington Mutual—WaMu—reaping a profit thought to be well in excess of $1.5 billion. Along with the sale came a seat on Washington Mutual's board of directors. Bonderman would serve in that capacity until 2002, but his relationship with the CEO of WaMu, Kerry Killinger, would last much longer, eventually leading to another investment in a troubled bank.

But that's getting ahead of the story. Flush with success from the American S&L deal, in 1993, Bonderman and Coulter decided to strike out on their own. The trigger for the decision was yet another potential transaction, this time in the aviation industry. Continental Airlines was in trouble, and for relatively little cash and a lot of debt, RBMG could own it. But Robert Bass thought the transaction was too risky and declined to participate. Seeing opportunity, Bonderman and Coulter resigned. The partnership they formed, aptly called Air Partners, the predecessor to TPG, raised the $66 million the transaction required, and the two men were on the way to their first successful deal.

The creation of Texas Pacific Group followed. Its name combines the hometowns of the two partners— Bonderman's home base of Fort Worth and Coulter's location in San Francisco—and the combination presaged how perfectly the two complemented each other, their differences adding up to something greater than the sum of the parts. Basically, Bondo was the aggressive risk taker, his younger partner the more cautious voice of reason. In time, they would be joined by a third partner, William Price, another well-educated attorney on whom they would rely to structure the transactions.

The Continental Airlines deal seeded an auspicious beginning for the partnership, but it would be a while before they were able to revisit their initial success. Indeed, the next few transactions were, at best, mediocre. Still, in due course, the trio experienced considerable success and grew big enough and solid enough to shorten their corporate name to the more efficient TPG. Then the hits just kept on coming, as TPG acquired interests in brand-name companies that would make any private equity professional incredibly envious. Throughout the 1990s, as endowments and pension plans allocated more and more of their investment portfolios to private equity, TPG was one of the largest beneficiaries of the trend, and this allowed Bonderman and his partners to pursue more and ever bigger deals.

True, other private equity firms were also experiencing success; the burgeoning economy was like the ocean's tide, lifting all financial ships. In time, TPG found itself competing for assets against similar firms in an increasingly crowded field. Given the size of TPG's asset base, Bonderman and his team were also forced to seek out larger transactions in order to impact the bottom line.

Shop till You Drop

The purchase of American Savings & Loan by Washington Mutual—the 1996 deal choreographed by Bonderman—was only one in a long string of acquisitions made by Kerry Killinger as CEO, whose own story is essential to understanding Bonderman's. A serial acquirer who believed bigger is much, much better, Killinger went on a shopping spree that would make the most addicted shopaholic look like a Tibetan monk. He bought such large thrifts as H.F. Ahmanson in California and Dime Savings Bank in New York; he swallowed up multiple mortgage lenders; he devoured credit card issuers, in the process making WaMu America's third largest originator of mortgages and ninth biggest credit card company. From the time Bonderman resigned from Washington Mutual's board of directors in 2002 through 2007, Killinger acquired more than 30 different financial entities, adding significantly to the potential liabilities on the bank's balance sheet. Lehman Brothers, Goldman Sachs, and others stood in his corner, abetting his growth strategy by leveraging their own balance sheets, finding customers willing to pay large fees in exchange for cash that would be used to absorb more companies. WaMu was no different from the indebted customer base it served, except that "subprime" was a term intended to be descriptive of individuals, not the country's third largest lender.

There was a plan behind these acquisitions, and Killinger made sure everyone knew about it. He wanted to make a signature mark on the credit industry, to change it forever and brand the change in the name of Washington Mutual. His goal was to become the "Wal-Mart of banking," and he said as much in a statement in 2003, unaware of the ultimate irony of his words: "We hope to do to this industry what Wal-Mart did to theirs, Starbucks did to theirs, Costco did to theirs and Lowe's and Home Depot did to their industry. And I think if we've done our job, five years from now you're not going to call us a bank."[5]

Like Wal-Mart, WaMu's strategy was to focus on the lower and middle class. This was hardly a novel or even a particularly original strategy; those segments of the population were the targeted market for a number of banks. After all, aside from mortgages on their homes, so-called high-net-worth individuals don't typically walk into their local bank branch and request a home equity loan, nor do they run up the balance on their credit cards. Such activities are more in the realm of the broad middle classes of the population. Moreover, with interest rates at relatively low levels during this period, there wasn't much of a profit margin on people with good credit ratings. So Killinger aggressively entered the subprime market, providing all forms of credit to those segments of the population that, because of poor credit scores, did not find it easy to secure loans or mortgages from other institutions.

In general, such people were living beyond their means, already had too much debt, or had a history of defaulting on prior obligations. What WaMu said to them was: *It doesn't matter*. This was the era of prosperity and excess in America, an era when people felt comfortable stretching their budgets to remodel their homes, buy flat-panel televisions, drive new cars, and move into bigger houses in new neighborhoods. Every other billboard across the country, every other ad on radio and television seemed to be an invitation from a bank, reassuring people that they were right to feel comfortable about all that budget stretching and urging them to come on into the local branch and walk out with a commitment. In fact, you could apply for a loan over the Internet.

WaMu became one of the most aggressive providers of credit to these subprime borrowers, often lending money without requiring any documentation of earnings or personal balance sheet. "No-doc" lending it was called, and WaMu was a past master at marketing it and providing it. The bank trademarked its somewhat annoying but attention-grabbing and very effective marketing campaign, and "Whoo Hoo" became a part of the American lexicon. (The more logical spelling, Woo Hoo, had been appropriated by Homer Simpson.[6])

It was all a highly profitable business for Washington Mutual, which was, of course, able to charge higher rates of interest to these troubled credit applicants who were desperate to borrow. As the profits rose and WaMu became one of the country's fastest-growing banks, CEO Killinger attained something approaching rock star status. From 2002 through 2008, his annual compensation averaged more than $12 million, peaking at $22 million in 2007. His name appeared on the *Forbes* listing of the country's highest paid CEOs. Investment banks fawned over Killinger, anxious to consult on his next acquisition and earn huge fees in the process. These firms provided WaMu with increasing amounts of liquidity so that the company could increase its ability to make more loans. In addition to providing leverage, Wall Street packaged the loans into asset-backed securities (ABSs), then marketed the securities to yield-starved investors anxious for an above-market return. It was all reflected in the price of Washington Mutual stock: In 2002, the year Bonderman left the board, WaMu's stock had been trading in the $30 range; its value reached a peak share price of $45 in 2007.

It sure must have looked like Killinger knew what he was doing.

Déjà vu All over Again

Economic bubbles are much like balloons. They keep expanding and expanding until the latex is so stretched that it pops. The demise of a bubble, like a balloon, is rarely unexpected; the excess, in substance or in shape, is in full view for all to see. Only the exact timing may be unexpected.

When a balloon pops, we jump involuntarily. No matter that we knew it was going to pop, no matter that our nerves are steeled, the loud noise and total collapse still cause us to react. When an economic bubble pops, the result is no less ruinous, only less audible. In fact, a bubble can pop before anyone notices, with only a hangover from the after-effects providing the evidence.

Kerry Killinger didn't notice that his bubble was about to pop. Throughout 2007, while a significant number of financial institutions were experiencing enormous losses from a decline in the creditworthiness of their mortgage portfolios, he still maintained that WaMu would not suffer the same fate, repeatedly making public statements about the viability of his company. He sat down with reporters from the *San Francisco Chronicle* in August 2007 to declare how pleased he was with the risk management changes recently put in place. He asserted that he felt comfortable with the loan portfolio and anticipated an end to the credit crisis in the next couple of quarters.[7]

Killinger's forecasting ability would turn out to be on a par with his risk management skills. The default rate on the mortgages, loans, and credit card debt held by the bank continued to sky-rocket. By the end of the first quarter of 2008, Killinger needed an infusion of cash, and he needed it in a hurry. But where he would get it was anybody's guess.

Bonderman's private equity fund, TPG, was brimming with cash. It recently had raised $26 billion from investors for two separate funds. The smaller fund, with $6 billion under management, was set up to acquire financial firms that stood to benefit from the government bailouts being proposed to deal with the worsening credit environment. Bonderman had seen this movie before. The script looked a lot like the success he and Coulter had enjoyed with American Savings & Loan almost a quarter of a century earlier. *Déjà vu*, he must have thought. The once-in-a-lifetime opportunity to acquire a top-tier financial institution at a fire-sale price was now a twice-in-a-lifetime experience. He probably couldn't believe his luck.

True, this time the government had not yet stepped in to provide a backstop for the transaction, but there was good reason to believe that the Treasury would not let WaMu fail. After all, only a month earlier, in March 2008, the government had brokered the sale of an insolvent Bear Stearns to J.P. Morgan, providing $30 billion in funding and a willingness to absorb all but a small portion of any loss that Morgan might realize from the acquisition.

The Bonderman-Killinger relationship, which dated back 12 years to Washington Mutual's acquisition of American S&L in 1996, had remained strong. Even after Bonderman left the WaMu board in 2002, after serving on it for six years, the personal relationship persisted even in the absence of the business tie.

It was April, the cruelest month, as the poet had called it—in another context, to be sure—and the Washington Mutual board of directors was feeling the pressure. The bank's lax lending standards were now coming back to haunt it in the form of write-offs against what assets remained. The government bank regulators, anxious to avoid another Bear Stearns debacle, were pushing WaMu's board to sell the company to J.P. Morgan, a willing acquirer.

But Killinger wanted to remain independent. He knew that if WaMu were merged into another company, he would be out of a job. He also thought the price being offered, $8 a share, which was lower than WaMu's 52-week low of $8.72 hit on March

17, was too low—and he spurned the J.P. Morgan offer. Killinger also had tried to raise money from sovereign wealth funds, state-owned funds that typically invest globally. To do so, he knocked at the doors of Singapore, Kuwait, and Saudi Arabia but was turned down—perhaps because these entities had already poured $100 billion into such failing financial institutions as Citigroup and Lehman Brothers and were in no position to lose more money. As the WaMu situation deteriorated by the hour and as the need to do something grew more acute, Killinger remained unwilling to concede defeat. Finally, he turned to an old friend.

By all accounts, David Bonderman and his partners at TPG had no more than a week to perform due diligence, an impossibly short amount of time for such a complex transaction. Instead, Bonderman relied on his relationship with Killinger, his instincts, and his prior history serving on WaMu's board. In all likelihood, he also derived comfort from his successful experience buying and selling American Savings & Loan during another period of extreme stress in the banking sector. The decision to invest in WaMu must have seemed like something of a homecoming for Bonderman. He would ride in as the white knight, but this time, instead of being the acquired, as he was with American in 2002, he would be the acquirer—of a much bigger and more important company.

This is not to say that emotion ruled. For David Bonderman, one of the industry's most successful private equity investors and a man accustomed to careful analysis, emotion would never be a driving force. On the contrary, there was sufficient reason—in terms of hard cold cash—to ante up both reputation and significant dollars for the WaMu investment. On April 9, 2008, just a week after J.P. Morgan's $8-per-share offer for the troubled company, Bonderman anted up both—in an offer that WaMu *did* accept. The structure of the transaction as it was finalized illuminated the reason for the TPG action.

In all, Washington Mutual received a total infusion of $7 billion in new capital—an extraordinary amount, considering that the entire value of the company at the time was approximately $9 billion. TPG led the transaction, negotiating a per-share price of $8.75, a one-third discount from the stock price at the time. A provision of the deal stated that if WaMu raised additional capital at a lower price within the next 18 months, the purchase price would be reset, entitling TPG to a refund of the difference. TPG invested $1.35 billion of its own money. Another $650 million came from TPG's co-investors, and unaffiliated investors contributed still another $5 billion. As part of the deal, WaMu agreed to cut its dividend to preserve cash and to exit the businesses that got it into trouble.

Of course, selling such a large part of WaMu required the approval of existing shareholders. On June 24, a shareholder vote ratified the board's decision to sell more than half the company to TPG and others. Bonderman rejoined the board of directors and would help lead the company back to profitability—or so everyone thought.

Traders definitely were of that mind. The day the deal was announced, the stock closed higher by almost 30 percent, essentially erasing the discount that TPG received. It wasn't just that WaMu was able to replenish its balance sheet; that was a secondary consideration. Foremost in traders' minds was David Bonderman. After all, he had served on WaMu's board for six years and knew the company intimately; he was thought to be close to Kerry Killinger, the bank's CEO; and he was also a brilliant investor. Arguably, the other investors placed their faith more in Bonderman than in the transaction itself because they also didn't have the time to perform the comprehensive due diligence that would have been appropriate. Instead, where smart money leads, others follow. Sometimes to their peril.

The Damp Seattle Weather Never Allowed the Ink to Dry

TPG's investment in WaMu began to sour quickly, declining with the housing market that spring of 2008, and Bonderman no doubt regretted making the investment. In June, barely two months after the transaction, Bonderman, in concert with other board members, removed Killinger as chairman, a post he had held for nearly 18 years. He would continue as CEO but would now have someone looking over his shoulder as he ran the company's day-to-day operations.

Maybe keeping Killinger in any position was a mistake—the bank's fortunes continued to decline at an alarming rate. The stock price plummeted, and the company sought additional capital to allay investors' and regulators' fears that it was running out of cash. TPG even agreed to forgo the reset provision, a gesture that could have cost it a fortune if the investment had ultimately worked out. As the summer heated up and TPG's investment cooled, the company found out what others had known—and what TPG should have realized from the outset. Bonderman and Coulter of all people, definitely should have realized it: Washington Mutual was a house of cards facing a gale-force wind.

Finally, David Bonderman had had enough; business was business and friendship was—well, not business. He had relied at least partially on Killinger when he made the investment in WaMu. Now that TPG's $2 billion was evaporating "faster than you can say option adjustable-rate mortgage," as one wag put it,[8] Bonderman and WaMu's board fired Killinger outright. The date was September 8, 2008—exactly five months after TPG had made its investment in WaMu. The dismissal of Killinger was equal parts necessary and symbolic, the intention being to restore confidence in company management.

It failed. On September 25, 2008, the Federal Deposit Insurance Company (FDIC) seized the assets of Washington Mutual. With more than $300 billion in assets, it was the biggest bank failure in history, almost eight times the size of the failed Continental Illinois National Bank a quarter century earlier.

And David Bonderman didn't see it coming until it was too late. Neither did those who followed him into the transaction. Seven billion dollars evaporated in less than six months.

Bonderman's WaMu Timeline

1984: On behalf of the Bass Group, Bonderman orchestrates the purchase of American S&L from the federal government.

1996: Bonderman arranges Washington Mutual's acquisition of American S&L, joins the WaMu board.

2002: Bonderman resigns from the WaMu board,

April 2008: Bonderman's TPG invests $2 billion in WaMu; Bonderman rejoins the WaMu board.

June 2008: WaMu chairman Killinger is forced to step down from running day-to-day company operations.

September 8, 2008: Killinger is fired.

September 25, 2008: FDIC seizes WaMu's $300 billion in assets—including TPG's $2 billion.

What Went Wrong

"You can't go home again," Thomas Wolfe said, titling one of his most famous novels and adding a phrase to the lexicon. While Wolfe surely didn't have billionaire private equity investors in mind when he coined the phrase, it aptly applies to David Bonderman.

Imagine you grew up in a modest two-bedroom bungalow, surrounded on all sides by open land, the structure a mere dot on the landscape. Years go by, you're an adult who moved away long ago, and one day you decide to take a drive to the old neighborhood. The sign tells you you're on the street where your childhood home was located, but you look at where you thought the house was and instead see a McMansion, rising three stories from the ground, extending a half block on either side, a forest of trees reaching for the sky. The only familiar marking is the number on the mailbox out front. Have you gone home again? Is a street address home?

Not in the case of WaMu. David Bonderman moved into a house he had never before visited. The address was the same, but the structure was different. And he, of all people, should have seen the difference.

Bonderman's billion-dollar mistake was rushing into a market that was deteriorating fast—and doing so on the basis of assumptions, not objective scrutiny of the facts. He substituted familiarity for due diligence and did not have the time to do the process right. (WaMu was failing fast and needed an immediate cash infusion.) In other words, Bonderman likely assumed this WaMu was not all that different from the WaMu he had always known and that Kerry Killinger was the same successful CEO. He thought he would be right at home at Washington Mutual, but home life at the giant bank had changed. Had Bonderman had the time to perform his usually rigorous process of examination and analysis, he would have realized that the Washington Mutual from whose board he resigned in 2002 resembled the 2008 version in name only.

"Washington Mutual built itself into America's biggest mortgage bank almost overnight. But this year, POW! Profits are getting hammered, and the CEO is apologizing to Wall Street."[9] That was the headline on a story appearing on CNNMoney.com about WaMu's troubles—not its troubles in 2008 but in 2004, two years after Bonderman left the company's board of directors. The issues the article referred to, however, were the same the bank would face three years later, although the magnitude of the problem was far less in 2004. Still, it seems a harbinger of bad things to come: The bank had lost money on its mortgage portfolio, and Killinger was apologizing for the company's performance yet not shouldering the blame for a failed acquisition strategy and subpar underwriting standards.

True, 2004 was admittedly a tough time for the economy and the markets, so perhaps Bonderman had been willing to give Killinger a pass for the problems recorded by CNNMoney. Even so, and even though the company had never recorded a loss during the period Bonderman was associated with it, he should have been scared off by the more than 30 acquisitions he watched Killinger champion over the six-year period that followed his tenure on the WaMu board, changing the direction of the company from a somewhat conservative thrift to one that set the standard for lax credit standards.

Investors cannot rely on a prior experience with a stock and assume they will derive the same experience from it, particularly after the passage of time. Companies are not stagnant. Markets change, strategies change, and the macroeconomic underpinnings change. Every investment must be treated as a brand-new investment—even if it's a stock you've invested in before—and a new due diligence process must be undertaken every time—even if you're "familiar" with the company.

That doesn't mean you should discard all memories. Instead, use your experience with the company to measure how it has changed. Why did you sell the stock in the first place? And did the circumstance that caused you to sell it change for the better? How has the company performed relative to the strategy it laid out when you were an investor?

That's just the kind of scrutiny Bonderman didn't have time to perform when TPG put up $1.35 billion to anchor the $7 billion investment in WaMu. There's a lesson there: Make the time to examine a prospective investment thoroughly, or forget the investment.

As for the co-investors who put up $650 million and the other $5 billion that followed him into the transaction, they had even less time for analysis. Instead, they assumed that Bonderman knew the company inside out, and perhaps they thought he got a nod and a wink from Killinger. Not a good idea. It's okay to rely on smart money to surface ideas for you to investigate, but it makes no sense to place complete reliance on others. For one thing, different investors have different risk parameters, so following others without taking risk into account simply flies in the face of a basic tenet of investing. In addition, the investment you find yourself following the "smart money" into may represent a very small portion of those investors' portfolios. TPG's loss of $1.35 billion, an enormous sum, represented only about 1 percent of the fund's value.

Of course, someone who has that much money can afford to roll the dice. The question is: Can you?

Lessons Learned

- *Don't catch a falling knife.* When a potential investment is deteriorating rapidly—the stock price is declining—don't feel compelled to get in on it. Wait till the speed of descent slows, allowing you the time you need to assess risk versus reward. Emotion or impulse buying, the feeling that *I have to do this now because it is so cheap* only clouds proper judgment that should be based on analysis. Additionally, don't allow the pressure of an impending deadline to force you into an investment before you are comfortable with all aspects of the transaction. It's okay to pass.
- *Every investment is a new investment.* Fresh examination and analysis are required every time. Markets and companies are not stagnant. If you have invested in the same company in the past, assess how the company or its end markets have changed—and if that change is for the better. Even if the company is basically the same as before, the operating environment for that company may have changed dramatically.
- *Review company performance.* Assess how the company has performed relative to the milestones of the business plan that was in effect during your previous experience as an investor.
- *Don't follow blindly.* When you see the "smart money" going to a stock, regard it as just one data point among many. Those investors may have a different risk tolerance from yours, a different allocation strategy, a different portfolio structure.
- *Don't squander gains.* Do not make an investment or stay in one because you're playing with "house money" (i.e., the profits derived from the same investment). The profits you have already made in an investment have been accounted for and taxed.

CHAPTER 3

Aubrey McClendon

FALLING ON THE WRONG EDGE OF THE TWO-EDGED LEVERAGE SWORD

As with any tool, leverage can do wonders if you know how to use it. But if you hold it wrong or get careless or look the other way even for a second, it can draw blood.

It did both for Aubrey McClendon; coming and going, he realized both the slicing effectiveness of leverage and its stabbing wounds.

Yet knowing how to wield leverage is essential in investing. Its importance rests in the simple fact that it can enhance—can increase—the return on an investment. When you borrow money to invest, and the investment then increases in value, you realize a greater return on the investment than if you had paid the purchase price out of your existing financial resources. Indeed, without borrowing the money, you might not have been able to afford the investment at all. Leverage therefore gives you access to benefits you might otherwise not have been able to realize, and then it magnifies the benefits.

The classic example of leverage is taking out a mortgage to buy your own home. Since most of us lack the ready resources to purchase such a significant and costly an asset, the bank lends us the money—with the property itself as the collateral—to supplement the down payment we are able to muster. With a relatively small amount of money, therefore, we are able to control a much larger asset. As the value of the property increases, the fact that we are using other people's money creates a greater return than if we had laid out the full purchase price from our own existing resources.

You and Aubrey McClendon

Do you own your own home? If so, chances are you leveraged your existing financial resources to buy it. That is, you took out a mortgage —a loan, probably from the bank—to supplement the down payment you had saved up over the years. As the value of your property increases, the leverage increases the financial return on your down payment.

For example, suppose you buy a house for $300,000 by putting down $100,000 and taking out a mortgage of $200,000. Over the first year of ownership, the house rises in value by 3 percent; this represents a gain of $9,000 on the price you paid for the home and a 9 percent return on your down payment. Even reduced by the interest paid on the mortgage, this is a substantially magnified gain. Few other investments offering such a large potential return are available to the average individual; that is precisely the power of leverage.

But as so many homeowners found out in the subprime credit disaster, leveraging—whether to buy a home or take out a home equity loan to finance improvements or for other purchases—can also greatly magnify loss. For example, suppose your $300,000 house is losing value instead of gaining, and you're feeling the full force of the recession's financial squeeze. Unable to make the monthly mortgage payments, you put the house on the market and are forced to sell for only $175,000. The result is the loss of your $100,000 down payment plus the $25,000 that is the difference between your selling price and your mortgage. In other words, your loss has been as leveraged as your gain would have been, but in this case, that amounts to everything: your entire investment and your home.

The Wall Street equivalent of the homeowner's mortgage is the individual investor's margin account, which enables the investor to borrow against his or her existing investment portfolio. Typically a broker provides the wherewithal for leverage, and the collateral that covers the lender's risk—usually, stocks or bonds—is called the margin. An investor must maintain a minimum margin requirement that protects the lender against any fall in the value of those stocks and bonds used as collateral. If and when the value of the margin falls below that minimum requirement, the broker issues a margin call to the investor to either provide more collateral or default. Just as a bank forecloses if you default on your mortgage, your broker will take ownership of your stocks-and-bonds collateral and sell them to satisfy your obligations if you default on your margin account. Different terms, equivalent action: Either way, you lose ownership.

And whether leveraging to buy a house or invest in a stock, what can boost a return as the investment increases in value can also intensify the loss if the value of the investment goes down. That is the risk; it is the other edge of the leverage sword. **That is why you should never risk what you cannot afford to lose.**

People risking what they couldn't afford to lose is about as good a definition as you can find for the subprime mortgage disaster of 2008 that led to the galloping home foreclosures of 2009 and that traveled through the veins of the world economy like a deadly virus.

And risking what he couldn't afford to lose is what tripped up master investor Aubrey McClendon when he got caught in what may have been the biggest margin call in history and went down for a loss of $1.92 billion, half his estimated fortune and almost all of his stock.

Wildcatter with a Taste for Bordeaux

There is little that is subtle about the public Aubrey McClendon. Tall, handsome, charismatic, McClendon is an Oklahoma business-man with pronounced likes and dislikes, an advocate of social and political causes who puts his money where his mouth is, and a born-and-bred oilman with an eye for the main chance. He is also the co-owner of the Oklahoma City Thunder, which means that you do not want to mention his name too loud in Seattle, from whose Sonics the Thunder evolved.

McClendon was almost literally born into a network of business and political connections that stretched from his native Oklahoma around the country. For starters, he is a great-nephew of Robert S. Kerr, who was once the governor of Oklahoma as well as its U.S. senator. Kerr was also the co-founder of Kerr-McGee, one of the granddaddies of the energy industry. But McClendon has his own friends in contemporary politics, most notably former Governor Frank Keating and former Senator Don Nickles, who sit on the board of directors of McClendon's company, Chesapeake Energy.

McClendon is a consistent and generous contributor to numerous causes, some of which clearly advance his business and political agendas. In an interview, he said that these days, those agendas "are focused entirely on trying to encourage the greater use of carbon-light natural gas in the place of carbon-heavy oil and coal." But there was a time when the agenda was political as well. Like most astute businessmen who make their living in commodities, McClendon is prone to hedging most bets—even when it comes to candidates for office. For instance, in addition to contributions to the 2008 presidential primary campaigns of Giuliani, Romney, and McCain, he also wrote checks to Clinton, Richardson, and Obama; the latter also got his vote. But in the past, McClendon's big money went to conservative political action committees (PACs) like the Swift Boat Veterans for Truth, which opposed John Kerry in 2004, and to such causes as opposition to gay marriage. Just when you think you've got the guy pegged as a Bible-thumping social right-winger, he turns up as the Finance Committee co-chairman for the unsuccessful 2008 county commissioner campaign of Democrat Jim Roth, the first openly gay individual ever to hold statewide elected office in Oklahoma.

McClendon now says he has "sworn off" all contributions to PACs, but he has not sworn off advocacy. He was vocal in his support for the Duke University men's lacrosse team, members of which were falsely accused of rape in a divisive case in 2006. He is also chairman of the American Clean Skies Foundation, a nonprofit advocacy group for natural gas and other alternatives to petroleum. In addition, he has supported the commercial campaign for natural gas usage of his friend and fellow Oklahoman, legendary oilman T. Boone Pickens. Of course, natural gas is responsible for McClendon's considerable wealth and is the main asset of Chesapeake Energy. That alignment of his public advocacy with his business interests doesn't mean that McClendon has no altruism; he can exhibit altruism in spades and has done so in many ways and on many occasions.

Perhaps because of his past social conservatism, McClendon has been referred to by some as a redneck; with a self-irony meant to sting those who call him that, he has even used the term on himself. But it's a dubious appellation for a man who is a loyal alumnus of one of the most prestigious universities on the eastern seaboard, Duke, the alma mater also of his wife, Katie, an heir to the Whirlpool appliance fortune. And it is perhaps particularly dubious for a man who owned a 75,000-bottle collection of exceptional wines, the vast majority of them French, valued at more than $100 million. A very small portion of the collection, less than 5 percent, was auctioned by Sotheby's in 2009, ostensibly to replenish McClendon's supply of cash following his nearly two-billion-dollar mistake. Figure in Sotheby's commission, and the gain from the wine auction couldn't have made more than a small dent.

Starting from Scratch

Despite his background and connections, McClendon started his own business from scratch, cofounding Chesapeake Energy in 1989 with his friend and fellow Oklahoma native Tom Ward. The two men plunked down an initial investment of $50,000 and named McClendon chairman and chief executive officer (CEO) and Ward president and chief operating officer. That structure persisted throughout the company's phenomenal growth, which peaked at a valuation of nearly $25 billion in 2008.

Few dispute that McClendon was the architect of the model that produced the growth—a model that other independent oil and gas producers soon copied as best they could. The model was simple: As energy prices kept going up, and as technology kept on finding and opening new reserves, thus partially tempering the risk of a "dry hole," Chesapeake—and the energy companies on its tail—kept on leasing or acquiring acres and acres of land, paying for new and better equipment, and drilling wherever they could set down a rig.

McClendon and Ward came to this strategy naturally, if not necessarily by original design, and certainly on a path that took some interesting turns. Initially, their business had been land acquisition—buying properties in order to sell them to gas producers. McClendon's idea that they should hold onto the land, acquire more, and drill it themselves would distinguish Chesapeake from the pack—and make it the leader others eventually would follow. It was a strategy that brought McClendon and Ward immense wealth and well-deserved recognition as brilliant businessmen. But along the way, it also brought them to the precipice of insolvency, for leverage was a cornerstone of the model—borrowing money and selling shares to pay for the acquisitions and the drilling activity. As their debt rose and gas prices declined, McClendon and Ward sometimes found themselves flirting with disaster—the kind of disaster that has made more than one oilman, and more than one businessman, simply give up. These two, however, persevered through the tough times, held firm to their analysis, and stuck to their conviction that natural gas prices would rise. Their perseverance would pay off handsomely—and then some.

But leverage continued to be an essential component of the Chesapeake business model. In fact, the company was generally considered to be one of the most highly leveraged in the industry. By year-end 2007, the company's debt-to-book capitalization—that is, the ratio of what it owed compared to the amount of capital it had available—was 47 percent.[1] That's a high number for any company, but it is very high for a company whose fortunes—and therefore ability to service the debt—could rise and fall with natural gas prices and with whether Chesapeake's hedges on forward pricing were good bets or bad.

But where shareholder value was concerned, the buy-and-drill strategic direction was all uphill—year after year after year. By the second quarter of 2008, Chesapeake was the largest producer of natural gas in the nation. And one of its biggest investors —and certainly its most persistent—was the chairman himself. Repeatedly, whatever the stock price—whether it hovered in the teens, moved into the $20 range, climbed into the $30s, or edged even higher—McClendon could be heard to state that he believed Chesapeake was a $100 stock. In business as in politics, he put his money where his mouth was—in this case, by buying the stock continuously. Perhaps no other CEO in any industry anywhere in the country was as renowned for insider buying—which is tightly regulated and extremely transparent—as McClendon. And he leveraged himself to the hilt to do it. Outright purchases of the stock are only one method of acquiring shares for an executive. The other, and perhaps more cost-efficient way, is to be "awarded" the stock as part of a compensation package. McClendon's awards provided him with the equivalent of more than 11 million shares in stock and option grants.

Of course, meaningful insider buying by senior management is always an endorsement. It evidences a bullish confidence in the company's mission, management, and people. That doesn't mean that McClendon's investments were simply an ego trip: Chesapeake's performance was exceptional, and it was considered a model company—an exciting growth company that was also named one of *Fortune* magazine's 100 Best Companies to Work For. So the strategy McClendon put in place was clearly a sound one, and his persistent buying seemed to echo the man's personality and his belief system: If you like something, double-down on it.

McClendon was also a great CEO for others to bet on. He was extremely well regarded by his energy industry peers as well as by the institutional investor community. Clearly, as substantiated by the performance of Chesapeake stock, he was a shareholder favorite. Through strength of personality, industry knowledge, and financial commitment, he occupied a singular position not just in his industry but in the business world as a whole, where few other individuals stood as tall.

But there *were* some nonbelievers. For as Chesapeake continued its aggressive leasing, it also continued to borrow heavily, racking up $11 billion in debt between 2002 and 2008 to acquire more and more properties. One skeptic, at least initially, was Wall Street energy analyst Charles Maxwell, a Chesapeake director, who was once heard to comment that it was the role of the board of directors to keep the chairman's enthusiasm under control. But then the chairman persuaded Maxwell that if Chesapeake didn't spend the money and get the land, another company would. Maxwell acquiesced. "We decided it would be us," he said.[2]

There were also a few skeptics among shareholders who wondered if the equity being issued in the form of secondary offerings to the public might be diluting the value of the stock too much. If so, of course, it would also be diluting the value of McClendon's stock, and as a major shareholder, to say the least, such dilution would hardly be in his interest.

Other skeptics hinted that the equity offerings might be aimed at benefiting the so-called founders' well-participation plan,[3] a unique coinvestment agreement that, as its name suggests, enables Chesapeake founders to invest directly in Chesapeake wells. But this unusual arrangement, one in which McClendon must personally pay for his share of the costs associated with the purchase, exploration, and production of the wells he participates in, might also be seen as further evidence of his all-in philosophy. In 2007 alone, for example, McClendon reimbursed the company $177.7 million for his participation in the plan,[4] a fact perhaps lost on his skeptical critics.

For the most part, indeed, shareholders and management were in agreement that the vigorous pattern of issuing equity and debt to fund acquisitions was a winner. That McClendon was the biggest winner of all was not in dispute. By 2006, the chairman owned more than $880 million of his company's common stock. The next year, more than three-fourths of McClendon's annual compensation of $18.7 million came in the form of more Chesapeake stock, and the *Forbes* 400 list of wealthiest Americans ranked McClendon 220th.

No wonder he saw little reason to depart from strategy. In fact, as Chesapeake kept on leasing land and setting up rigs, it gained the title of the nation's most active driller and set a record for rig count not seen since the 1984 oil boom.

Setting up rigs wasn't all McClendon was doing. He and Ward were also hotly pursuing the Seattle Sonics basketball team, although a gag order prevented them from talking about it. McClendon, however, had a little trouble holding his tongue and was fined $250,000 in June 2008 for saying out loud what everyone knew—that he had bought the Sonics to move the team to Oklahoma City. McClendon was also deeply involved at the time in the launch of his American Clean Skies Foundation, which promoted cleaner energy—like natural gas—and in congressional lobbying for legislation that would do the same.

That year, 2008, McClendon seemed to step up his insider buying. Starting in February, as natural gas prices continued to rise, and as Chesapeake stock also moved steadily upward, McClendon bought in on a regular basis—at least monthly. It's a level of conviction—of confidence in his company—that seems nothing less than admirable.

McClendon Buying Spree 2008: Timeline[5]

February 26: 7,600 shares cost range of $46.47 to $46.55
February 26: 192,400 shares cost range of $45.65 to $46.55
February 27: 148,700 shares cost range of $45.61 to $46.07
February 27: 51,230 shares cost range of $45.68 to $46.16
February 28: 100,000 shares cost range of $46.06 to $46.21
February 29: 100,000 shares cost range of $45.24 to $45.40
March 5: 306,000 shares cost range of $46.13 to $46.41
March 6: 53,800 shares cost range of $45.77 to $45.91
March 6: 46,200 shares cost range of $45.54 to $45.76
April 2: 500,000 shares at a cost of $45.75
May 23: 203,000 shares cost range of $54.70 to $55.05
May 23: 446,000 shares cost range of $52.45 to $53.05
June 11: 200,000 shares cost range of $59.99 to $60.08
July 15: 750,000 shares at a cost of $57.25

By early July, when the stock peaked at nearly $70—McClendon, exercising his usual savvy, waited till the price dropped again before buying big—his holdings amounted to nearly 30 million shares, worth more than $2 billion. He kept going. By September 30, his stake registered at 33.4 million shares—5.8 percent of Chesapeake's common stock. The *Forbes* 400 list moved him up 86 slots—sending him from the 220th richest American to the 134th in one year.

But by then, gas prices and Chesapeake stock had begun their downward slide, and Aubrey McClendon was about to make news in a whole different way.

"Substantially All"

The headline came on October 10, 2008. The meat of the story was contained in the simple statement issued by the office of the chairman of Chesapeake Energy to the effect that McClendon had sold "substantially all" of his holdings in order to meet margin calls.

The statement tersely asserted that the sales were "involuntary and unexpected." It blamed the "worldwide financial crisis." And it added the usual disclaimer that the action "in no way" reflected Chesapeake's financial soundness or the chairman's view of "future performance potential."

The sales had come quickly—seemingly in a second. In fact, over the course of a mere three days—from Tuesday through Thursday, October 7 through 9—Aubrey McClendon was forced by his lenders to sell 31.5 million shares of stock. That represented 94 percent of his 5.8 percent stake. Valued at $2.2 billion at the stock's peak in July 2008, the shares sold for $569 million three months later. McClendon's holding in his company was down to shares worth a mere $32 million—a loss in net worth of nearly $2 billion.

Chesapeake itself, mirroring the position of its CEO, was of course incredibly leveraged to gas prices. Gas prices were falling and shareholders were heading for the exit, concerned that Chesapeake's hedging contracts wouldn't protect it against the plunge in natural gas prices. And as Chesapeake's stock price declined precipitously, eroding the value of the collateral McClendon had staked against his borrowings, he had to sell to meet the margin calls from nervous counterparties. The total bill for these margin calls came to roughly $700 million.

But while this two-billion-dollar mistake may have seemed like a sudden spasm, it was really a long time coming—and a long time building. "I got caught up in a wildfire that was bigger than I was," McClendon told a *Wall Street Journal* reporter the day after the announcement of his stock sale.[6]

True, but Aubrey McClendon himself had set the fire. His strategy to go anywhere and everywhere to buy and drill had been the driving force in Chesapeake's growth. And the policy of issuing equity and debt to fund the acquisitions had been the fuel of that growth. It looked like a brilliant strategy while natural gas prices were rising. It certainly created value and was seen by shareholders, with the exception of a few cautious naysayers, as a winning strategy. Nobody had ridden the strategy to a bigger win than Aubrey McClendon himself. He had done it by his own hand, by repeatedly—even aggressively—borrowing against his holdings to amplify those holdings. It was the other edge of the leverage sword, and it cut deep.

McClendon's mistake wasn't that he set the fire, however. His mistake was that he neglected to take precautions against getting burned by the heat of that $700 million margin call.

What Went Wrong

Too much leverage, too little diversity.

Those were Aubrey McClendon's two basic investing mistakes, but his example offers three lessons for investors. Two of the lessons are *not* to do what he did: Do not let yourself become overleveraged the way McClendon did, and do not put all your eggs in one basket, as he put all his in Chesapeake Energy. (And certainly do not do what McClendon also did when he leveraged the bet further with additional, sizeable investments in natural gas properties.) The third lesson for investors is that insider buying and selling do not necessarily mean what they seem to mean.

First, leverage. As we've seen in this book, and as is evident on any given day on Wall Street, it's as powerful a tool of investing as you can find. It does the hard work of making the investment possible, then magnifies the profit on the investment's return. Maybe its very power blinds investors to this fundamental fact about leverage: Buying on margin is borrowing money, and, eventually, the loan must be repaid.

Yes, that is all too easy for the average investor to forget—especially in the midst of that heady feeling you can get when an investment's value keeps going up, up, up. But Aubrey McClendon is not the average investor; he is the ultimate insider, the savviest of the savvy, a businessman who built a $50,000 start-up venture into the biggest natural gas producer in the nation and reaped a personal fortune in excess of $3 billion. He is a man who should have known that no bubble lasts forever, that no investment goes up without end, and that leverage therefore should be used in moderation. That's basic. It's Investing 101. And it should have been second nature to McClendon.

Second, diversification. This too is Investing 101. Don't put all your eggs in one basket is as sacred a tenet of investing as buy low, sell high. If anything, buying on margin makes diversification even more important, for if leverage is borrowing and borrowing is risk, diversification is a way of dispersing the risk. The principle is simple: Some eggs in the basket will lose, some will win. Margin calls on some investments can be offset by big gains on other leveraged investments. Again, this is basic investment wisdom. McClendon's persistent and heavy investing in Chesapeake may have shown loyalty. It may have been good public relations. It may even have been sound investing based on careful analysis leading to McClendon's passionately held conviction that Chesapeake stock was undervalued and that natural gas would evolve to become the dominant energy source for the United States. But even factoring all those things together, and with the best will in the world, the sheer size and volume of his stake in his company flew in the face of investing common sense.

Had Aubrey McClendon not been leveraged to his eyeballs, and had his leveraged position not been solely in one stock, he would have been far better equipped to confront the world financial crisis that he cited—not without justification—as the trigger of his $700 million margin call.

Why did it happen? Why did so brilliant, so shrewd, so well connected and well advised a businessman as Aubrey McClendon make these mistakes?

McClendon attributes it all to the world financial crisis. "I did not see the greatest economic downturn in 70 years coming around the corner," he has said. "I wish I could have been able to do so, but I was hardly alone in my inability to see it." In public statements, he has further described the crisis as a set of "extraordinary circumstances" that left him "very disappointed" to have been "required" to sell his Chesapeake stock. That is an apology; it is not an explanation. We have to look elsewhere for causes, and they are not too difficult to decipher.

One obvious reason is financial ambition. Even at the stratospheric levels of wealth achieved by an Aubrey McClendon, it seems it is always desirable to have more. That appears to be an inherently human response and probably had something to do with McClendon going hell-for-leather after more land, more rigs, and more personal holdings. But since desire for financial gain is at the heart of virtually all investing, it does not supply much of an explanation. That is, financial ambition may be why people invest, but it isn't why people invest in such a way as to fly in the face of history and common sense to their ultimate detriment.

Ego is another possible cause. Sure, you say to yourself, leverage is something people should be careful with—that is, *other people*. But it doesn't apply to me. Ditto with diversification: That's for novices; me, I've got it nailed. Arguably, no one has ever been in a better position to predict the outcome of an investment strategy than Aubrey McClendon, yet he didn't have it nailed; no one does.

McClendon's willingness to evidence his devotion to his company by buying its stock—virtually to the exclusion of all other stocks, or so it seemed—was somewhat unusual and was remarked on frequently. He liked answering the remarks. "I am frequently asked why I continue to buy Chesapeake's stock in the open market, and my reply is pretty simple," McClendon told investors back in 2006. He then reiterated his consistent position: "Chesapeake's stock has . . . substantial and largely unappreciated upside, and we have successfully mitigated many of the traditional risks associated with our industry."[7]

That's a perfectly sound reason for buying the stock. But buying it to the extent McClendon did—and with the leveraging he took on to do so—goes a bit beyond making a sound investment. It's a matter of amount; McClendon's was excessive. And perhaps it was ego that played a role in pushing the investing a degree too far. This is not a swipe at the merits of ego. Sometimes ego is constructive. But it is rarely constructive in investing and never when it clouds judgment and inserts an additional component of risk.

A third possible cause is that McClendon may have been either too close to the situation to see it straight on or perhaps was distracted by his other pursuits. The year 2008 was a busy one for him. McClendon was involved, at least through contributions, with a number of congressional races. He was lobbying existing congressional representatives for passage of the Natural Gas Act. His American Clean Skies Foundation was launching its CleanSkies.tv network, and

McClendon was on hand for the press launch and other activities. A number of these pursuits, particularly the latter two, had a direct bearing on Chesapeake's business prospects; the aim was to spread the gospel of natural gas as clean, less expensive energy—and then watch the price of the commodity soar. Perhaps, consumed by these endeavors and by the eroding price of natural gas—a function of increasing production and lessening demand amid a global financial crisis—he was unable to focus on the twin evils of margin and its consequences.

Do these answers explain why McClendon got blindsided by the financial and credit tsunami that caught so many by surprise? Maybe not. Maybe, as he contends, neither he nor anyone else could possibly have seen over the horizon of global prosperity to the perfect storm that would act like a plague on the world economy. That may be true, but only to a certain extent and not to the extent of absolution. But absolution from what? From whom? Certainly McClendon was entitled to do what he did. Unlike 99.9 percent of the rest of the world, however, he could lose everything he had invested in Chesapeake and still be wealthier than that 99.9 percent. Financial tsunamis rarely emit a warning signal; for the average investor—if not an Aubrey McClendon—that most certainly argues for moderation of risk.

And therein lies the heart of the matter: Going all in and assessing the risk of doing so if things turn ugly are well within an individual's control. The worldwide financial crisis is not. Yes, Aubrey McClendon should have seen that the amount of leverage he was assuming was simply not sustainable. He should have seen that Chesapeake could not continue endlessly to finance that level of debt. And it is easy enough to say that had Aubrey McClendon been more risk sensitive, as opposed to risk averse, he would have seen all that, and then his company would have been better able to withstand the onslaught of counterparties caught in the credit crunch. That onslaught cost the company where it hurt, requiring it to sell some of the natural gas–producing assets that it had accumulated over the years. McClendon's answer to this is to insist that "If I had been risk averse, Chesapeake would not exist today, and I would be quietly toiling in someone's accounting office." As to being "risk sensitive" versus "risk averse," McClendon doesn't comment.

Investing in Chesapeake the way he did seems entirely in accord with McClendon's personality and with his history in business and politics: If you approve of something, bet on it big. McClendon had a lot of money to bet with: Worrying about whether you can afford to lose just may not have anything to do with it.

Following Insider Moves

And that brings us to the third lesson that McClendon's experience provides. In addition to controlling your investing behavior so you don't over leverage yourself or put too many eggs in one investment basket, the Chesapeake debacle teaches investors to be wary of following insider moves.

The investment transactions of corporate officers, directors, or major shareholders vis-à-vis their own company must, by law, be publicly disclosed. Many professionals track and monitor these moves as a matter of course, then simply mimic them. But the fact of the matter is that insider moves may not always mean what they look like they mean. So while it may make sense to look at what insiders do, their moves should be regarded less as prescriptions to be followed than as tea leaves to be sifted and read carefully for clues.

Conventional wisdom has it, for example, that insider buying means that a stock is going up—therefore you should buy it too; insider selling means that a stock is going down—therefore, you should unload your supply of it quickly. But in fact, even when insiders buy stock and it does go up in value, that may not be why they bought it. The correlation may be entirely coincidental. So what counts is to explore the context of and the motivation for the buy or sell transaction to see what signals it may be giving.

Context and motivation figured to some extent in McClendon's insider buying, to take just one example. Under the terms of his employment contract—the context—he was required to own Chesapeake stock equivalent to five times the combined value of his salary and bonus. Of course, his holdings far, far exceeded this level, so there was another motivation at work. But knowing the context sheds light on the motivation: Here's how much McClendon had to buy, here's how much he did buy, draw your own conclusion.

After all, when McClendon sold his shares of Chesapeake, the company's stock was indeed trading down, but McClendon didn't make the sale because of the market action. It was because he was margined. If you're an investor in Chesapeake, it's important to know that. Knowing it doesn't mean you won't decide to sell your shares of Chesapeake; you very well may. But you will have done it not in slavish imitation of a business leader but rather with a full understanding of the situation.

Or suppose a CEO buys 10,000 shares of his company's stock at $10 a share. On its face, that looks like a good buy. But if it turns out that the CEO actually draws down an annual salary of $5 million, his $100,000 investment in the company looks cosmetic. And if that is the case, then it is worth asking (a) whether you should follow this CEO in this or any other matter and (b) why the CEO of the company is applying makeup.

Rule 10-5-b

Rule 10-5-b is the Securities and Exchange Commission (SEC) regulation prohibiting insider trading—that is, trading by individuals who have access to information about the company that is not available to the public at large, which is considered ipso facto unfair. Insider trading has been officially outlawed since the Securities Act of 1934, but it was "clarified" in 1942 to answer the case of a corporate executive who was bad-mouthing his company publicly at the same time that he was buying its stock. Over the years, the rule has consistently been revised and adjusted to call for more disclosure of information to more people. The rule today prohibits acts of both commission and omission that may constitute fraud or deceit with regard to both the buying and selling of a security. Here is what the law says:

It shall be unlawful for any person, directly or indirectly, by the use of any means or instrumentality of interstate commerce, or of the mails or of any facility of any national securities exchange,

(a) To employ any device, scheme, or artifice to defraud,
(b) To make any untrue statement of a material fact or to omit to state a material fact necessary in order to make the statements made, in the light of the circumstances under which they were made, not misleading, or
(c) To engage in any act, practice, or course of business which operates or would operate as a fraud or deceit upon any person, in connection with the purchase or sale of any security.

It is why officers of a company typically must reveal publicly any trades they make in the company's stock.

A Kind of Epilogue

McClendon was down but not out as a result of his sell-off—by no means stopped in his tracks. The loss of $2 billion from a fortune of $3 billion is statistically catastrophic and may well be psychically stunning, but it probably did not affect the daily life of the McClendon family in any material way.

Even the announcement of the debacle in October included news about a number of drastic cost-cutting measures Chesapeake had put in place—along with the sale of some key assets, including the company's stake in certain undeveloped natural gas sources. Two months later, in December 2008, McClendon was holding a press conference to proclaim that Chesapeake was back from the grave. The cost cutting and asset selling had worked, he asserted. Chesapeake's stock at the time was trading at not quite $14, but the company had liquidity, it was hedged, and it was financially sound and stable.

By January 2009, McClendon was back buying shares in Chesapeake, whose board of directors renewed his contract as CEO for another five years. The terms of the renewal: an annual salary of $975,000, McClendon's agreement to stay on for the full five-year term of the contract, and a once-only retention payment to the chairman of $75 million. That payment was aimed not only at seducing McClendon away from pursuing what the company described in the SEC filing as "other entrepreneurial opportunities"; it also helped him defray some of that $177.7 million reimbursement for his ownership stake in the company's wells. **The renewal contract brilliantly highlights the difference between privileged, cosseted CEOs of humongous energy companies and the average investor; when the latter makes an investing mistake, no bonus payment is forthcoming to soften the blow.**

In February 2009, Chesapeake announced that a substantive write-down on the value of its assets had pulled it to a loss for the fourth quarter of 2008. Chesapeake stock fell another 8 percent. By March, the company was calling itself "the largest independent producer of natural gas in the U.S.," a come-down from being the largest producer—period—of gas in the nation, but only a slide from number one to number two. If history is a guide, Chesapeake may well reclaim the top spot at some point.

The wine auction was held in two sections: Half of what was sold was offered at Sotheby's New York; the other half was shipped in temperature-controlled containers to the Hong Kong convention and exhibition center for sale under Sotheby's auspices there. It is one way, if not perhaps the preferred way, to liquidate assets when you have leveraged more than you could afford to lose.

Lessons Learned

- *Don't buy what you can't afford to own and can't afford to lose.* Buying on margin allows you to increase your investment by borrowing against the security you are positioning, but the strategy doesn't leave much "margin" for error. The penalty for being wrong in this situation could be the loss of your entire principal; unleveraged, you would lose a smaller amount. Margin is not always a bad tactic. In fact, if used responsibly within the context of what you can afford to lose, it can increase your return. Thus, it may be wise to assess what a plausible downside target is and to keep enough additional collateral on the side in case you have to shore up the requirement. This way you are less likely to be sold out of your position.
- *Margin concentrates a position.* You may be better off buying multiple securities with some margin. That lets you leverage your return while diversifying your holdings.
- *Margin can take a decision out of your hands.* When you buy on margin and the security declines in value, the decision to sell is not necessarily yours. When the security declines to a certain level, the collateral is called in and liquidated unless you provide additional capital. Again, to avoid this outcome, you may not want to use the entire margin available to you.
- *Insider activity is only one data point.* Ignore buying and selling by senior executives unless you can understand the rationale for the action. For example, insiders may have to buy stock because of their employment contracts, or they may have to sell because of financial pressures unrelated to their company's business—as in McClendon's case. His sale of Chesapeake stock had nothing to do with the prospects for the business, which were extremely positive. Insiders generally have a much longer investment time horizon. Their financial circumstances may make them more or less willing or able to hold the stock through downturns. When their stock is declining, some CEOs will buy a token amount of stock relative to their financial means. Don't fall for this tactic. Make sure their purchase is financially significant to them before using it as a data point.

4

Bill Ackman

DETOUR FROM DISCIPLINE

The *American Heritage Dictionary of the English Language* defines discipline as "control obtained by enforcing compliance or order; a systematic method to obtain obedience; a set of rules or methods, as those regulating the practice of a monastic order." If there is any parallel to be drawn between the world of investing and the world of the cloister, it is that both investors in the tumult of Wall Street and monks in the quiet of the cloister try to live by holy rule. On Wall Street, it is called investment discipline, and, not unlike the vows of behavior to which monks submit, it is a set of standards and prescriptions that define practice and behavior. Make no mistake: This discipline bears no relation to government regulation. Investment discipline is something that investors themselves generate and define—for their own purposes and within their own individual investment styles. Yet on Wall Street as in the cloister, experience shows that deviation from discipline can be costly indeed.

That may be especially so in the world of *activist investing*.

You've heard of *passive investing*. That's where you invest in an index fund, then go home, pull the covers over your head, close your eyes, and let the market do what the market will do.

And you've also surely heard of *active investing*, in which the investor or fund manager works the market daily, performing virtually round-the-clock research and due diligence and buying and selling day after day in response to or in anticipation of world events or emerging data.

Activist investing is something else altogether. What the activist investor does is buy a large enough position in a company's stock to be able to influence or control the company's strategic direction.

Where the passive investor mitigates risk through diversification and the active investor mitigates it through relentless focus, the activist investor limits risk through taking charge—or at least, trying to.

Since this chapter is about one of the most formidable of the current crop of activist investors, Bill Ackman, and since Ackman is a man who enjoys playing tennis, think of the differences in tennis terms: The passive investor is the baseline player, hanging back and waiting for the ground strokes. The active investor is the volleyer, hitting shots off a short bounce while trying for a wide range of angles And the activist investor? He's the one charging the net, ready to dictate play, and applying pressure with bulletlike shots.

Tennis player Ackman describes a mistake by investor Ackman as "an unforced error." On the court, an unforced error is a shot the player would normally execute, either keeping the volley going or scoring the point. The key to any shot, say tennis experts, is to maintain the disciplines of time and position. If you let either discipline slip even a little—if your timing is off or if you're wrong-footed or off-balance or not in the right place—you simply miss. In a close match, even one miss can make you a loser.

In the investment arena, discipline may indeed involve timing and where you put your feet, but above all, it is there to mitigate risk. Within an investment style, investment discipline drills down to identify and quantify risk, then to define the parameters of risk for the varied instruments of the investment game. Maybe your investment style is that of seeking out perceived low-risk value stocks. You might define a discipline for that style that targets companies with a certain price-to-earnings ratio or that sets a debt limit on the balance sheet of any company you'd consider a candidate for investment.

Whatever the particular criteria, the discipline is there to be adhered to. That's what discipline is for. Detour from it even briefly, and you may be paying for the mistake for some time.

I Love You, You're Perfect, Now Change

Activist investing of the type Bill Ackman engages in is a simple and powerful tool. Activist investors look for opportunities to "unlock the value" they believe a company's current strategic direction is failing to maximize. The hint that there may be value to be unlocked is that the company's stock is trading at a low price; if the investor can ascertain that the price represents a discount in terms of the intrinsic value yet to be unlocked, that company is probably a good investment. An underperforming stock is also a hint of potentially widespread dissatisfaction among the shareholder base. Dissatisfied shareholders ipso facto create a formidable ally for those pressuring management for change—and represent fertile ground for activist investors.

So activist investors usually troll among companies that have poor share price performance, looking to see if they have strengths that are not obvious and/or weaknesses that can be profitably rectified. Different investors establish different disciplines for this selection process, and the focus and emphasis may vary from investor to investor. But whatever the specific net an investor casts, it is likely to haul in such catches as large and possibly undervalued real estate holdings, business activities that may not be achieving scale or synergies, management teams that have failed to meet their own strategic objectives. Almost all investors want to reel in companies that have a strong balance sheet with low debt levels and underused cash, especially if the company is not already controlled by a single, powerful shareholder or doesn't have a strong management presence among the shareholder base. To different investors with their different selection disciplines, any and all of these may be signals of intrinsic value that may make the companies candidates for investment.

Once a company is targeted, the investor begins to purchase stock. When the investor's position exceeds 5 percent of the company's outstanding shares, he or she must file with the Securities and Exchange Commission either a 13-G form indicating that the investment is passive or a 13-D, possibly indicating an active—read: activist—investment.

The 13-D activist investor then typically undertakes any of a range of activist measures. Usually, he'll start with a private meeting with the management of the target company, during which he is likely to propose initiatives designed to unlock shareholder value and receive ratification in a higher stock price. One such initiative might be to use the company's cash balance to repurchase shares, thus increasing the value of each remaining outstanding share. Other initiatives might be for a range of cost-cutting measures—from firing staff to shutting off the lights at night to reducing use of the company-owned fleet of jets. The activist might suggest that a pending acquisition is not advisable, or that the company should put itself up for sale in whole or in part. Or he might try to replace existing management, a move said existing chief executive officer (CEO) and staff would certainly not favor and probably would seek to avoid at all costs.

In one form or another, activist investing has been around since the 1980s. Its first appearance was as greenmail, an unsavory but often effective tactic in which a single shareholder looks for a payoff *not* to take over a company. Today, there is a range of activist investing motivations and intentions, and it is possible to debate whether the activist's aim in bending the will of company management is altruistic—for the benefit of all shareholders—or selfish—for the sole benefit of the activist. Whatever the motivation, however, the goal is the same—a higher stock price as the end game.

And activist investing is on the rise. FactSet Research Systems, the financial data and software company, reported that from 2006 to 2007, the last year for which figures were available as of this writing, the number of activist investing "campaigns" increased 17 percent—from 429 in 2006 to 501 in 2007, including 138 activist debuts by institutional investors and hedge funds.[1]

The increase was noticeable enough to have spurred a new industry of lawyers and financial public relations consultants who advise companies on how to avoid being targeted by activist investors or, once targeted, how to defend against the campaign. Needless to say, these companies and their advisors see activist investors not as players of a game typically associated with strawberries and Champagne enjoyed on manicured lawns but as predatory beasts. It is not coincidental that FactSet calls its database on activist campaigns SharkWatch. And it is perhaps instructive that SharkWatch maintains a list of the *crème de la crème* among the predators it tracks; somewhat akin to a pop radio station's list of biggest hits, the list has been dubbed the SharkWatch 50.

On the Rise

William A. Ackman surely ranks among the top activist investors of the day. Ackman is the founder and president of Pershing Square Capital Management—with hedge fund assets under management of approximately $6 billion. Launched in 2004, Pershing Square is Ackman's Act Two. Act One was Gotham Partners, which he and

Harvard Business School classmate David P. Berkowitz founded in 1993, when Ackman was just 26. At the time, the fund's focus was pretty much on commercial real estate, an interest Ackman inherited—perhaps genetically—from his family's generations-long involvement in the business. Out of the gate, Gotham had seed money of $3 million, which it managed to grow to $568 million by 2000, the peak of its success. By 2003, however, style drift, illiquidity, and some rescue moves that backfired brought the firm tumbling down. The collapse was exacerbated by an investigation by the then Attorney General of New York, hedge fund hunter Eliot Spitzer. The investigation yielded no findings. Although both Gotham and its principals were exonerated of any wrongdoing, and the wind-down of the business eventually delivered to investors a threefold increase on their capital, the curtain was definitely down on that act.

For a man unaccustomed to failure, it was perhaps a sobering experience. It was almost certainly a learning experience, and it is fair to assume that Ackman brought its lessons to his new venture.

Bill Ackman went into investing because when he was working for his father's commercial real estate company right out of college, "the people clearly having the most fun were the people making the investment decisions." For a man of such obvious intellectual rigor, surely part of the fun is the discipline of the decision-making process—choosing the businesses in which to invest, then shaping the structure of the investment. The particular Pershing Square discipline—the way Ackman goes about the process—is his signature in the world of activist investing. It is what distinguishes Pershing Square from the pack.

What Ackman is looking for, as he himself has written, are businesses "for which we can predict with a high degree of confidence their future cash flows—not precisely, but within a reasonable band of outcomes."[2] To identify such businesses, Pershing Square has articulated six selection criteria:[3]

1. The business must be a mid-cap or large-cap company.
2. It should not be controlled by a single shareholder.
3. It should be minimally dependent on the capital markets.
4. It should have low financial leverage, if any, and modest economic activity.
5. The asset base should contain hidden value.
6. It should be a catalyst for value creation that Pershing Square's involvement can unlock.

In addition, of course, the price must be right; that is, the company must be trading at a large discount to the intrinsic value the selection discipline has uncovered. And in fact, Ackman concedes that he may bend or even waive one of the six selection criteria if the price is particularly good. In other words, he might detour from discipline if he is confident enough of the rewards of doing so.

In any event, once candidates are selected, the discipline of the process then requires analysis of the reasons for the undervaluation. This means that the Pershing team looks hard at governance structure, management skill and expertise, concentration of ownership, and of course the balance sheet—they really don't want to see leverage there—to assess "whether we can effectuate change in order to unlock value."[4]

It is a process that takes time and care as well as skill and savvy. And that is one reason why Pershing's portfolio is so highly concentrated; the limited number of positions in the portfolio—only from 10 to perhaps 15 stocks at any one time, often no more than a dozen—offers the luxury of very deep due diligence, which is a distinguishing characteristic of Ackman's brand of activist investing. Of course, the highly concentrated portfolio also enables ownership positions large enough to make the management of targeted companies sit up and take notice. And big positions can lead to big returns. All the more reason to do the kind of very deep diligence for which Ackman is noted. Former Pershing analyst Richard "Mick" McGuire likens the process to "turning over rocks." You do it slowly, one rock at a time, drilling down to whatever depth of granularity is necessary. "You have to be patient," says McGuire, "and you have to be absolutely disciplined in your focus on the kinds of business you want." Once you've found the kind of business you want, McGuire goes on, "you have to be willing to be an activist, a catalyst to close the value gap." That's the beautiful part about activist investing: Activists don't have to weigh probabilities about what would happen if a certain course of action were followed and about what the business would then be worth. Instead, activists can make it happen and realize the premium. That must be fun too.

In 1995, for example, Ackman became an activist investor in Wendy's and nudged management to spin off its doughnut chain, Tim Hortons Inc., reckoning that the parts were worth more than the whole—that is, that the value of Tim Horton's had been obscured by the much larger corporate parent. When Wendy's followed Ackman's suggestion and sold off the doughnut chain, the value of Wendy's stock more than doubled.

Perhaps emboldened by this success, Ackman in 2003 went after McDonald's, seeing not just a global brand but a lot of valuable real estate under all those golden arches. Pershing Square wanted the giant chain to spin off its real estate holdings into a real estate investment trust (REIT), then borrow to finance a massive share repurchase and debt refinancing. Ackman estimated the plan could boost the stock price by 40 percent. McDonald's, however, persistently said no to the sale of its real estate, but it undertook other actions that just as persistently raised the stock price. By the time Ackman sold his stock in December 2007, its value had pretty much doubled.

By that time, he had already moved heavily into retail, investing in such big-box stores as Sears as well as in the Barnes & Noble bookstore chain. Given the retail sector's declining performance, Ackman looked to the balance sheet—the value of legendary brands, real estate assets, receivables, and credit cards—to find hidden value his active involvement could unlock. Perhaps it was the zeal to do so that made him bend, perhaps even waive, the selection criteria discipline he had so carefully and assiduously created. Whatever the reason, the deviation from discipline laid the groundwork for that unforced error in the book business and for a very big loss in the big-box megastore sector.

Betting on Books

Barnes & Noble was the "starter" investment for Pershing Square in the book business. The world's largest bookseller, Barnes & Noble had the dominant market share, highly capable management, an enduring brand, enormous amounts of net cash, and was trading at a 20 percent discount. It seemed an obvious candidate within the Pershing Square discipline. In time, however, Ackman would sell his Barnes & Noble position and would instead make Borders, Barnes & Noble's distant competitor, his standard-bearer in the book business.

As businesses go, the book trade didn't constitute a particularly "sexy" investment, but it looked to Pershing Square like a good one. Ackman noted the bizarre publishing tradition in which booksellers can return their unsold inventory to the publisher for a total refund—not helpful if you are the publisher, but attractive to an investor as a signal of low inventory risk. Mick McGuire, who had been following the book business for Pershing since 2004, loved the fact that "the depreciation of the fixtures in a bookstore is bigger than the reinvestment to maintain them"—another plus for cash flow, which, if not growth-oriented, was nevertheless steady. Add in the relatively low cost of generating the cash flow and the resilience of books as a low-cost form of entertainment, and you have the chance for an investment that, while not transformational, could prove of incremental value. Sometimes simple is good.

Ackman was also impressed by the fact that "the customer spends an average of an hour or more in a bookstore." In his eyes, bookstores constituted that rare retail species, the destination store—a place to which people travel for the express purpose of spending time there. In fact, his vision of bookstores was that they weren't actually bookstores at all but were mini-shopping malls. Stock them with a range of higher-margin products in addition to books, and you could give the affluent, educated consumers who enjoy the bookstore "experience" lots of high-dollar-value buying choices during their hour or of browsing. That is likely the vision Ackman would have tried to realize at Borders if there hadn't been the mistake of that unforced error.

It was while doing due diligence on Barnes & Noble that the Borders opportunity first manifested itself. It was an obvious connection: The two companies were not only of the same breed but represented essentially a duopoly—*the* bricks-and-mortar bookselling chains. Borders seemed to possess similar investment attributes as Barnes & Noble: cash generation, low inventory risk, a proven form of entertainment, and so on. But the parallel did not track perfectly; as Mick McGuire puts it, "in a series of areas, Borders was lagging Barnes & Noble."

It seemed then—and in retrospect, with acute 20-20 vision, it is blindingly evident—that on every point on which Barnes & Noble hit the mark in terms of Pershing Square's selection discipline criteria, Borders fell just a shade short. Barnes & Noble was well managed, stable, achieving high margins, and unburdened by leverage. Borders was, concedes Mick McGuire, "undermanaged, underearning, facing a series of challenges—or opportunities, and operating with a levered balance sheet."

An important signal of the quality of Barnes & Noble management was the set of strategic actions the firm had taken back in 1999 and 2000 in the face of declining fortunes. The thrust of those actions was to retrench and restructure. Seeing that locating their stores within shopping malls produced a subpar return on capital, Barnes & Noble aggressively reduced its roster of more than 500 mall stores to a mere 50. Barnes & Noble also carefully reviewed the diversity of products offered in its stores and committed to purging from the shelves those that were not profitable. Reading the tea leaves on digital media—the downturn in consumer interest in CDs versus MP3 downloads—the firm reduced its exposure to such media and focused instead on product categories that could not be handled via Internet and iPod.

The Borders response, by contrast, was to try to grow its way out of trouble. It reduced the number of its Waldenbooks mall stores only minimally, and where Barnes & Noble reaffirmed its identity as "bookseller," Borders, reluctant to shrink the digital media portion of its offering, continued to define itself as a purveyor of books, music, and movies. Moreover, the firm had expanded overseas into the United Kingdom with both superstore and small-format concepts, and management continued to invest substantively in these stores, despite the fact that they did not perform well. It was a case of continuing to throw good money after bad; it would have made more sense to pay down debt and streamline operations to increase operating margins.

Still, it seemed to the Pershing Square analysts that Borders was the same core business as Barnes & Noble, that—potentially, at least—it presented the same mini-shopping mall paradigm that Ackman envisaged in his overall assessment of what the "bookstore experience" could become. Deconstruct Borders into its separate elements—superstore, mall business, international reach—and, says Mick McGuire, "it looks like a Barnes & Noble that is underperforming its potential." Rationalize and monetize each segment of the business, and for the price at which Borders was trading, it becomes an attractive investment—certainly if the challenges can be met successfully, and maybe even if they're not. And of course as activists, unafraid to engage managements of their portfolio companies if need be, Pershing Square was willing to help lead Borders down the same evolutionary path that Barnes & Noble had taken.

So, while Barnes & Noble offered little downside as an investment but also, as a pretty well optimized business, less upside, the upside on a Borders bet could be really exciting, even though it had a much bigger downside. Barnes & Noble, with its much tighter risk/reward scenario, presented a potential upside of only some 20 percent, with a downside also limited to that amount. Few if any investment professionals think it advisable to enter into an investment in which the risk/reward equation is in balance, however; it's essential to do an additional calculation that assesses the probability of the outcome. In the case of Barnes & Noble, a mature, almost boring company, the probability of achieving the upside was far greater than the chance of a loss in the stock. With Borders, however, as with most troubled companies, the potential return on investment was much higher—but entailed significantly greater risk. Or as McGuire puts is: "One won't grow; the other might double if you do the business right." In a portfolio as highly concentrated as Pershing Square's, where no investment represents more than about 10 percent of the total portfolio, might it not be worth it—a "fundamental value play," in McGuire's words—to take a position in Borders and go for the dynamic upside reward if it succeeded?

A couple of other factors seemed favorable in terms of that essential additional calculation on outcome probability. For one thing, a new management team was now in place, and this group seemed to have the right sense of what needed to be fixed—in Ackman's words: "bloated inventories, bad systems, and weaker margins than Barnes & Noble." The new team was headed by CEO George Jones, who "grew up in the Target franchise," as McGuire puts it—a franchise that Pershing Square had assessed as very well managed indeed. As Pershing's point man for the Borders investment, McGuire sat down with Jones, and the two came to a meeting of the minds. In addition, some months earlier, a number of private equity firms had expressed interest in purchasing Borders at prices well in excess of where the stock was trading. A seemingly good new management team, potential purchasers, and the prospect of a hot reward if everything gelled: All these factors nudged the Pershing Square analysis toward the positive until it all seemed to come down to a simple equation—either fix it for what McGuire calls "an exciting upside," or sell it.

"So," says Ackman, in 2006, "we bought a passive stake and sat back to watch what happened." Significantly, Pershing Square's passive stake in Borders was not an all-in bet; Ackman limited his investment to a smaller percentage of the portfolio than McDonald's or Wendy's had occupied.

That would turn out to be prescient, for what happened was not very reassuring. The new management team, to put it as simply as possible, was not very effective. Yes, they sold some overseas subsidiaries, but they still didn't rationalize the enterprise in any strategically meaningful ways. Meanwhile, a year in, the company announced a plan to issue convertible bonds. Pershing Square analysts thought the proposed transaction would be disadvantageous to shareholders—it would dilute their ownership interest—and would further encumber the Borders balance sheet. The deal was eventually withdrawn, but, says Ackman, the fact that it was tried "was the signal that management didn't know what it was doing."

Confirming that assessment, Borders next entered into a price war with Barnes & Noble, virtually its only non-Internet rival. This struck Ackman as plain foolish. "Amazon is cheaper than either of them," he contends. "People go to bookstores to hang out, not to buy a cheaper book." The price war had the effect of driving margins down even further as the firm spent heavily on promotions and, in an effort to prop up its falling stock, raised its dividend— another ill-advised move for a levered company. As if all that weren't enough pressure, a major shareholder announced the launch of a proxy war. At that point, CEO Jones asked Pershing Square to take on a more activist role in the business, and it did so, filing a 13-D and recommending one director in 2007 and another, Mick McGuire himself, in January 2008.

In its new activist role, Pershing Square quickly saw that the financial situation was dire. Ackman therefore put together a financing proposal under which Pershing would infuse cash into the company. In return for putting more money on the line, Pershing laid out a number of requirements, the most important of which called for the Borders board of directors to put the company up for sale. This was the last recourse—the if-all-else-fails safety net of the investment thesis. Unfortunately, the timing was bad: Retail mergers had ground to a virtual halt in an economic environment so uncertain that potential acquirers had all they could do to stay focused on their own business, much less consider taking over somebody else's. As Ackman says simply: "We missed the market, so the sale failed." Under the terms of the financing agreement, Borders turned over more stock to Pershing Square.

In January 2009, Ackman held 33.62 percent of Borders stock and helped recruit a new CEO, Ron Marshall, an expert at turning around failed companies. Mick McGuire left Pershing Square to serve as chairman of the board of directors of Borders Group.

At the time, Borders stock was trading at 30 cents a share. Said the new chairman shortly after taking over: "Our break-even valuation—that is, where the stock would have to go for us to recover all our investment capital—would be $10 a share." At the time, that looked like a long way up.

The bet on books had failed.

Betting on Books: Timeline

October 2006: Pershing Square takes initial 3 percent stake in Borders Group Inc.'s shares.

November 2006: Stake is raised to more than 11 percent; the stock value rises.

October 2007: Pershing Square files 13-D declaring activist intentions.

March 2008: Under agreement, Pershing Square, with an 18 percent stake in the company, loans Borders operating cash while Borders puts itself up for sale, begins sell-off of foreign assets, and attempts to reduce debt.

October 2008: As agreed, after failing to find a buyer, Borders issues 5.2 million stock warrants in a compelled sale to Pershing Square.

January 2009: Amended 13-D notes "beneficial ownership" of 33.62 percent of Borders shares. New management brought in. Stock sinks to 30 cents a share.

Source: Pershing Square Capital Management.

Aiming at Target

Target, the anti–Wal-Mart, the so-called upscale discount retailer that had once bought all the advertising space in an issue of *The New Yorker* magazine, looked like a very different ball game from Borders. On paper, at least, it did not seem to conform to the popular notion of a value investment. In April 2007, when Ackman first began buying shares, the price ranged from $58 to $67 per share— not particularly a fire sale. Notably, Ackman bought the stock as it was rising. In fact, the price had increased 45 percent during the previous 12 months. That rise was no doubt fueled by the company's superb performance, for which its management received plaudits from numerous sources. One of them was *Chief Executive Magazine,* which had named Target's Bob Ulrich CEO of the Year.

Bill Ackman was the first to acknowledge the skill of Target's management. In fact, in asserting his belief that the stock was undervalued, he paid homage to Ulrich and the rest of the team, equating his investment in the company—a 9.6 percent stake by the summer of 2007—with a vote of confidence in their managerial abilities. He made it clear that Target's management and Pershing Square's financial professionals would together be able to unlock substantive further value from the Target proposition.

To that end, Ackman created a special entity, Pershing Square IV, as the vehicle for his Target stake. The stake cost Pershing Square $1.98 billion—$158 million for nearly 2.5 million shares and $1.6 billion for options on 79.2 million more shares. Yet even as he announced his 9.6 percent stake, in July 2007, it still was not clear exactly where Ackman intended to find the value he intended to unlock.

In August, Pershing pros and Target managers got together for a meeting, and Ackman made it at least partially clear. First on his list was a partnership deal on Target's credit card business. Ackman saw the business as an asset that could be sold to pay for maximizing Target's capital structure through the repurchase of shares, which was the second item on the Ackman agenda.

Target management, however, was inclined to view the credit card portfolio as an integral part of the company's relationship with customers. They were not eager to share the portfolio or give up control over it, but they did agree to review the Ackman suggestion. Meanwhile, in November 2007, Target management announced a $10 billion share repurchase authorization; it eventually spent half of the authorization to buy back nearly 11 percent of its shares.

In May 2008, Ackman first broached to management the third plank of his Target program: real estate. Simply put, Ackman saw Target's 85 percent ownership of its 1,500 stores nationwide, many occupying highly desirable pieces of geography, as a prime asset that could be sold—again, to maximize capital and raise the company's share value.

Target's much-praised management may have gulped, but they listened. Ackman invited Goldman Sachs to participate in crafting a formal proposal on selling off the real estate assets, and Pershing and Goldman staffers worked throughout that summer and fall of 2008 to prepare the proposal. In the interim, Target announced the sale of a 47 percent interest in its receivables to J.P. Morgan Chase. The deal was not structured as the partnership arrangement Ackman would have liked; the reason, says Ackman, was Target's "desire for control."

The real estate proposal was presented at the end of October. In its broad outline, it was similar to what Ackman had urged of McDonald's, Wendy's, and others—a formula that was by now virtually an Ackman signature: Spin off the real estate assets into a tax-free, publicly traded real estate investment trust so as to increase the value of Target and its shares. Under the terms of the proposal, the spin-off REIT would own only the land under the stores, with Target retaining ownership of the buildings; the REIT would rent the land back to Target under a 75-year lease.

"There is a very large real estate company, one of the largest in the country, inside the [Target] business," Ackman asserted in making the proposal.[5] Indeed, the resulting REIT would be the largest such entity in the nation and would become the 62nd largest company in the Standard & Poor's 500—if it existed.

But Target management balked at the idea. They expressed concerns over what the impact of such a sale of key assets might be on their debt rating, their borrowing costs, and their liquidity—especially in a credit market growing increasingly tight.

So Pershing Square amiably went back to the drawing board to work on a revised transaction that would address the company's concerns. Since 2008 was drawing to a close, Ackman and his staff decided that it would make more sense to present the revised transaction after the 2008 holiday season—the peak of the year, of course, for retailers.

But the 2008 holiday season was anything but a peak for retailers, including upscale discount retailers. Target's sales fell 4.1 percent—not unexpected, given consumer reluctance to spend—but the needed markdowns diminished profits. Defaults on credit card payments further eroded margins. In January 2009, Target's stock sank by nearly 10 percent.

Pershing Square IV, however, lost 40.1 percent of its value. In a way, it was even worse than that. Because the fund primarily had used stock options to bet that Target's stock would rise, the loss was magnified. In fact, by the end of February 2009, the Pershing Square IV fund had declined by 90 percent, a far worse performance than if Ackman had purchased the underlying shares. "It's a disaster," he told the *Wall Street Journal* on February 8. That was a Sunday; the *Journal*'s reporter found him in his office at night. He was there writing a follow-up letter to his investors. "I apologize profusely," Ackman wrote, and he added: "Bottom line, Pershing Square IV has been one of the greatest disappointments of my career to date." (There was more disappointment to come: In March, Ackman launched a proxy fight to gain seats on the Target board. He lost the fight two months later.)

The real disaster of Ackman's billion-dollar Target mistake is that the company was, as he clearly saw, a quality company that outperformed most other retailers, as both a retailer and a stock. It may even continue to do so. Indeed, by the end of the first quarter of 2009, Pershing Square's Target fund had inched up 48 percent out of its 90 percent decline—still neither a win nor a recovery, but perhaps a sign of better times ahead. *But it doesn't matter.* It didn't matter that Ackman bet on a horse that was definitely a winner, because the jockey paced himself for a mile and a half on a course a mile long. His timing was off, and so was Ackman's, as he rolled his 2010 option calls into 2011. When the aim is to realize a return on your investors' money, timing counts.

Aiming at Target: Timeline

April 2007: Ackman starts buying Target shares.

July 2007: The Pershing Square stake is at 9.6 percent of Target shares.

August 2007: Pershing meets with Target management to discuss credit card partnership and share repurchase ideas.

November 2007: Target announces a $10 billion share repurchase authorization.

May 2008: Ackman broaches idea of a real estate transaction; Target announces the sale of a 47 percent interest in its receivables to J.P. Morgan Chase.

July 2008: Pershing meets with Target and representatives of Goldman Sachs to discuss the real estate opportunity.

October 2008: Pershing presents its real estate solution to Target's board, which expresses "concerns."

January 2009: Pershing Square IV loses 40 percent of its value.

February 2009: Ackman apologizes to investors.

March 16, 2009: Ackman launches proxy fight to gain board seats for hand-picked representatives.

May 29, 2009: Ackman loses proxy fight.

What Went Wrong

Blame Archimedes.

"Give me a place to stand," the inventor of the lever is reputed to have said, "and I will move the earth." In a nutshell, that's what levers do: For little effort, you can achieve great gains—gains that otherwise would not be possible. That's the case when a small gardener levers a huge rock out of her perennial patch, and it's the case when an investor uses money he doesn't have to make an investment that, if it pans out, will return a greatly magnified amount on the money put in. The only question for the investor is where he gets the money he doesn't have. The usual answer, of course, is that he borrows it. But there's another answer people sometimes forget: options.

In a very real sense, options are a more esoteric and correspondingly riskier form of borrowing. What you buy when you buy an option is the right—but not the obligation—to buy a particular asset. That's quite a difference from the leverage gained by borrowing. When you borrow money to buy an asset, you own that asset; its intrinsic value is yours, for better or worse. If you buy an option, you have a contract to buy a specified quantity of the asset at an agreed-on price—the so-called strike price—at some time on or before the expiration date of the contract. On that date, you either exercise the option—that is, buy the asset at the strike price—or walk away and let the contract expire. And along the way, that *right* that you own may depreciate in value, even as the underlying stock stays flat or increases in value.

Either way—whether by going into debt to buy the asset or by contracting yourself to buy it at a certain amount at a certain time—it's leverage. It's trying for a big gain with least effort, a big return on money that you haven't actually put on the line or that you may not even have.

And it had always been part of the Ackman discipline to avoid leverage—whether on the balance sheets of companies he invests in or on his own balance sheet. **Ackman's billion-dollar mistake, therefore, is that he departed from his own investing discipline.** The differences in how this detour from discipline played out between Borders and Target are just variations on a theme.

In the case of Borders, Ackman could assure himself that he was not bending the discipline of his selection criteria all that much, although bend it he did—without advertising the fact. At its core, after all, Borders really was equivalent to Barnes & Noble. True, it was not as well managed, it was somewhat levered, and it faced a number of strategic challenges. But if you could fix those inadequacies (and after all, that's what activist investors do—they fix things) the reward could be terrific. So the discipline got bent, and when the reward was not forthcoming, there was no discipline to fall back on. Even a bend is as good as a break when investment discipline is at stake.

In the case of Target, Ackman directly and unequivocally advertised that he was bending his selection criteria discipline—versus his off-the-record detour from discipline in the Borders deal. Certainly he and he alone had the power and authority to waive the rule on leverage—once he judged that the case was sufficiently compelling—and he did so with a kind of flair one can only admire. One must equally admire the elegance of the leverage he allowed himself—namely, the heavily optioned structure of the Pershing Square IV fund. Through such leverage, Ackman was able to own 81.76 million shares of Target for a cash outlay of only $158 million—the price of a mere 2.5 million shares. The rest of the stake— 79.2 million shares—was provided thanks to options valued at $1.6 billion. In fairness, the leveraged strategy was fully disclosed, and Ackman estimated that approximately 60 percent of the investors in Pershing Square IV were other hedge funds, while 90 percent were investors in his other funds. So all these investors had either made money with Ackman—who of course had a history of super performance—or they understood the downside of leverage.

But options are tricky. You have to guess right on three often-elusive factors: time value, direction of movement of the stock being optioned, and market volatility. The option's strike price has to be less than the market price of the underlying asset before you can be in the money and can make a profit by exercising the option. Ackman bought $1.6 billion worth of options because he believed he could get Target to make certain value-accreting moves, such as selling off its real estate assets; at that point, the strike price of the options would be less than the market price of Target stock, and he would be in the money. When the real estate sale didn't happen, and the stock price and the market for retail stocks tanked, the value of the options declined more steeply even than the stock. The leverage he had hoped would magnify his gains on the upside in fact amplified his losses on the downside.

In the long run, the value of Ackman's Target options could possibly put him in the money again, or perhaps fall again, but in any event will continue to fluctuate going forward. It is equally likely that Ackman, again taking the long view, will exercise the options and convert them into shares. What is unlikely is that Ackman will ever fully recover the value of the original options; it is simply past the time when that can happen.

Options: Being Right May Not Be Good Enough

Investing in options is a double-edged sword: If you're right, the return can be substantial, but if your analysis is even slightly flawed, the entire principal might be wiped out.

An option is a leveraged means of investing in a stock, but what is often overlooked is how that leverage works. Simply put, an option is an investment in a financial instrument that, unlike a stock, has no intrinsic value other than the contractual right to *call* (or buy) a stock at a predetermined price or to *put* (or sell) the stock to someone at a lower price. The option buyer is thus synthetically either going long or short, respectively, on the underlying stock—you're long on a call option when you believe the value of the stock will rise, short on a put if you think the value will fall.

But here's the catch. Options have a cost called a premium. The premium is based on such factors as how close it is to the strike price, the price at which the option is to be exercised (the farther away the stock price is from the strike price, the less expensive the premium); time value (the longer the expiration period, the more expensive the premium); and the volatility of the underlying stock (the more volatile it is, the more expensive the premium, since on any given day the stock can be up or down through the strike price). Of course, the general condition of the market is usually a factor as well. Here's how it all works:

In June, an investor purchases a call option on Google with a $400 strike price for July. Google is trading at $370 a share at the time, and the investor, who doesn't want to tie up all her capital, pays a premium of $40.00 for the option. That's clearly a leveraged purchase—that is, the investor is paying slightly more than 10 percent of what it actually would cost to own a share of Google. On the day in July when the option expires, Google trades at $405 a share. Bottom line: Google had to reach $440 on the day the option expired for the investor to break even—that is, the strike price plus the cost of option, or premium. But at $405, the share price fell well short, and the investor took a loss of $35.00. She guessed right on the direction of the stock but paid too much for the time value and volatility. Her five-dollar "win" on the price is wiped out by the cost of the premium.

Had Ackman rationalized the risk in departing from his discipline? Maybe. If so, it was understandable. His activism had succeeded with others—McDonald's, to name just one—and success is a persuasive argument. Moreover, there were all those other hedge funds that were invested with him; they too must have seen the attraction not just of the investment but of using options to leverage it.

Of his Borders mistake—the one he himself called "an unforced error"—Ackman has much to say, and he says it simply and a bit wistfully, ticking off the misjudgments and wrong assumptions. "We thought anyone would be better than the old management," he says, "but it wasn't true." What he calls "the activist investor versus the public company CEO" is not necessarily a winning proposition for the activist investor, who, it turns out, is more limited than one would have thought in fixing what's wrong at a company. "Turnarounds are hard," Ackman says. "Turnarounds that are levered are very hard. And turnarounds where you don't know the management aren't worth taking."

Then the assumption that "if all else failed, we could sell" vaporized, and that put the final flourish on the failure.

In the investing business, says Ackman, "you don't get paid for degree of difficulty. It's not like the Olympics." The Borders investment, he suggests, was the triple Salchow of investing. "The degree of difficulty was too hard," he says. "The stars had to be aligned, and they weren't."

But isn't that what discipline is for? It's the thing you turn to because the stars are aligned only very rarely—and because you can never be sure when they may slip out of alignment.

No leverage, Ackman's discipline said. And as events proved, discipline was right.

Lessons Learned

- *Know the investment discipline established by your fund manager.* And find out whether and when the manager has deviated from the discipline.
- *Review the positions.* Examine the positions taken by your investment manager or mutual fund, and look for warning signs. For example, if the fund prospectus states that the fund will invest only in healthcare and consumer equities, but the fund's quarterly report shows a 10 percent weighting in financials, it is time to look for another manager. Financial stocks require a different analysis and a different discipline.
- *Discipline means discipline.* The end does not justify the means. The law of averages almost ensures that deviating from a discipline does not always lead to an investment mistake, but the odds are there will be a mistake at some point. So don't be tempted to invest or stay with a manager who changes tactics when a deviation from discipline results in a winning trade. Doing so only will provide that manager with greater motivation to be undisciplined—which is sure to end in financial disaster.
- *Good investors are made, not born.* Becoming an astute investor is an evolutionary process. Analyze your good investments to understand which disciplines were hallmarks of the outcome. Analyze your losing investments with the same goal.
- *Develop a checklist.* Keep a record of investment criteria that have worked for you and those that have not. This checklist is the backbone of your investment discipline. Stick with it.
- *Use options to hedge.* Options are best used to hedge, not to express a view as to whether a stock will rise or fall. Option investing requires you to be right both on the stock's direction, sometimes with absolute precision, and on the time frame in which it will reach that price, again precisely. And then there is the general market. Ask yourself if you can tolerate the risk.
- *Allocate your investment dollars wisely.* Weight the investment of riskier companies appropriately, as Ackman did with Borders. It's okay to gamble every once in a while if you are financially able to handle the risk, but make sure gambling is a very small part of your portfolio.
- *It's okay for you to speculate.* While it may be okay for you to knowingly violate your investment discipline—at least within the speculative portion of your portfolio—it is not okay for your mutual fund manager to do so.

CHAPTER 5

Nick Maounis

"TRUST, BUT VERIFY..."

Nicholas Maounis knew just about everything there was to know about being a professional investor when he founded Amaranth Advisors in 2000. The fund was his chance to put into practice ideas about infrastructure and integration that he had honed over decades of working for others, ideas tempered in the crucible of market realities. It was his opportunity to realize his own vision of how to structure a fund and imbue it with a culture that could, in his words, "add alpha." And it succeeded brilliantly, growing by leaps and bounds.

Were the leaps too big, the bounds too high? Did ideas that were once central get shoved over to the margins? Maybe. But one thing is for sure: Nick Maounis was an extremely accomplished and skilled investor. If he did not know everything there was to know about investing when he started Amaranth in 2000, there is no question that he survived its collapse in 2006 with much more knowledge.

"There is no substitute for experience," Maounis is reputed to have declared. "This one"—the experience of failure—"makes me a better investor."

The tuition costs were high, but the lesson was a valuable one: If an investment can yield big gains, it also can create sizable losses. Maounis either forgot that or didn't realize it or allowed profits to cloud his judgment. By the time it all became clear, it was too late.

Trading in the Blood

With a father who was head of trading at the prestigious Arnhold and S. Bleichroeder Advisers, LLC, and a mother who ran the order room for Gruntal & Co., one of the nation's oldest brokerage houses, Nick Maounis almost literally grew up in the financial markets. We can imagine the dinner-table conversations in the Maounis household—the parents exchanging the details of their workdays, discussing the highs and lows of stock movements and commodities futures and all that transpired in between the highs and the lows. The Maounis boys—Nick and his brother—must have absorbed financial trading through a process of osmosis. Or maybe it was just there from the beginning, coded into Maounis's DNA, then augmented and enriched through the dinners, the chats with both parents, the mentoring by a loving father who enjoyed teaching this apt and eager pupil.

So it was probably not surprising that young Nick was making options markets on bowling scores in high school when his classmates were making nickel bets on NCAA basketball brackets. It sounds like a little thing—a kid's quirk—but in fact it was great early training for Maounis—the kind of hands-on training no business book can teach, which may be one reason why Nick Maounis is not a great fan of business books. Instead, by making markets on bowling scores, he was teaching himself the skill of handicapping both the probability of an outcome and the correct value of the risk associated with betting on that outcome. It's a skill that most great investors and traders possess; Maounis clearly came by it naturally.

"You can't shop for caviar in the supermarket," Maounis senior told his son in the pre–Whole Foods, pre–Wild Oats days. It was a message akin to the answer Willie Sutton gave when asked why he robbed banks. "That's where the money is," Sutton said. Similarly, Maounis's father was telling him that if you want to make the big money, you must go where the big money is. So right after graduating from the University of Connecticut in 1985, Maounis joined L.F. Rothschild as a currency trader. When a seat opened on the convertibles desk, Maounis applied but was told he did not have the proper training. "My father will train me at home," Maounis replied—and got both the job and the promised training from his father.

Back then, convertible trading was part of arbitrage, and the desk at Rothschild was run by two experts in the field, John Angelo and Michael Gordon. Maounis flourished under their tutelage, building out the convertible arbitrage business, earning 20 percent for investors on his trading, and becoming the youngest senior vice president in the history of the firm. Rothschild had its troubles, however—mostly consisting of some bad blood among senior management—and it suffered serious losses in the 1987 stock market crash. Angelo and Gordon opted out of the mess to form their own hedge fund, the extremely successful Angelo, Gordon & Co., in 1988, and they brought Nick Maounis with them.

He was there for two years until lured away by Donald Sussman, founder of Paloma Partners, innovators in various forms of quantitative, relative value investing like computerized statistical arbitrage, which seeks to profit from any discrepancy between the price of related securities and their historical norm. Paloma also pioneered an innovative investment approach—providing capital to multiple traders and combining their performance into one fund—and it was equally ahead of its time in gold plating its systems of operations and controls. Perhaps the firm recognized that lack of infrastructure is one of the two primary causes for hedge fund failures—the other being, of course, lack of performance. Sussman offered Maounis a choice: either his own group or participation on a team. Maounis chose the latter, possibly assuming it to be a better learning experience, and when the team leader left in 1991, he was more than ready to take over.

Maounis expanded the focus of his investment mandate to include numerous strategies, creating a comprehensive multistrategy fund. In his view, the single-strategy model—for example, investing only in stocks or only in bonds—was fundamentally flawed. Subject to the ebbs and flows of one market, such a fund couldn't guarantee that there would always be a moneymaking opportunity to exploit. Within a multistrategy model, by contrast, if investment ideas were not apparent within one strategy, almost by definition, you could find some in another strategy. In a way, it was the ultimate realization of his father's advice to go where the money was to be made; in a multistrategy model, there was always a place where money could be made.

But there was something else about a multistrategy model that particularly appealed to Maounis—the ability to cross-fertilize investment ideas, with each strategy in the model nourishing the other. For example, currency traders with their view of how the dollar is valued against other currencies can help stock traders understand whether exports by U.S. companies will be more or less attractive to foreign buyers and thus may either increase or lower those companies' revenues—and thereby impact the stock price. What could really make this kind of cross-fertilization happen, Maounis believed, was a level of optionality in people—that is, a team whose members could transpose their skills. In Maounis's concept of this, an analyst who could understand equity markets should also be able to understand credit markets; Maounis believed that expanding expertise in this way increased the analyst's effectiveness. He tried to make it happen both in his recruiting at Paloma and by adding still more strategies to his playbook: credit arbitrage in 1994, for example, and, in 1999, energy trading.

Actually, it was a magazine article that first turned Maounis on to energy trading and to thinking about energy derivatives. The article prompted further research on Maounis's part—significant research, until he had learned just about everything he could about the commodity and the markets it traded in. He discovered NordPool, the world's first multinational exchange for trading electrical power derivatives exchange and, eventually, European Union emission allowances, and he began looking for expertise in the energy trading sector. By serendipity, when Enron collapsed, Amaranth was already geared up, thanks to Maounis's early line on the wide spreads and scarce opportunities that constituted the energy trading potential.

But for now, all that was a few years away, and Maounis was still busy building a formidable track record at Paloma. It was formidable indeed: From 1992 to 2000, his fund netted 22 percent, a far better return than the average market indices.

The time seemed ripe to put into practice all that he had learned about building a hedge fund. In 2000, with $600 million, $300 million of it in a managed account from Paloma, Maounis launched Amaranth Advisors LLC.

How to Build a Hedge Fund

Amaranth is a Greek word that means "unfading." It is perhaps best known for the purple flower that grows from the amaranth herb, but Nick Maounis first confronted the term when he bought an antique pool table for his home. Hearing that the word was Greek, like the

Maounis family, and that it refers to something that does not wither, he thought it would be the perfect name for his hedge fund.

At first, the fact that Paloma was involved as a managed fund made it difficult to raise money: Other investors balked at the notion of one investor constituting such a large portion of the fund. Moreover, as a managed account, its funds remained under Paloma's control, which meant that Paloma could pull its $300 million from Maounis at any time. This was not the case with Maounis's other investors; their money constituted actual hedge fund investments and were subject to an initial quarterly lock-up and other restrictions regarding redemption. In other words, the situation meant preferential liquidity for Paloma—and preference for one is typically not a good marketing tool among investors. Nonetheless, after the first year, the fund had $350 million in assets outside of Paloma—largely the result of organically grown gains. The fund's core strategies were distressed and credit trading, global convertible arbitrage, merger arbitrage, long and short equity—initially utilities and technology. Knowing that the model is only as good as its inputs, the firm added fundamental research to the mathematical determination of opportunities—an edge, as Maounis saw it, over the rest of the industry.

Nick Maounis was a man who had thought long and hard about what makes a successful hedge fund. He was a student of business in general and of investing in particular. He was a guy who valued culture as one of the most important factors in an organization and who set out to build what he believed would be a winning culture.

The building blocks were what Maounis had determined were the four pillars of success for hedge funds—as embodied in one or more well-known funds: fundamental long/short equity, credit (as embodied by Appaloosa), quantitative (as embodied by D.E. Shaw and Citadel), and commodities and energy trading. His aim was to combine the benefits of all of them and gain an extra plus through the synergistic magic of integration.

Integration, wrapped in an alpha-adding infrastructure, was the key, and, thought Maounis, it should go every which way: across activities, functions, processes, markets, skills, talents, intellects. It was the cross-nourishing, cross-fertilizing possibilities of such integration that Maounis believed could constitute the winning culture he was aiming for—the culture he believed was essential for succeeding at an optimum level in the often-challenging business of managing money.

It is important to note that this belief—certainly when translated into a modus operandi—sharply distinguished Amaranth from most other hedge funds. Other funds saw themselves not so much as scalable businesses but as investment management vehicles seeking to capitalize on the investment expertise of the founding partner. Maounis saw a much different, much more enduring opportunity—and this was the opportunity he was trying to realize in Amaranth.

His starting point was people. Maounis was interested in finding people with the right risk philosophy and the right skills to create the culture he envisioned. He was taken by something Jim Collins had written in *Good to Great*—the notion that you should see who is on the bus, then decide where to drive it. It clearly codified what had long been a standing philosophy for Maounis: Find the right team, build the infrastructure around their skills and talents, don't ask them to do what they are not equipped to do but optimize what they are equipped to do, then go!—add alpha.

As Maounis saw it, this also meant starting the firm's own stock loan and portfolio finance department, being a self-administered fund so as to have the ability to turn on a dime if events warranted it, maintaining an internal recruiting effort, and ensuring that the risk management function looked at the correlation of strategies not normally thought to be correlated. All of this he implemented.

But integration-wrapped-in-infrastructure remained the driving mantra of the organization Maounis was building. It is why Amaranth continually added to the investment platform in terms of both activities and geographies: statistical arbitrage, healthcare, real estate investment trusts (REITs), financial services, Canada, Europe, Singapore. It is why Maounis copied the likes of Google and Cisco and built an on-site fitness center, a soundproof music studio for impromptu jam sessions, and a recreation room with an antique pool table, video games, and chess sets. Instead of people leaving the office to socialize with others outside the Amaranth environment, why not make socializing—integration—part of the natural order of the workday? Maounis often would grab people from the growing staff in the Greenwich, Connecticut, headquarters and haul them off to lunch together—people who barely knew one another, who worked on entirely different strategies: the Singapore guys talking with the quantitative guys, a risk manager chowing down with a REIT trader, a bottoms-up stock picker lunching with a top-down macroeconomic trader. From this cross-fertilization of experience and knowledge and thinking, ideas would emerge, Maounis believed, and if even just one good idea emerged in the course of a year, it would be worth it.

The structure worked; indeed, it worked well. Most of the investment portfolios were successful most of the time, and because success and failure did not correlate—the strategies had different investment attributes and were not mirror images of each other—the returns were very good. Amaranth grew—from its initial staff of 20 or so at launch in 2000 to some 425 people at the peak in 2006. Sixty percent of the staff at headquarters were in operations; 40 percent were investment professionals, of whom some 25 individuals at most were authorized to make investment decisions. Investors in Amaranth paid the industry standard rates of a 1.5 percent management fee and a 20 percent incentive fee.

Growth meant change. For one thing, Maounis himself, despite having been brought up with trading in the blood and having shown himself to be virtually an instinctive trader, no longer had time for that activity, much as he loved it and much as he excelled at it. Instead, he was managing his growing business, holding meeting after meeting on risk and other issues, taking three- to four-hour-long phone calls a day from Amaranth investors. He migrated away from one core strength, the ability to produce return in any market, to another, that of businessman, visionary leader, and, importantly, a portfolio manager overseeing a broad range of investments.

The very look of the fund was changing as well, its original allocation shifting as opportunities presented themselves. This is what successful multistrategy funds are supposed to do: Assess what the best investment opportunities are and reallocate funds to take advantage of them. Merger arbitrage had represented 40 percent of the fund's original allocation, but that shrank as more trading activities were integrated into the fund. Energy was one of the newer businesses. The magazine article Maounis had read about the deregulation of electric utilities stayed with him, and, early on, he had correctly predicted that there would be an opportunity to profit from the trading markets that would arise. One way for Amaranth to seize the opportunity was to trade natural gas, the feedstock for electricity produced by a number of utilities. But first Maounis needed someone who could lead the energy trading effort.

Harry Arora, a former trader with Enron, was the first person he hired to run the energy team. A couple of years later, a headhunter introduced him to Canadian Brian Hunter, a young but by no means inexperienced trader, who resigned from his position as head of the natural gas desk at Deutsche Bank (DB) and brought his 10 years of experience with him to Amaranth in 2004. Hunter had a reputation for understanding optionality, knew the implied boundaries in natural gas trading, and immediately began making money for Amaranth in both up and down markets. This was no doubt partly because he understood risk so well; the downside volatility on energy trades—that is, negative returns below an acceptable rate—was only 10 percent, which is considered very low indeed.

But then, risk management was an important function altogether at Amaranth. It was headed by a Harvard-educated risk management expert and peopled with more than 15 highly credentialed managers, 3 of whom were focused exclusively on energy. This wasn't a function that looked solely at value at risk (VAR), the standard probability measure of what you might lose on a mark-to-market basis over a fixed time horizon, assuming normal markets. Maounis also wanted to know what the fund could lose out of the uncertain tail that's left after the VAR is calculated; tail loss, he believed, was the most dangerous. It is very much to Maounis's credit that he knew this danger existed and tried to measure it, for so many of his peers paid it little attention.

Moreover, in the case of Amaranth and energy trading, this focus on risk management appeared to pay off. With three risk managers sitting on the trading desk and concentrating on energy trades, and with Hunter himself careful to keep the risk in line month to month, energy trading managed to achieve single-digit downside volatility on a yearly basis—an impressive achievement, especially when combined with the profitability record Hunter was racking up.

The Energy Wager

Hunter's success with energy was particularly notable because 2005 was not a great year for other sectors of the fund. Convertible bonds were down, and, in the midst of difficult market conditions, so was credit. Against that dismal news, Hunter's energy wager was scoring big.

"Wager" is a quick and simple word for an energy strategy that was actually exceedingly complex and that had been worked out after much thought and research. But at the simple level, in its essence, it was a wager: Hunter was betting that the natural gas price spread would widen between the winter months, represented by March delivery contracts, and summer months, represented by April contracts. He had been making the bet since joining Amaranth in 2004, when the spread was about 40 cents, and it had indeed continued to widen, returning big bucks to investors.

So in April 2005, when Hunter was offered a job at SAC Capital Advisors, headed by the preternaturally secretive and wildly successful Steven A. Cohen, an offer sweetened by a seven-figure signing bonus, Maounis was loath to see him go. Maounis countered Cohen's offer with a sweet one of his own: He offered Hunter a level of money and authority on a par with the firm's top earners. But given the size of the pool of assets that Hunter traded, the offer would effectively make him the most highly paid person at Amaranth. Maounis also arranged for Hunter to move his family back home to Calgary, Alberta, and run the energy book out of an eight-person office there. Hunter stayed with Amaranth—but moved back to Canada—and in September 2005, in the wake of hurricanes Katrina and Rita, his energy bet paid back huge money as the price of gas soared upward on the belief that the hurricanes would significantly damage the natural gas production facilities on the Gulf Coast. That payoff alone seemed to justify Maounis's faith in Hunter.

And the bet kept on working—strategically adjusted on occasion by the energy team to capture changes in the market. In fact, by the end of April 2006, Amaranth's energy book had earned $1.2 billion in six weeks. For the first four months of the year, the fund's returns were estimated at 30 percent, way above other multistrategy funds, and most analysts believed it was because of Hunter's energy trades.

Then in May 2006 came the first sign of trouble.

Spring and Summer 2006

The tables turned in May. Price spreads between the warmer and colder months narrowed. The markets seized up. There was massive producer selling. Over the last two weeks of May, Hunter's energy bet lost $1 billion—virtually everything it had won in the previous six weeks. Then came the margin call and the pressure on cash.

By the end of May, Maounis called an all-hands meeting of the six partners. Volatility was much higher than anticipated, much higher than the assumptions on which the fund's risk numbers had been predicated. The question was whether this was a once-only volatility event or a signal to reassess their risk management situation altogether. The partners determined they had three options, each dependent on what the market offered:

1. Add cash and reduce leverage.
2. Trim the size of their positions by selling—albeit into a weak market.
3. Hedge more of the position.

They decided to do the second—to reduce their exposure in other strategies by selling those positions and allocating more cash to the energy business to slash the volatility.

By that time, of course, the market had begun to notice Amaranth's footprint, so in June, the decision was made to "play dead." The idea was to stay below the radar, making sure the Amaranth energy strategy was not revealed to the markets. The team would liquidate positions as they could while allowing the fundamentals of seasonal changes play out. It looked like that might work: The fund as a whole was up 6 percent that month. At the end of June, Bloomberg could report that Hunter's energy book, combined with other commodity positions, controlled 56 percent of Amaranth's risk capital and accounted for 78 percent of its performance. But there was little liquidity for trading, and other portfolios of the fund were trimmed once more in order to feed cash to energy trading.

Then in July, a rare event—indeed, a virtually unprecedented event—exacerbated volatility: the first-ever summer drawdown on natural gas. Drawdowns, when gas storage providers require gas companies to reduce the amount of gas they hold in storage, typically occur during the heating season as a way to avoid downward pressure on the spot price of natural gas—i.e., too much storage supply might bring down the price. Applying this price risk mitigation mechanism at virtually the height of the non-heating season that runs from April to October threw the market into a tizzy and considerably complicated the situation at Amaranth. It became harder and harder to cut risk since the market for natural gas couldn't absorb the volume of Amaranth's position. Maounis told Hunter it had to be done, and if it wasn't done quickly, he and his team would need to return to Amaranth headquarters in Greenwich and work the issue there until the energy exposure was cut.

The team moved from Calgary to Connecticut. They were there for the rest of the summer. Their daily task was to cut risk. By the end of August, Hunter had put together a final risk-cutting plan, the culmination of months of ongoing planning and risk management actions. Among other things, the plan entailed moving positions away from trading on the New York Mercantile Exchange (NYMEX), which was pressuring Amaranth to cut its risk, and instead trading them on the Intercontinental Exchange (ICE), which was more liquid and where positions are cash settled. This move was set for the end-of-August expiration, which typically takes place over a period of a few days. At the time, Amaranth's assets totaled some $9.5 billion.

On day 1, Amaranth made money.

On day 2, August 29, 2006, Hunter was ready to settle the ICE position when an anonymous e-mail arrived saying, in effect: "We're coming after you." Meanwhile, NYMEX ordered Amaranth out of the market for the last 30 minutes of the trading day because, said NYMEX, it was worried that the fund was too big and might be the target of market manipulation by other traders.

There was an odd irony to this NYMEX worry; Amaranth, having previously noticed some irregularities in the market, had asked NYMEX to investigate what was going on. Yet at the moment when manipulation seemed a possibility, NYMEX decided to keep Amaranth out of the market. It seemed a little bit like victimizing the whistle-blower.[1] Nevertheless, Amaranth of course complied—and lost $550 million in that half hour. For Hunter and his team, for Maounis and his partners, it must have felt like an amputation, as their traders' instincts and business skills were rendered impotent while all they could do was observe the carnage. The mysterious e-mail they had received now made sense.

And when the day was over and the loss was complete, there came an accusatory phone call from NYMEX asking why Amaranth had ignored the order to do nothing for the last 30 minutes of the trading day. Fortunately, stacks of trading records proved that the firm's personnel had done exactly as NYMEX had decreed. If there was manipulation in the market, it wasn't at the hands of Amaranth but rather at its expense. Something had happened, but Amaranth, stilled by order of NYMEX, had been restrained from stopping the bleeding of $550 million—a loss that still left the fund up 5.5 percent on the month.

That evening, Maounis suggested to Hunter that he contact Goldman Sachs and put together a deal that would get Amaranth out of the mess it was in, even at a loss on the portfolio. After all, the fund was still 25 percent up on its portfolio of $9.5 billion. Hunter argued against the suggestion: They had come into the month of August with $3 billion in cash, equal to 30 percent of the fund—which should be enough liquidity; Hunter believed the fundamentals were still in their favor; a good portion of the risk had already been reduced; and he felt they still could work it out. Hunter asked for two more weeks.

Maounis was scheduled for a mid-September business trip to Las Vegas with Goldman Sachs president Gary Cohen and Dan Och, founder of the Och-Ziff Capital Management hedge fund. Many other high-profile money managers would also be attending. Under the circumstances, Maounis was disinclined to go; he felt strongly he should not be away from Greenwich—not take his hand off the wheel—at this critical time. But Hunter persuaded him it would be okay: he should go ahead. With rumors already swirling about Amaranth's exposure, not showing up to such an important event with a who's who of Wall Street expecting his arrival would have been tantamount to Maounis mailing a copy of his portfolio to every competing hedge fund. Very reluctantly, Maounis flew west and was at an outdoor event on a pleasant September Monday, his fellow money managers congratulating him on how well Amaranth had done for the year, when his cell phone began ringing with the news that natural gas prices were in free fall and that Amaranth was losing $350 million. Maounis spent the rest of the day in his room, on the phone, trying to stave off the inevitable.

What had happened? In market movements that Maounis would later tell his investors were "highly remote," the weather turned cool enough for people to turn off their air conditioners, there was little hurricane action that year, and with inventories of natural gas surging, the spread that had been $2 at the beginning of the month narrowed to 63 cents. It was an eventuality that any risk management team, even Amaranth's, might easily miss. Yet the Amaranth team had not missed it. They had vetted even this scenario, outlandish as it was, and assessed the odds of its occurring as "vanishingly small." Yet occur it did.

It was unprecedented; both the collapse itself and the rate at which it took place were statistically anomalous, and Brian Hunter's energy wager unraveled with the velocity and destructive force of lightning. The next day, Maounis stayed in his Vegas hotel room, still on the phone, feeling as if the walls were closing in on him. They did close in on him—figuratively, anyway. He flew back to Greenwich to try to save what he could.

But it was too late. That week, Hunter's actions lost Amaranth some $4.6 billion, and the fund began selling positions at a loss to raise money. On September 22, Maounis was expressing "regret" to Amaranth investors. By the end of the month, the loss was $6.6 billion. In dollar terms, it was at the time the biggest implosion of any hedge fund ever, producing a 60 percent loss for the year. (Losses by Citadel Investment Group in 2008 would eclipse the Amaranth "record.") Day after day, night after night, the Amaranth partners gathered to discuss their options. In what certainly must qualify as a credit to the culture created by Maounis, there was no finger pointing; partners and employees held together as a team. If they hadn't, the damage, already devastating, could have been total. In the end, Nick Maounis was forced to do what he most earnestly did not want to do—wind down Amaranth and return cash to investors.

Within weeks, J.P. Morgan and Merrill Lynch had taken over the energy book, paid billions to do so by Amaranth; in fact, approximately half of the September loss of $6.6 billion was in concession payments to J.P. Morgan, which simply added Amaranth's energy book to its own already substantial one. Then Morgan flipped the book to Citadel Investment Group. Amaranth investors were left with about a third of their money. While not a great economic result, it was nonetheless a credit to decisive action by the operations and trading team Maounis had recruited. Other funds similarly afflicted by major market reversals in leveraged instruments—Peloton, for example (see Chapter 8)—had been completely wiped out.

The Securities and Exchange Commission, suspecting some form of market manipulation, demanded to see all Amaranth's records, reviewed them all, and after review, never pursued any action. In an August 2009 letter issued by the enforcement division of the SEC Amaranth would ultimately be absolved of any wrongdoing.

Amaranth never had a trade fail because of the energy exposure. There was no margin call it did not meet. Only one investor—a public pension fund—sued.

The Federal Energy Regulatory Commission and Commodity Futures Trading Commission of the U.S. government charged Amaranth Advisors with manipulating the market and Brian Hunter with attempted manipulation, expressing conflicting views on how this was done. But by this time, Maounis, who was never personally charged by any regulatory agency, was tired of having to defend his firm. He struck back.

Nick Maounis was convinced that the decision to force Amaranth into failure was made at the highest levels of J.P. Morgan, the investment banking arm of J.P. Morgan Chase. Indeed, he believed the decision had been made by two of chief executive Jamie Dimon's lieutenants, Steven D. Black and William T. Winters, who headed the division that dealt with Amaranth. A lawsuit filed by Amaranth on November 13, 2007, alleged that the firm and its investors were in fact the victims of deliberate actions by J.P. Morgan, which, as Amaranth's prime broker, was responsible for settling all its trades. According to the complaint filed before the New York State Supreme Court,[2] J.P. Morgan deliberately derailed two transactions that would have saved Amaranth from collapse. The first was a trade in which Goldman Sachs, for a fee of course, would take over Amaranth's energy book and thus mitigate the hedge fund's exposure. The second was an offer from Citadel Investment Group of a trade and a bridge loan. The lawsuit alleged that Morgan severed both lifelines by making false claims about Amaranth's exposure and solvency. In the case of the Goldman Sachs lifeline, Amaranth also contends that its contract with J.P. Morgan allowed the firm to make risk-reducing trades but that Morgan prevented Amaranth from doing so. The result of these actions by J.P. Morgan, according to the complaint, was a loss to the fund of at least $1 billion. The lawsuit also accused Morgan of leaking details of Amaranth's energy positions to other traders—there had been periodic rumors to this effect—further pressuring the portfolio. Perhaps not coincidentally, after J.P. Morgan derailed both transactions, it essentially foreclosed on Amaranth's energy book, making an estimated $750 million over a period of weeks. It will likely take years before the allegations in the lawsuit are either proven or defeated.

Nonetheless, by the end of 2006, Amaranth, contravening the essential character of the plant that was its symbol, had faded.

Rise and Fall: September 2005–September 2006 Timeline

September 2005: Amaranth energy strategy, piloted by Hunter, realizes a huge payoff in wake of Hurricanes Katrina and Rita.

April 2006: Amaranth's energy book earns $1.2 billion in six weeks.

May 2006: Amaranth's energy book dives, giving up previous gains.

June 2006: Amaranth's trim-and-play-dead strategy is on target.

July 2006: There is an unprecedented summer drawdown on natural gas; Amaranth team readies plan to move positions.

August 28, 2006: Amaranth's plan is launched, seemingly successfully.

August 29, 2006: Mystery e-mail arrives, NYMEX orders Amaranth out of the market 30 minutes before closing, Amaranth loses $550 million.

September 2006: Natural gas prices plummet. Amaranth's losses eventually will exceed $6 billion.

September 22, 2006: Maounis expresses "regret" to investors, begins to unwind Amaranth.

Life of Brian

Brian Hunter grew up near Calgary, the energy boomtown of western Canada, with an interest in working on Wall Street. The son of a father who poured concrete for a living, Hunter had a knack for numbers, studied physics at the University of Alberta, graduating in 1998, then obtained a graduate degree in applied math and wrote his thesis on commodity pricing. It was enough to get him to TransCanada, the large pipeline company, as a junior analyst energy trader working on how to profit from anomalies in energy prices. And that was enough to get him to Wall Street, where he went to work for Deutsche Bank in 2001, arriving in New York with his wife just after September 11.

Neither of them liked New York, and Hunter didn't care for his job. Although he had made millions for the bank over the period of years, but lost millions in a single week on one wrong bet, Deutsche Bank refused to pay Hunter a bonus that year. In his first brush with the U.S. legal system, Hunter sued DB. (In what must have seemed a footnote to his other troubles, the court found for DB in 2007.)

That's about when Amaranth stepped in, hiring Hunter in 2004—with the implied promise that he could move back to Calgary, which he did.

After the Amaranth collapse in 2006, Hunter tried to start up his own hedge fund, Solengo Capital Advisors, raising a reported $700 million and hiring four ex-Amaranthers among his staff. Solengo was swamped, however, by a rising tide of legal and regulatory scrutiny—specifically, by an enforcement action from the Federal Energy Regulatory Commission that took up so much of Hunter's time and effort that none was left over to launch Solengo. Investors apparently were concerned enough about the legal issues that they hesitated to provide the committed capital.

Enter Peak Ridge, the Boston-based asset management firm, which hired Hunter to advise its Commodity Volatility Fund and at the same time bought Solengo's assets. In the first quarter of 2008, the fund returned 49 percent—at a time when many other funds were posting losses; by August 2008, the fund was up 230 percent for the year.

But Hunter's legal troubles continued. As of this writing, he was still the target of allegations from three sources:

1. The U.S. Senate's Permanent Subcommittee on Investigations charged that the large positions Hunter took in the natural gas market inflated the prices paid by consumers and businesses.

2. The Federal Energy Regulatory Commission (FERC) charged that Hunter manipulated down the closing prices of the New York Mercantile Exchange (NYMEX) natural gas futures contract to benefit the short position on the Intercontinental Exchange (ICE), thus harming consumers.

3. The Commodity Futures Trading Commission leveled the same charge as FERC but only on the grounds that Hunter compromised market integrity, not that he harmed consumers.

What Went Wrong

You could compile a good-size list.

Maybe it was relying primarily on one among the 10 prime brokers that served it, J.P. Morgan alone, whose own desire to make money may have been in conflict with its desire to see a troubled client survive. That could be why, as the lawsuit alleges Morgan ultimately pursued a tactic that gained it a greater return than the fees from Amaranth would have provided. A hedge fund is supposed to be able to trust its prime broker; perhaps in this case, it was a mistake to place so much trust and give so much power to one single entity.

Maybe it was a matter of letting the tail wag the dog. Maounis was aware of the tail risk of energy trading, but the tail eventually overcame the fund, causing its demise.

Style drift, explored in Chapter 8 of this book in the case of Geoff Grant and Peloton Partners, may also have been an issue. (Perhaps not coincidentally, Peloton's prime brokers raised the price on their collateral, forcing Peloton into bankruptcy, then—like J.P. Morgan—flipping the positions they had called in to make a hefty profit in a short time.) In the Amaranth example, a multistrategy fund seemed to let itself drift into what was primarily—even predominantly—an energy trading fund. Yes, other strategies still existed at the fund, but, as we can see clearly in retrospect, these other strategies were functionally neutered; they became mere offsets.

Perhaps **it was a mistake to rely on a single talent,** even one as luminous as Brian Hunter seemed to be. And perhaps, where money is concerned, there really is no such thing as luminous talent.

Or maybe it was the weather.

If I had to pick just one cause of Nick Maounis's $6 billion mistake, it would be **risk management.** To paraphrase Sir Isaac Newton, investment positions that go up could very well come down, and while all objects, regardless of weight, fall to Earth at the same rate of speed, riskier trades seem to decline a lot faster than more mundane investments.

Yale lecturer and onetime Paloma Partners executive Leon M. Metzger has put it succinctly. "Exceedingly high returns," Metzger is quoted as telling a *New York Times* reporter the week Amaranth lost its shirt on energy bets, "can suggest a very high risk/reward profile."[3] Such a profile, Metzger went on to say, "can lead to exceedingly high losses, too." That would seem to be an elementary reality of investing, even though, as this book suggests, it is a reality that investors test—and prove—over and over again.

Granted, Amaranth had established a fine risk management function. Headed by the highly respected Rob Jones and including risk professionals who were both expert and experienced in the field, Amaranth's team probably was as well educated in the subject as a team could be. It was careful to look beyond the VAR and to scan correlations not usually scanned. And it did a good job in ensuring that Amaranth—and specifically Brian Hunter in his highly volatile world—got the risk back in line month after month after month.

In short, Amaranth's risk management process was well thought out, well staffed, well organized, and worked very well indeed— until it didn't.

There's an inherent fallacy about risk management. For one thing, nobody really *manages* risk; all you can do is try to measure it—to take its dimensions and express those dimensions in numbers. But all you are ever really measuring is what has happened in the past. And while you might extrapolate probabilities from that, there is absolutely no guarantee that the past predicts the future. That, precisely, is the risk.

The first question that comes to mind vis-à-vis risk and Amaranth was the allocation of assets to energy trading. This was supposed to be a multistrategy fund; Maounis is a man who can wax truly eloquent on the subject of integrating diversified strategies to achieve synergistic results of which a single strategy is simply not capable. The concentrated position on energy, which bid fair to overwhelm the other strategies in the fund, undermined that diversification and raised the risk: It simply put way too many eggs in the energy basket.

Brian Hunter was betting those eggs on offsetting positions, going long on natural gas to be delivered in the winter and shorting the deliveries for the fall of 2006. Doing so inevitably exposes a trader to quick correlation changes, and it is fair to ask whether the controls Amaranth had in place to correct for such changes, if any, were adequate to the task.

It is also fair to ask what happened to the controls in place to moderate Hunter's use of leverage, which is surely a core risk in any hedge fund operation. Clearly, what started as acceptable leverage turned unacceptable as the market went against Amaranth and as its ability to sell the harmful energy contracts without impacting the market dried up. What was missing from the set of controls that brought the firm to that position of impotence?

Nick Maounis did not personally commit these sins of omission and commission. But he was in charge. Amaranth was his baby. And he is the one responsible.

Of course, you don't have to tell that to Nick Maounis. Nobody knows better than he what went wrong or who bears ultimate accountability for what happened. For the risk management function of his new fund, Verition Fund Management LLC, launched in Greenwich in late 2008, Maounis adopted as a governing mantra the Russian proverb that became a favorite with Ronald Reagan: "Trust, but verify." To put that into practice, Maounis devised a risk management process that combines external scrutiny with internal scrutiny and adds the requirement that members of the risk management team demonstrate trading experience and acumen as well as quantitative and analytical skills. In other words, you have to have "been there, done that" as well as having a pedigree of academic credentials for managing risk.

Maounis then gave the new process real teeth by putting Verition's external risk manager on the board of the fund. Such a move ups the ante on the risk management stake because it establishes an arm's-length distance between the risk management function and the operation. An independent board member answers to the other members of the board, not to the chief executive. He is liable to the investors for his judgment—for bad decisions as well as good—and he knows it. An outside risk manager as an independent board member answerable to investors is a real hedge against risk, and Maounis is to be commended for having seen that clearly. He also saw what happened at Amaranth as a playbook for avoiding meltdown. He believed that having lived through the experience of loss made him better at the profession. A number of investors agreed and have put their money on the line at Verition to evidence their faith in Maounis.

What Maounis did not change was his belief in integration and infrastructure—integration every which way wrapped in an alpha-seeking infrastructure. It had worked at Amaranth—at least for a while. And this time, Nick Maounis knew how hard it would be to keep integration whole and how the infrastructure can come tumbling down if you don't.

Lessons Learned

- *Understand risk.* Nick Maounis was an extremely successful and brilliant trader who surrounded himself with similarly smart and savvy people. If he was unable to completely understand the "tail" risk, then an individual investor stands little chance when dealing with esoteric or inherently risky investments, particularly those with imbedded leverage.
- *Leave commodity markets to the pros.* Commodity markets are the bastion of professionals, not of casual investors. They are not "physical" markets like the stock market; the only way an individual investor can

partake in a commodity market is through the use of such leveraged instruments as future contracts. By definition, this kind of leverage ratchets up the risk.

- *Hedging commodity risk is imperfect.* Brian Hunter had traded energy for 12 years before he lost it all. He came from Calgary, Canada, where energy is the primary industry. Yet despite this background, and despite his insights and training, he was unable successfully to mitigate the downside to his investments through hedging.

- *Know your broker.* Make sure you understand his or her motives in servicing your account. Amaranth alleges that J.P. Morgan's motives were to profit from Amaranth's difficulties, that the bank gained more from the fund failing than it would have gained had the fund succeeded. (NB: The author takes no position on this claim.) To an individual investor, this should also be a concern. Disreputable brokers make more money by convincing you to trade often—it's called churning—because their earnings derive from commissions and not from the money that you might earn from a buy-and-hold strategy.

- *Check credentials.* Ask your broker and/or fund manager about their investment track record. What was their biggest mistake, and what safeguards have they put into effect to ensure that it doesn't happen again? Nick Maounis is a much better investor now because he learned from his mistakes; think of it as wisdom gained. For one thing, the only natural gas he will ever buy again is to heat his home. Others have not been as wise. When John Meriwether ran Long Term Capital Management, the firm spectacularly imploded, losing billions and nearly taking down the global bond market. Meriwether started another fund, JWM, and again lost billions pursuing essentially the same strategy. Victor Niederhoffer ran his first hedge fund aground when he made an ill-conceived bet on bank stocks only to have a similarly ill-conceived bet on bank stocks put his second fund out of business. Same mistake for both; same result.

- *Mistakes can be a learning tool.* Don't invest with a fund manager or broker who claims not to have made any mistakes. First, it is probably a disingenuous claim, and second, even if it is accurate, you don't want to be part of the first misstep. And there is sure to be one. Successful professional investors will tell you that they have learned more from their mistakes than from their successes. The size of the mistake is less important—it didn't have to be fatal to their business—than the lesson learned.

CHAPTER 6

Leon Cooperman

THE PIRATE OF PRAGUE MEETS THE PRINCE OF PRINCETON—AND THE BOY FROM THE BRONX GETS SQUEEZED

Two realities shape the context for the story of this chapter and the lessons it provides. One is the disclaimer found in every investment prospectus, every mutual fund advertisement, every come-on from every bank: *Investing involves risk. Investment returns will fluctuate. It is possible to lose money by investing.*

The other reality is the well-worn Wall Street axiom that if investing is risky, investing in emerging markets is particularly risky.

It's one thing to accept these realities intellectually. After all, it is clear that the nature of investing is hypothetical—that is, the outcome depends on assumptions that may or may not prove out. When those assumptions are about places and people and institutions that have no investment track record—as in the emerging markets—the burden of proof becomes even heavier.

Our rational minds can embrace those realities, but it can be quite a different thing when loss actually occurs. Yet loss *will* occur. Sometime, someday, in some way, on some investment somewhere, you will lose money. It happens to professional investors, and it will happen to you. The awful truth is that it has a better chance of happening to you if you invest in emerging markets than if you stick to familiar, more mature, more open and easily accessible markets.

Professional investors know this. That is why they take extra precautions, do extra due diligence, exercise extra prudence when they invest in markets that are just being born or are just coming forth into the light from obscurity.

But sometimes, even if and when you take every precaution, do all the due diligence, and exercise every bit of forethought of which the human species is capable—even then, sometimes an investment simply blows up in your face, and you take the loss. It happens.

It happened to the best of them, Leon Cooperman of Omega Advisors, one of the most upright, learned, circumspect, and savvy investors in the world. And what may have hurt the most was that it happened at the hands of a once-trusted employee who defrauded him. Caught in a vise of greed and gluttony, Cooperman saw his four-decade track record of success and a lifelong reputation for probity threatened. Emerging markets can offer large profits, but they are opaque and prone to fraud—a dangerous place to invest. The gains are sometimes reserved for the cheaters, not the investors.

Can fraud be avoided? If so, then it is clearly a mistake not to uncover the deceit before being injured by it. Or is being ensnared in a hoax sometimes unavoidable and the unfavorable outcome happenstance? It's a legitimate debate. The result, however, is the same.

Wall Street's Professor

Throughout the years when Goldman Sachs was enjoying its incredible run to ascendancy in the world of finance, one of the key reasons was Leon G. "Lee" Cooperman, who for 25 years ran the firm's investment research department and was later chairman of Goldman Sachs Asset Management. For nine years straight, *Institutional Investor* magazine, the bible of the investment banking press, rated Cooperman the number-one portfolio strategist in its putative All-America Research Team. That was uncommon recognition for what was already commonly understood on Wall Street—namely, that research under Cooperman was a key component of Goldman's exceptional performance.

Unlike many of his colleagues and certainly many of the younger generation he mentored, Cooperman came from a modest background. A city boy, Cooperman was born and raised in the Bronx, the son of a plumber. He attended the public Hunter College as an undergraduate, then went to work for Xerox as a quality control engineer. That career didn't seem to be quite enough for young Cooperman, so he enrolled in Columbia University's Business School. At the age of 24, Cooperman took a job in Goldman's research department, and there he stayed for nearly a quarter of a century, creating the Cooperman legend and establishing the Cooperman fortune.

In 1991, Cooperman struck out on his own, founding Omega Advisors, Inc., with $450 million in capital. Here's how Cooperman described the core strategy of the fund to *Fortune* magazine in 1996: "We're a value-oriented, research-driven firm that buys undervalued stocks, shorts overvalued ones, and participates in selected overseas debt and equity markets. May not be an exciting approach, but it works."[1] And for the most part, so it did; the fund was up nearly 27 percent for that year, and it had done nearly as well for the other years of its existence. But while Omega is at its core a value investing fund, it also has been shaped by the activist, often outspoken, nature of its founder.

In 1999, shortly after retiring from Goldman, Steve Einhorn joined Omega as vice chairman, thus creating a double-barreled center of excellence at the top. Einhorn originally had been hired into Goldman by Cooperman, had headed the firm's Global Investment Research, and had been named to the All-America Research Team for 16 consecutive years.

But Einhorn missed Omega's most challenging year. In 1998, the markets were roiled by the collapse of Long Term Capital Management, a hedge fund that held bond positions so big it had to be bailed out by the government when its strategy failed, threatening to take down the global markets. That same year, a default in Russian debt that Omega owned prompted its exit from emerging-markets investing.[2] Three years later, in 2002, the fund lost 11 percent, a rare occurrence. But, in general, under these two legendary leaders representing two generations of investing genius, Omega has succeeded brilliantly: The fund had as much as $6 billion in assets under management before the worldwide financial crisis hit and halved its assets, as it did for most funds, leaving Omega nevertheless with a solid basis for rebuilding. That is precisely the sort of thing at which Cooperman excels.

Always direct, opinionated, his views formed by careful analysis and pinpoint logic, Cooperman also has been known to be volatile, evincing a temper seemingly more Bronx than Goldman Sachs. He otherwise exemplifies the consummately responsible wealthy entrepreneur. A bit portly, sometimes bespectacled, with thinning hair, Cooperman has never allowed his billion-dollar net worth to overcome his values, has never been caught up in the high-profile game of showcasing his wealth or his status as a member of the hedge fund elite. In the small New Jersey town in which he lives, a place where consumption often can be conspicuous, the Coopermans still occupy the same modest home where they raised their children. Some sharp-eyed neighbors may notice that they are visiting the Leon and Toby Cooperman Jewish Community Center in the neighboring town, and family members sitting anxiously in the waiting room at Saint Barnabas Medical Center may find themselves gazing at the print on the wall announcing that the donor of the room was Leon Cooperman. But few people know that their neighbor Mr. Cooperman sits on the boards of the New Jersey Performing Arts Center, the Crohn's and Colitis Foundation of America, the Damon Runyon Cancer Research Foundation, and his alma mater, Columbia University's Graduate School of Business. He is also chairman of the Saint Barnabas Medical Center Foundation, philanthropic support arm of New Jersey's oldest and largest nonprofit hospital. But Cooperman is not the kind of guy to leave a milestone with his name in lights at every step along his career, even though the distance from the South Bronx where he was born to the house in Short Hills, New Jersey, where he now lives, while not great in terms of miles—under 40—represents a significant journey of achievement and reward. What counts rather is that Cooperman traveled the distance under his own power and on his own terms the whole way.

Thousands of miles away, another individual was traveling his own route under his own power and on his own terms—terms very different from those that guided Lee Cooperman. Yet eventually the lives of the two would intersect—the professorial Wall Street investor and the man who seemed to combine the vague underworld aura of Jay Gatsby with a farcical movie plot by Woody Allen.

The Pirate of Prague

Whatever Viktor Kozeny was selling, he made people feel they wanted in on it. Czech born but now an Irish citizen living in the Bahamas—and still wanted by the authorities in both his native land

and the United States—Kozeny was dubbed the Pirate of Prague by no less an authority than *Fortune* magazine. And by all accounts, he fits the label, coming off as the kind of swashbuckling buccaneer you secretly can't help rooting for, even though you know he perhaps does not have your best interests at heart and may indeed have larceny on his mind. A born promoter, Kozeny is gifted with the ability to charm and beguile his way into—and for the most part, out of—absolutely any situation in any language on just about any continent on the planet.

At the age of 19, he charmed his way into the heart of an American physics professor, who gave Kozeny a place at the university and convinced a colleague to give the young Czech student lodging in his home. Kozeny proceeded to run off with his landlord's wife. She left him two years later, but not before he had gotten her to bankroll his next upward step—a Harvard education. From Cambridge, Kozeny proceeded to London and a job at Flemmings, the renowned investment bank, from which he was soon fired for failing to do the job for which he was hired; instead he was on the phone a lot, "doing deals," he explained. It should be noted that at each of these way stations, Kozeny compiled glowing recommendations from professors and principals, even when they had to send him on his way.

The turn of the decade in 1990 found Kozeny back in Czechoslovakia with a new wife he soon dumped—more or less abandoning their child as well—and a new identity as a "business consultant." Vaclav Havel had just led the Velvet Revolution, and the postcommunist government was eager to privatize the nation's state-run industries. To jump-start the process, every citizen was offered the chance to buy a booklet of vouchers that could be tendered for shares in the newly privatized companies. Each booklet cost $35, and they were slow to sell. After all, these newly "capitalistic" citizens were utterly unfamiliar with the practices of a market economy—and with the idea that it could be profitable to get in on the ground floor of a financial opportunity.

Then Kozeny stepped in. He set up a group of closed-end mutual funds—which he named the Harvard Funds after his alma mater, no doubt hoping to capitalize on the value of such a revered brand. He then embarked on an aggressive advertising campaign, the likes of which the citizenry had not experienced in seven decades of communist ideology. It worked. Kozeny convinced nearly a million Czechs to turn their vouchers over to him to invest for them; in turn, he would pay them 10 times their money if they wanted to cash out after a year. Before long, Kozeny controlled some 15 percent of the Prague stock market, and when he swapped the vouchers for stakes in key companies, he made a fortune—hundreds of millions of dollars through management fees of up to 7 percent and a brokerage fee of 1 percent, until the value of the Harvard Funds hit $1 billion. He augmented this wealth even further through shrewd investments in Russia and the Ukraine. As promised, those Czechs who cashed out after the first year made a fortune. Those who didn't, however, were left with nothing when the fund collapsed.

Kozeny wasn't on hand for the collapse; he had already left the country. His immense wealth in what was still a poor country had elevated him to celebrity status and had stirred the curiosity of the Czech government. Then the press began to inquire into the genesis of Kozeny's wealth and the tangle of his vast holdings. The alarm bells sounded particularly loud when a former member of the Czech secret police was arrested and found to possess embarrassing information about some Czech officials as well as state secrets. Viktor Kozeny was alleged to have bought the damaging information, and an investigation was launched. Kozeny claimed that he too was a victim of the blackmail scheme, although it is doubtful that anyone took this claim seriously. Serious or not, Kozeny began to think that his celebrity status was starting to shrink.

The Czech government, inexplicably slow to confront its most famous symbol of the new society, put him on the wanted list, but it was way too late. In fact, in their pursuit of Kozeny, the Czech authorities would continue to play catch-up for years. True, they did catch him a couple of times, but for relatively minor offenses with relatively mild "punishment." Once Kozeny used Harvard's assets, instead of the large fees he earned for managing the portfolio, to pay for an advertising campaign. By Czech standards, it was a serious infraction. The penalty? Repayment of $6.8 million and a fine of $37,000, the maximum the law allowed. Given the wealth Kozeny had reaped from the republic, that was small potatoes.

Meanwhile, Kozeny had decamped. He became an Irish citizen and resident of the wealthy tax haven, Lyford Cay, in the Bahamas, an island nation allergic to extradition entreaties. Secure in his Bahamian refuge, Kozeny was free to enjoy his wealth and plan his next financial conquest.

There were lots of options. The Bahamas are legendary—to some, perhaps notorious—as a haven for international financial titans, mega-millionaires, and those who follow the money. Kozeny set out to network among them—and he succeeded brilliantly. One early contact was Michael Dingman, a generation older than Kozeny but similarly "entrepreneurial." Dingman, a onetime member of the boards of Ford Motor Company and Time, Inc., was best known for turning companies around and selling them while retaining a healthy portion of the value for himself. His last big deal in the United States had culminated in a very large initial public offering (IPO) of the stock of Henley Group. The IPO led to a series of shareholder lawsuits charging that the company never made any money and that Dingman had enriched himself at the expense of others. Embittered by the personal attacks and legal troubles, Dingman renounced his U.S. citizenship and headed for friendlier climes.

In Lyford Cay, the two self-exiles, Dingman and Kozeny, had time and space to create a business plan for restructuring Czech industry—the start, the two men were certain, of a massive investment plan for Eastern Europe. Their efforts garnered significant interest and generally good reviews from the financial media and from others with an interest in emerging-markets investments. Dingman declared that he was anteing up $140 million of his own money. But it wasn't just his money that generated the business buzz; despite the Henley debacle, Dingman was a well-regarded businessman, and his presence in the project lent it credibility. The Czechs looked forward to his bringing the lessons of western-style capitalism to their country along with American management teams. Meanwhile, Kozeny would bring to bear his intimate knowledge of how things worked in his native country—and he would contribute some of the Harvard Funds' money.

Not long after the plan was launched, however, it was announced that the Harvard Funds were no longer an investment vehicle; instead, they were being transformed into an industrial fund. Kozeny began selling the assets of some of the funds and consolidating his interest in others. In some cases, he sold the Harvard Funds' assets to himself and Dingman at below-market prices, allowing the two men to realize significant gains. The two also bought into other companies in which Harvard had no interest, usually selling out as the stocks rose when their ownership interest became known.

The share prices of the companies Harvard held began to crumble, and its investors fled for the exits.

It was all presumably legal. It would not have been in the United States, for example, where any ownership interest above a 5 percent threshold must be disclosed, but in the embryonic regulatory environment of Czechoslovakia at the time, no disclosure was required.

Then came the final play of this inside game. The new Harvard industrial fund was merged into a holding company jointly owned by Kozeny and Dingman, Sklo Union Teplice. Next, this company was merged into a Cyprus-based company owned by Dingman—Daventree, Ltd. If the infant Czech securities regulations seemed murky, they were as transparent as a picture window compared to the opaque operating environment in Cyprus, where nothing ever needed to be disclosed. With no requirement to file financial reports or any other form of documentation, the Czechs were out of luck in trying to track down who owned what. Somewhere between Prague and Nicosia, the grandiose plan to restructure Czech industry was lost.

The Dingman-Kozeny venture caused the rest of the world to rethink the idea of investing in Eastern Europe. Thanks to an American tax exile living in the Bahamas and a Czech-born, newly minted Irish citizen who was his neighbor, the economic awakening of Czechoslovakia would be put on hold. Even educated and experienced emerging-markets investors experienced significant losses. The bottom line was that the risk/reward equation for investing in Eastern European markets had to be repriced. It would be a while before outside capital would flow back into the borders of the Czech Republic.

The Dingman-Kozeny alliance also fell apart. Dingman decided it was too difficult to do business in such an environment. Kozeny decided it was time to move on. Although the details of what really happened between the two—and at their hands—are difficult to navigate, they were explored in court in that trial Kozeny did not attend, courtesy of his Bahamian hosts, who were unwilling to part with their wealthy citizen. Kozeny, meanwhile, was busy writing chapter two of the conceivably epic novel of his life.

This is the part of the story in which Viktor Kozeny, armed with his increased wealth, began a period of spending on a lavish scale and with a global reach that outdid anything Jay Gatsby might have come up with. From London to Lyford Cay to Aspen, Kozeny partied extravagantly and picked up every tab. There were $20,000 dinners and bottles of wine that cost more than what a Czech worker made in a year. In Aspen, the house he bought set a record for high prices in a place where high prices were de rigueur. Next door in Aspen was Frederic "Rick" Bourke, scion of the luxury handbag company Dooney & Bourke. Bourke was charmed by the younger man and was delighted to accompany him on a worldwide tour, on Kozeny's private Lear jet, in search of opportunities for what Viktor Kozeny called "excess returns." They found what Kozeny assured Bourke was the opportunity for excess returns of a lifetime in Azerbaijan on the western shore of the Caspian Sea.

Oil was of course the name of the game in Azerbaijan, where, it was whispered, untapped reserves aplenty were under the Caspian Sea just waiting to be freed. What Kozeny saw as the opportunity, however, was not the oil so much as the privatization vouchers that might one day purchase the giant state oil company, SOCAR. Under Azeri law, foreigners could buy the vouchers only if they also bought a corresponding number of options from the government. Kozeny's aim was to gain control of SOCAR—the sale price of which Kozeny maintained would be undervalued—through the vouchers, then sell it in a public offering for billions. "Another sleeping beauty has emerged," he wrote of Azerbaijan, a brazen reference to the earlier privatization in Czechoslovakia, and he set out hell-for-leather to awaken her.[3]

Kozeny dispatched people with suitcases full of cash to buy vouchers on the streets of Baku. Back home in Aspen, the party went on, and Kozeny kept talking up his "great opportunity," promising potential investors a return of "20, 50, 100 times" when SOCAR was flipped. Bourke bought in. So did Florida money manager Aaron Fleck; Boston developer Richard Friedman—a confidant of the Clintons; and the onetime majority leader of the U.S. Senate, George Mitchell, globally respected as the negotiator of peace in Northern Ireland. With such top-flight names on board, Kozeny headed for Wall Street to look for institutional investors.

Fleck, well respected and well connected, lent credibility to Kozeny's quest for more investors and opened some doors for him, including the door to Lee Cooperman's Omega Advisors. Cooperman put Kozeny in touch with the Omega partner who oversaw the firm's emerging-markets portfolio, Clayton Lewis.

The Prince of Princeton

Lewis is, in a sense, the shadiest character in this story—not just because he is a self-confessed felon but also because so little is known about him. Suspended in a kind of legal limbo—awaiting a sentence that will not be handed down until he has testified against Kozeny, who continues to fight extradition—Lewis seems a man without a future. Of his past, little has been disclosed. A Seattle native, he cultivated a reputation as an extreme sports athlete, drove a souped-up Porsche 911 and raced it—rarely successfully—and was not well thought of on Wall Street. "Balding and arrogant," said one observer, adding that he nonetheless never expected Lewis to be a crook.

Even Lewis's present is unclear. His whereabouts as of this writing are unknown; rumors place him in Hawaii, but they are only rumors. Perhaps his location is best defined as "limbo," a place in which he is likely to remain until his work as a witness for the U.S. government is complete. Prosecutors have no interest in seeing Lewis sentenced lest he be further tainted in the eyes of the jury, as if his admission to a felony would not have already limited his effectiveness. For despite his freshly minted criminal record, Lewis is still the best available option for corroborating the case against Kozeny.

Yet unlike Kozeny, whose misdeeds are as extravagantly technicolored as his charm, Lewis appears to be a garden-variety swindler: He cheated the guy who trusted him, but it was his own greed that got the better of him—unfortunately taking down a lot of other people along the way.

A graduate of Princeton, Clayton Lewis went to work for Goldman Sachs, *the* plum job for anyone interested in investment banking. He was there for 10 years, then left, miffed, after a year in which the firm's performance had been less than stellar and everyone's bonus, including Lewis's, was down. He was on his way to Lehman Brothers when a friend of Cooperman's recommended him for the Omega staff. Cooperman duly met with Lewis, found him intelligent and eager, and made him a deal: Lewis would start with a modest salary but would be entitled to a percentage of any profits he generated. The two shook hands, and Lewis joined Omega in 1995.

And at first, Cooperman was very pleased with Lewis's performance. Lewis made emerging markets his forte, developed that arm of the business for Omega, and became a star performer for the firm, earning something on the order of $500 million for the firm over three years with take-home pay for himself of about $30 million. So when, in February 1998, Lewis came to Cooperman with what he claimed was "the best investment ever," Cooperman was willing to listen.

Lewis's pitch was Viktor Kozeny's Azerbaijani venture. Lewis told Cooperman he had personally visited Azerbaijan twice, had met with the president, had conferred with the World Bank, and was convinced the investment was a terrific opportunity. He suggested to Cooperman that the investment effectively would let them buy oil reserves for pennies when the market price hovered at $6 or more. But since Kozeny's venture constituted a private investment—that is, there was no true public market for Azeri vouchers, so it was not a trade per se—it was not within the purview of Lewis's own investing authority and required review by Cooperman and the investment committee.

That is standard practice at firms like Omega. Senior investment professionals are given extensive creative latitude as well as investing authority up to a certain dollar amount—approximately $150 million in Lewis's case. In other words, he could invest up to that amount on any investment idea or in pursuit of any investment thesis he liked without requiring approval from anyone. But for a dollar above that amount or in the case of a private investment, the investment idea had to undergo exhaustive due diligence and to pass muster in a hearing before the full investment committee— complete with comprehensive documentation.

Lewis duly made his presentation before the nine-member committee, which of course included Cooperman. Naturally, because emerging-markets investments are by definition riskier than those in developed countries, the returns on investments there must be well above average in order to attract capital, and the investment committee wanted to be certain the venture could yield such returns. They peppered Lewis with questions—about the terms of the investment but also about Kozeny. Lewis assured them that Kozeny, while certainly colorful and aggressive, had never done anything illegal, and he persuaded them that the opportunity was real and that Kozeny had the process well in hand. Later, court proceedings would make it clear that Lewis and Kozeny had cut their own deal, in which Lewis would receive a substantial percentage—40 percent—of Kozeny's take on the venture—an agreement that was likely in Lewis's back pocket as he was making his presentation to the investment committee.

To be sure, the committee already understood that Clayton Lewis faced the possibility of making 100 times his own money if Omega invested in the Azerbaijani deal. Like a professional poker player with four aces, Lewis held a hand that, if not a guaranteed winner, nevertheless allowed for very few ways to lose. It was the fund's money he would be wagering, but he stood to benefit personally. If the trade went bad, he wouldn't be affected very harshly because his own stake in the fund was minimal. But if the investment returned even just a fraction of what Kozeny had promised, Lewis stood to make a fortune, for the bulk of his compensation was based on how much money his portion of the portfolio earned. Lewis was ready to bet heavily. He had a separate fund, approved by Omega's attorneys, from which he wanted to allocate 15 percent for the Azeri vouchers. In addition, approved by no one because no one knew about it, he had $20 million in vouchers and options that Kozeny had given him, and these Lewis sold directly to two of Omega's investors—a university and a Fortune 10 company—pocketing the proceeds for himself.

To the investment committee, he made a convincing case, although he did not get as much as he asked for. Lewis wanted a 3 percent allocation from the fund for the venture, but that request hit a Cooperman veto: Cooperman simply would not commit that much money to an illiquid investment in an emerging market. Moreover, Cooperman wanted a complete separation between Omega and Kozeny and had rigorous contracts drawn up for Kozeny to sign. The contracts stipulated that Kozeny would get nothing until Omega had received a targeted rate of return, that Kozeny could not sell anything to Omega from his own inventory, that Omega would pay cost for the options and vouchers and cost only, and that the options and vouchers would have to be kept in a separate, secure location. In fact, Kozeny stored them in a fortified bunker on the premises of the Minaret Group, the western-style investment bank he had founded, housed in the most expensive office building in Baku, the Azeri capital. The vouchers reputedly filled the bunker. The options for the vouchers—critical to the investment since foreigners could not hold vouchers without them—numbered a mere 20 or so and were also held by Minaret. In addition to these stipulations, Kozeny was required to affirm that he knew the rules laid down in the U.S. Foreign Corrupt Practices Act addressing accounting transparency and bribery of foreign officials. Kozeny signed, and the investment committee gave its stamp of approval.

Cooperman is reputed to have told a friend that he anticipated a "10-bagger"[4] from the investment—perhaps 10 times the money Omega put in. It was not an unreasonable assumption—unless of course the deal went sour or the facts were not as they seemed.

Waiting for SOCAR

By 1998, everything was in place. Cooperman, Lewis, Bourke, Fleck, and Mitchell were on the boards of two advisory groups established to promote the SOCAR purchase in the United States. Lobbyists were at work promoting the foreign policy benefits of a privatized SOCAR. Public relations consultants had been hired. And Viktor Kozeny kept assuring investors that the SOCAR privatization was "wired"—that is, that everyone in the Azerbaijani establishment who had to give consent had done so—especially, if not exclusively, the president, strongman Heydar Aliyev, without whose approval nothing in Azerbaijan went forward. Nothing.

In February of that year, Clayton Lewis went to Azerbaijani and sent back a confidential memo concurring that the venture was moving along smoothly, that privatization would likely happen ahead of the October presidential elections, and that Aliyev's approval was a done deal.

But then October came and went. No privatization. The investors were told that it would occur after the elections, but the elections came and went. No privatization. The year 1998 came and went. No privatization. The investors became a bit uneasy, then more than a bit uneasy.

Over at Omega, Lewis was gone. Cooperman had fired him in August after he had blown through the firm's risk limits on Russian investments and had lost almost half a billion dollars in that country, equivalent to the amount he had made for Omega in the three previous years. In his wake were the Azeri vouchers Omega was carrying at cost, and Cooperman decided he wanted a fresh look at their value. After all, he was earning a 1 percent fee on the assets under his management, and he wanted to be sure he was marking the vouchers' value to market correctly, that he was not overcharging the very investors who placed those assets in his care. He dispatched in-house attorney Eric Vincent to Azerbaijan to check out the vouchers and options in Minaret's care; Vincent's brief was to get an on-the-ground understanding of the investment and of the value that remained.

One of the meetings Vincent attended as part of gaining this understanding was with the head of the State Property Commission, the agency responsible for the privatization process and for the voucher program. As he was leaving the meeting, Vincent was handed the usual packet of "take-away" materials these meetings ritually require, and he just as ritually stuffed them all in his briefcase. It wasn't until he was on the plane for home that Vincent pulled the materials out and began to read the State Property Commission's book, given to him in all innocence, about the privatization program.

What he read was stunning. The book stated clearly that the options for the SOCAR privatization vouchers had been issued in 1997—before Omega had invested in the deal. So where did Omega's options come from? It looked very much like they must have come from Kozeny, and if that were the case, it would be in direct contravention of the agreement that Omega had made Kozeny sign—which had specifically stipulated that Kozeny could not transfer any vouchers or options from his inventory to Omega.

Even more unsettling to Vincent, as he sat reading at 35,000 feet, was the stated price of the options. The government price back in 1997 had been 25 cents, not the $25 Lewis had quoted Kozeny as claiming. When Vincent presented this evidence to Cooperman, it suddenly looked like Kozeny had paid 25 cents for the options and sold them to Omega for $25, pocketing some $90 million—much of it, in Cooperman's mind, Cooperman's money. He had been robbed. In the words of someone who saw it happen, Cooperman's famous temper was suddenly and fiercely on display. The walls did little to muffle his rage. He went "ballistic."

He phoned Kozeny—repeatedly. When Kozeny finally called back, he said he had no time to talk to Cooperman. (Later, Kozeny would claim that the difference between the 25-cent cost and the $25 price tag was money for bribes, and Clayton Lewis, after denying knowledge of the bribes, eventually would confess he knew about them all along.)

Out of his own pocket, Cooperman then hired a major law firm to interview every member of Omega to see what each of them knew about the Azerbaijani investment. It was an expensive exercise, costing Cooperman more than $500,000, but since the attorneys determined that Lewis had worked alone, perhaps the money was worth it. Cooperman also called the New York District Attorney, the legendary Robert Morgenthau, asserting that Omega had been the victim of a fraud and promising cooperation.

After that, it was a lawyer's game.

In 1999, Omega and the two investors who had been approached separately by Clayton Lewis all sued Viktor Kozeny in a London court, claiming that he had defrauded them of $180 million and seeking more than $100 million in damages.

In 2003, Kozeny was indicted in a New York state court for stealing $180 million from investors including Omega and Cooperman.

In 2004, Clayton Lewis pleaded guilty in U.S. federal court to investing on behalf of Omega with the knowledge that Kozeny had bribed Azeri officials. Lewis is cooperating with federal prosecutors and as of this writing has yet to be sentenced.

In 2007, Omega agreed to pay $500,000 to resolve the U.S. bribery investigation; it "acknowledged responsibility" for Lewis's behavior but, in the standard legalese, neither admitted nor denied wrongdoing. Cooperman had felt almost literally mugged by the federal government for the $500,000. Federal prosecutors never charged him with anything, had Lewis's confession, and could not extradite Kozeny, but they could hold up Omega Advisors for half a million bucks and register a "win"—or so it seemed to Lee Cooperman. He fought the payment for years until he was persuaded by his legal team that going to trial would be a disaster for Omega and all its employees. It would, the lawyers said, cost enormous time, money, and focus; would generate bad press; and was likely to gain little. It finally seemed better to Cooperman just to let it go.

Logic would dictate that if there were any basis to implicate Cooperman or Omega, Lewis would have done so as part of his plea arrangement. And indeed in yet another plea agreement, the government absolved Omega of guilt. It is likely that the firm's biggest misstep was hiring Clayton Lewis—a regrettable act, as it turned out, but not a criminal one. The only criminal at Omega was Lewis himself, and Lee Cooperman tried to prove as much by bringing suit against Lewis. Cooperman's goal is to recover the $30 million in compensation he paid Lewis, a sum more representative of principle than useful as reparation.

In January 2009, Omega settled its London suit against Kozeny, freeing his assets held in Britain. The settlement came on the very day Cooperman was scheduled to testify on the subject of Omega's responsibility for bribery in the matter.

In July 2009, Rick Bourke, the handbag magnate, charged in federal court with helping Kozeny bribe Azeri officials, was convicted of having violated the Foreign Corrupt Practices Act.

Kozeny is still wanted in the Czech Republic as well as in the United States.

In the Bahamas, where he served a brief stint in the local jail, Kozeny lives "imprisoned" in the golden cage of his oceanfront mansion in Lyford Cay. He claims to be broke Azerbaijani never sold SOCAR.

Cloak, Dagger, and Lawsuits: A Timeline

1997: As Kozeny's proxies buy up SOCAR vouchers, Kozeny woos prestigious U.S. investors.

February 1998: Lewis presents the investment to Cooperman. Lewis sends reassuring reports from Azerbaijani, predicting the SOCAR privatization by October.

August 1998: Cooperman fires Lewis, dispatches Vincent to Azerbaijan, where he coincidentally uncovers Kozeny's options fraud.

October 1998: Azerbaijani elections: no privatization of SOCAR.

1999: Omega sues Kozeny, *in absentia*, in the United Kingdom.

2003: Kozeny, *in absentia*, is indicted in New York.

2004: Lewis pleads guilty to knowing about Kozeny's bribes and turns government witness.

2007: Omega settles with the U.S. government on the matter of Lewis's behavior.

January 2009: Omega settles the U.S. suit against Kozeny, still *in absentia* in the Bahamas.

July 2009: Bourke convicted of violating the Foreign Corrupt Practices Act.

What Went Wrong

If investing is risky, and investing in emerging markets is even riskier, then surely investing in Azerbaijan is riskier still. In fact, at the time Omega entered into the agreement with Kozeny, there was no public market on which to trade securities; the Baku Stock

Exchange would not commence operations until 2001, three years later. Without a stock exchange and without any regulatory oversight or transparency or financial controls, the risk quotient was sky high, almost intolerably so. **The unmistakable lesson from history is that markets not subject to public oversight or government regulation are prone to corruption. That is the mistake.**

Arguably, Cooperman unwittingly compounded the mistake by allowing the due diligence process on the investment to be overseen by an interested party, Clayton Lewis, who was already committed to the fraud.

For openers, the whole enterprise had the air about it of a movie script: Viktor Kozeny as Hyman Roth and Clayton Lewis as Michael Corleone divvying up the Havana casinos among lesser Mafiosi in *Godfather 2*—except that the divvying up was taking place in a country with a somewhat violent history and one that had only recently emerged as its own political entity.

Even a cursory glance at that nation's politics would have shown that President Aliyev ran a government reeking with corruption. A former Soviet strongman who had cut his teeth in the KGB, Aliyev was forced to rebuff coup after coup in Azerbaijan, which he did with little attention to the niceties. The one main asset Aliyev and the people of Azerbaijan could count on was SOCAR, which prompts one to ask why on earth they would ever sell it. They didn't, of course, and when Aliyev died in 2003—of natural causes—he was succeeded by his son, a former SOCAR vice president, who garnered an impossible-to-believe 77 percent of the vote. No wonder Cooperman made sure that Omega Advisors dotted every "i" and crossed every "t" in its contracts with promoter Kozeny before it sank a penny into Azeri vouchers.

For despite the comic-opera aspects of the venture, there were precedents for thinking that this newly emerging market just might yield an investment opportunity. The nearest and most obvious precedent was Russia, a country also ruled with an iron fist; it too had used a voucher system to privatize Gazprom, one of the largest gas companies in the world, and its various oil companies. So perhaps it was not entirely unreasonable to think that SOCAR too might be privatized. It wasn't even unreasonable to assume that a shady character with a blemished track record might be involved. Similarly shady, similarly blemished types had been involved in Russia's privatization—including former KGB officers.

There is a new term for these people now; they're called billionaires. The presence of Kozeny was therefore not necessarily a bad sign, as long as Omega's lawyers locked him in as well as high-priced lawyers can.

So where did this episode break down for Omega and the others? If a forensic analysis were to be performed, it would no doubt point to Lewis, the greedy bantamweight who always thought he deserved more than he was getting and just couldn't wait for whatever he was getting to arrive. Between the greed of Lewis and the guerrilla tactics of Kozeny, even Lee Cooperman couldn't avoid being squeezed. Cooperman did everything an investor can do to protect himself, his firm, and his investors' money. He took extra precautions—rightly so, in light of the nature of the emerging market and the nature of the guy promoting the investment venture. But when the viper is in your own nest—your own well-compensated, well-treated star performer—no amount of precautions can protect you. The bottom line is simply that some time or other, somehow or other, even brilliant and experienced global investors lose. And so can you.

Clayton Lewis perpetrated a fraud, but he also made a mistake. He wanted too much from the deal—and for that greed, he not only lost everything, including his future, but he also brought down an awful lot of other people with him.

Omega completely pulled out of emerging-markets investing. The opaqueness and inherent difficulty of investing in this sector, murky enough to begin with, was only made worse by the Pirate of Prague with his appealing promise to shed light on it all and the Prince of Princeton with his second-rate theft.

Yet the truth is that while the amount of money that Omega and Cooperman lost in Azerbaijan is significant, it represented but a small portion of Cooperman's net worth and an even smaller portion of Omega's capital. For Lee Cooperman, it really wasn't the size of the loss that hurt; it was its shape: fraud born of greed, by a person he had hired, worked with, been good to.

Maybe emerging-markets investing attracts that kind of fraud. Maybe such investing just makes it easier to perpetrate and therefore too seductive not to try. One thing is for sure, however: Even though every investor has to lose sometime, it's awful to lose at the hands of someone you trusted.

Lessons Learned

- *Emerging markets are extremely risky.* Investing in emerging markets contains greater risk than investing in developed countries and therefore should be a very small part of any portfolio. There is a real chance that the investment could be completely wiped out.
- *Check for the existence of regulatory safeguards.* The opportunity to invest in a ground-floor opportunity like the privatization of a public company, is tempting, but sometimes the urge must be resisted because the regulatory infrastructure—the rules that protect investors—are likely very thin or nonexistent. For example, if the highest levels of the Azerbaijani government were complicit in the Kozeny affair, what would be an individual U.S. investor's recourse if securities laws were broken? Certain emerging markets offer little or no protection to the individual investor. This makes for a very uneven playing field. Investing in the markets of such countries may be akin to responding to a plea for money from an anonymous e-mail. Stay away from emerging markets that do not have a track record of regulation that protects an investor.
- *Make sure rules are enforced.* Even when regulatory oversight exists in an emerging market, the safeguards may be deficient. Kozeny was able to engage in significant self-dealing by buying and selling sizable interests in companies without disclosing the acts to investors. As a result, when these transactions ultimately were revealed, the Czech stock market was hit hard, and investors had virtually no chance of protecting themselves against significant downside. In the United States, a 5 percent stake in a company qualifies that entity or individual as an insider, requiring filing a document with the Securities and Exchange Commission (SEC) any time shares are bought or sold.
- *Ditto for mature markets.* Even some mature markets and economies lack the kinds of regulatory oversight familiar in the United States. In Germany, for example, it was possible for Porsche to acquire approximately 75 percent of Volkswagen stock without public disclosure. (See Chapter 9.)
- *Know the other players.* If possible, perform due diligence on others who are involved in the investment. If the person or entity is of dubious character or has a history of securities violations, stay away.
- *Explore the SEC Web site.* Go to www.sec.gov for a listing of enforcement actions against individuals and entities that you should be cautious about investing with. It may take some patience to go through the site, but it's worth it. You also can use the Web to research the regulatory situation in other countries. You don't have to become an expert,

but keep in mind that emerging-market investments require greater market knowledge precisely because typically there is less protection for investors.

- *Allocate your investments intelligently.* Some financial advisors believe that every portfolio should have an allocation in emerging markets because of that sector's potential growth. While not a bad strategy, timing is important so that you don't find yourself "top ticking" the market. That's what happened to many investors with the Chinese market. With every newspaper, magazine, and business broadcast exclaiming over China's hypergrowth, it became the classic momentum investment, attracting a lot of capital. Those who invested late, however, lost almost 50 percent because they bought high just before the stock dropped in value. Review recent performance of the market or security you're targeting to make sure you're not the last one to invest.
- *Spread the risk.* If you do invest in emerging markets, spread the risk through mutual funds that specialize in those markets.
- *Be prudent.* Remember that wherever and however you invest, someday, in some way, you will lose. Therefore, never invest more than you can afford to lose, and stay diversified.

CHAPTER

Richard Pzena

FASHIONS CHANGE, HISTORY
PERSISTS—OR DOES IT?

How do you argue with history? You can't. History tells what happened, and there's no talking back to what happened—even in the arcane realm of money and investing.

Richard Pzena is a student of history and a man who believes what it tells him. He made that belief a core principle of his investing practice as head of Pzena Investment Management, and it made him immensely successful.

In a profession in which there are no certainties, where nothing is ever 100 percent, and where any one of the variables can start slipping out from under you at any time, history is something you always can turn to.

History never failed Richard Pzena. Until it did.

A Learning Experience

Pzena does not look like a scholar. Not that scholars have a particular look, but Pzena's demeanor suggests something altogether different. Think genial host. Simultaneously, think perfect guest at your next dinner party. That's the kind of guy Pzena seems. A man of ready affability, more scamp than speculator, Pzena is bright eyed, gracious, quick to laugh.

Along with the affability, however, is an intensity that can take you by surprise. Pose a question to Pzena, and you can almost see the pistons fire behind his eyes as you sense him framing his answer, a well-conceived response that is likely to shift the issue to a different dimension altogether, taking your inquiry a step up to a point you wish you had thought of yourself.

So, scholar he is. And driven. Scholarliness and drive constitute a rare combination in the investment world, where academics more often occupy a seat in the background rather than engaging on the front lines of portfolio management. In fact, Pzena tracks the start of his value investing career to a research project he undertook during his school days at Wharton, from which he graduated summa cum laude. Pzena was in his last year of the prestigious joint bachelor's-master's program, and he and two fellow students collaborated on a paper "redoing" the original research by Graham and Dodd on net-net working capital. The paper was, he says "a pure-pure value approach in which we did a screen of companies that were selling for effectively less than the working capital on their books." This revision of the classic analysis predated the era of widespread computer use, so the three authors did it the old-fashioned way, poring over stacks of stock guides, booklets containing vital financial statistics on thousands of publicly traded companies. It was time-consuming work, unappreciated—probably unknown—in today's era of online stock tickers and data feeds cut any way you like at the touch of a button. Whatever the means, the end result was good enough to be published in the *Journal of Portfolio Management* in 1981, and all three authors—Joel Greenblatt and Bruce Newberg were the other two—seemed well launched on careers in the field. (Greenblatt became an investor, author, and professor; Newberg became a bond trader at Drexel Burnham Lambert and eventually crashed and burned with Michael Milken.)

Maybe reading all those stock guides proved to be a turn-off for Pzena, for, upon graduation, he "rejected the whole Wall Street investment banking thing" and certainly the idea of becoming a security analyst. Instead, like many young men before him, he went west—at least as far as Chicago, where he joined the oil industry. It was 1981, and oil was at its peak. Pzena went to work for Amoco, which, until its 1998 merger with British Petroleum, seemed the quintessential American oil company.

He spent about a year at the corporate headquarters in Chicago then was sent south to New Orleans to make auction bids for offshore oil leases. In 1983, the government had introduced area-wide leasing in the Gulf of Mexico, opening up 2.5 million under-sea acres to competitive auction bidding. Oil companies were lining up to bid on those blocks of the acreage their geologists had identi-fied as containing robust oil reserves. The auction process spawned a Wild West atmosphere, and Pzena, in his own words, "got to expe-rience firsthand how you can get carried away in business." It was his introduction to *momentum investing*, aptly described by some as a "greater fool" process in which buying by one begets buying by another, driving the price higher and higher until valuation and expectations are so stretched that the next big move for the stock is a complete reversal. Momentum investing is the antithesis of Graham-and-Dodd style portfolio management, and it is anathema to classic value investors whose process is functionally rooted in the psychology of buying when others are selling.

Pzena saw this kind of investing early on in the oil-lease bidding process, and it made a lasting impression on him. Amoco's geolo-gists had found a patch of acreage they believed contained signifi-cant oil reserves. The bidding team on which Pzena served, after performing the usual due diligence on the property and its pros-pects, settled on a price they thought could win the bid. The price, however, exceeded the dollar amount they had authority to bid, so they kicked the issue up to their superiors in the management hierarchy. That group, in turn, grew even more excited about the property's potential to produce crude oil, and they increased the bid price accordingly—to a value that exceeded *their* bidding authority as well. They followed the same protocol as the others and passed the process up to the next level of management. And so it went—up and up the corporate ladder, with each succeeding tier of management becoming increasingly carried away and raising the bid price to levels they weren't authorized to offer. Eventually the journey ended at the top of the management structure, Amoco's board of directors. They added to the bidding momentum and pro-vided Amoco's final price for the acreage. By the time this offer was tendered, it was more than 100 times higher than the next highest bid—and, says Pzena, "produced zero return for the company."

The lesson learned? "You see these bubbles, and it's very hard to make money when you overpay for something—particularly in an environment of euphoria." In other words, beware abnormality, beware emotion, and beware momentum investing.

The "Wall Street Thing"

The bubble didn't last long. Neither did the Wild West lure of auction bidding, which Pzena was beginning to find overrated, even in the seductive atmosphere of New Orleans. Amoco management wanted him to come home to corporate headquarters and take up a planning function, but, says Pzena, when oil companies say "planning," what they really mean is arguing "about moving a well 200 feet." Since the only real strategic variable is price, planning did not strike him as a particularly interesting exercise.

Enter a headhunter from Sanford C. Bernstein & Co. Bernstein had two businesses under its corporate umbrella: a brokerage firm that provided research and trading services to a large selection of mutual funds and hedge funds and an asset management division. The firm had built a strong reputation for performing extensive research on value-type investments, and unlike other Wall Street firms, it preferred to hire analysts from the industry rather than train business school graduates. Bernstein's view was that significant knowledge of an industry is more important to the investment process than a degree in building earnings models. Where the latter was a generic discipline that could be taught, the former required the kind of immersion that produced insight.

Pzena found himself assessing the job offer as intellectually challenging: It seemed to marry the Graham-and-Dodd valuation work he had done as a Wharton undergraduate with his acquired knowledge of the oil industry. Despite his anti–Wall Street bias, it seemed that now might be the time to get into the investment game. Taking the lessons he had learned in New Orleans with him, he went to work for Bernstein Research as an oil industry analyst—writing reports for what he calls "the sell side," or brokerage part, of the business. It would be Pzena's job to market his research to the investment funds on the "buy side."

Research was then and is now the Bernstein calling card; the signature of the process is the legendary Bernstein Blackbook, known not just for comprehensiveness to the nth degree but for depth and context as well. Every new recruit, says Pzena, spends at least his or her first six months on the job doing nothing but working on a single Blackbook.

Pzena paid his Blackbook dues and began writing reports on the oil industry. He researched and wrote about the U.S. refining industry; he wrote about domestic production; he developed a framework for valuing oil companies. Two years into the work, however, he began to feel that being a sell-side equity analyst was not his calling. Just as Pzena was coming to that realization, Bernstein offered him a new opportunity.

Management had been making moves to expand beyond the firm's traditional large-capitalization value investment product and had decided to start up a small-cap fund. Pzena got the job. The fund was launched in the middle of 1990, and almost simultaneously, Bernstein asked Pzena to become director of research, a responsibility that would also include overseeing the research for the large-cap portfolio.

Just about the time these new opportunities were coming his way, Pzena experienced a gentle epiphany that convinced him to reach out and grab them. It was the summer, and, still wearing his oil-industry analyst hat, he was making a presentation on Middle East oil to a typical audience of fund managers and investment professionals. The concern that summer was Saddam Hussein's saber rattling. Pzena assured his listeners in the most positive terms that there was no chance at all that the Iraqi leader would invade Kuwait. Two days later, Saddam Hussein did exactly that, and Richard Pzena finally decided he really wasn't adding much value to the kinds of discussions fund managers wanted to have. It seemed the right moment to move to the buy side of the investment business.

He persuaded management to keep the small-cap fund, although he relinquished responsibility for it, and he launched himself into a new career as a large-cap value investment manager.

He continued in that job for five years. His title changed from time to time—director of research, director of U.S. equity investments, and so on—but basically, Pzena was in charge of the firm's flagship strategic value product, its U.S.-concentrated large-cap value portfolio. The five years were, he says, "a good environment for value." In particular, the era offered a learning experience in financial stocks. The fund's portfolio at the time was 40 percent financials—"it was," says Pzena, "the last time financials were cheap"—and he watched the portfolio skyrocket in defiance of conventional wisdom and the assumptions then in vogue.

Still, the incident offered a lesson in how financial institutions behave and how investor psychology works. That, plus what he learned in the oil bubble, would stay with Pzena as he made the decision, in 1995, to "venture out on my own." He was ready to put to practical use the lessons he had learned about momentum investing and his own version of Graham-and-Dodd value investing, a version that had been gradually evolving and maturing in his brain.

The Value Investor: Contrarian? Courageous? Or Both?

Investing is more like the fashion business than anyone wants to admit. Like fashions, industry sectors go in and out of vogue. One year, bank stocks are as hot as a narrow Hermes tie in gray and black. The next year, you wouldn't be caught dead wearing either; it's biotech stocks and Dolce & Gabanna ties with shocking splotches of color. Students of fashion will tell you to hold onto that narrow tie, however; one of these days, it will be back in vogue.

Ditto with investing. In fact, that's pretty much what value investing is all about—buying the out-of-fashion stocks, then waiting for them to come back into favor. It requires patience, vision, and the fortitude to stand alone. Value investors are a little like junk collectors. They sift through other portfolio managers' discards to find the lamp they can dust off and make work—the one fixture that turns out to be a valuable antique.

Before the 1990s, bank stocks were regarded as widow and orphan safe, metaphors for financial stability—as opposed to the dubious speculations of investing. And why not? What could be a safer investment than this simple, easily understood business model: Collect deposits on which you pay a rate of interest, lend the deposited funds to creditworthy individuals and institutions at higher rates, and capture the spread as earnings for shareholders. To make the investment even more attractive, pay shareholders a dividend on the shares of stock they own. From the neighborhood bank on the corner to the huge "money center" banks, an appellation reserved for only the largest institutions, banks were austere, solid, and utterly reliable recipients of your money—not just your deposits, but your investment money as well.

Then came the 1990s. That's when the unsightly wrinkles on this austere face began to be revealed, and bank stocks went tumbling out of fashion. The economy as a whole had begun to fade, and as Rich Pzena recalls it, "Every bank was in trouble." The Third World debt crisis of the 1970s and 1980s—when the less-developed countries were unable to service their outstanding debt to U.S. commercial banks—had taken the banks to the cleaners. Close on the heels of this disaster—and compounding it substantively— was the commercial real estate disaster, in which banks that had made both construction and mortgage financing loans suffered widespread losses. With mortgage delinquencies soaring and construction slowed to a crawl, banks had to write off their bad loans. Capital ratios, the measurement of a bank's fiscal health, tightened.

A Primer on Capital Ratios

How do you measure whether a bank has enough capital to meet its obligations—that is, pay its depositors and creditors and absorb unexpected losses? The primary measure is the institution's capital ratio.

In its simplest and most basic definition, capital ratio is capital divided by assets, expressed as a percentage. But in order to provide a common "language" banks can use to operate internationally, the Bank for International Settlements, established in 1930, created a standard framework for weighting a bank's assets based on risk sensitivity. The framework is embodied in the so-called Basel Accords, which govern the calculation of risk weights, while empowering each nation to set its own terms for measuring capital.

As a general rule, the higher the bank's capital ratio, the better.

The media poured out an increasingly ugly torrent of negative news, which in turn prompted investors to liquidate more holdings in the banking industry. The then-giants of the industry—Citicorp, Manufacturers Hanover, Chemical Bank, and others—appeared daily on the list of stocks achieving new lows. As the negative momentum accelerated, the selling grew indiscriminate. Whether you were in trouble or not, if you were a bank, your stock tumbled. The baby was being thrown out with the bathwater.

And as Pzena notes, although there was no run on the banks, "They stopped lending." It gave him pause. "I cut my teeth as a research director visiting banks and trying to understand the mentality of an industry that loaned money frivolously when there was no spread, and when the spreads opened dramatically, stopped lending." And Pzena claims he "never got an adequate answer as to why banks did this."

Against the background of this market slaughter, value investors like Pzena were doing their research, sharpening their analyses, trying to determine which banks would survive. Even more important, they were trying to figure out which bank stocks had been so indiscriminately oversold that their current price represented a steep discount to the actual worth of their ongoing business. Put another way: Which banks had such strong intrinsic value that the price at which their stock was selling could be seen as a bargain?

To ascertain that intrinsic value, the actual worth of the underlying business, value investors had to make certain assumptions about the potential earnings power of the bank under scrutiny. Different value investors came up with different ways of making these assumptions. Pzena's forte—and the way he put his own signature on value investing and carved his own value investing niche—was assessing a company's normalized earnings power. That is, what would this bank earn if it weren't for this current glitch—this particular crisis in the market and the economy? The reason he asked that question is that he believed the crisis was temporary; when it was over, no matter how long it took, everything would return to normal. Pzena believed that because it was right there in black and white in history.

And it was precisely his assessment of the normalized earnings power of banks that persuaded Pzena in the 1990s to defy fashion and buy out-of-vogue bank stocks. At the time, few were more out of vogue than Citicorp. In 1990, the holding company for Citibank—and later, of course, part of what would become the Citigroup behemoth—was trading as if it were going out of business, creating panic in the market. Late in the year, with nowhere else to turn, then chief executive officer John Reed turned to the oil-rich Middle East for help. His Royal Highness Prince Al-Waleed bin Talal bin Abdul Aziz Al Saud of Saudi Arabia responded, investing $550 million at a price of $2.98 a share—adjusted to reflect the stock's splits—a level it would not see again until the 2008 bank crisis. As the war in Iraq raged, the Saudi Arabian prince continued to increase his stake in the troubled institution—up to 14.9 percent of ownership. His investment helped create a floor for all stocks in the banking sector and propelled Pzena's holdings, which included Citicorp stock, much higher.

Indeed, all bank stocks eventually came back into favor, and their return to fashion laid the foundation for Pzena's stellar reputation as a preeminent value investor. Nearly 20 years later, in 2007 and 2008, the banks, including a far larger Citigroup, presented Pzena with what looked like the same sort of opportunity he had seen in 1990.

Looks can be deceiving.

Pzena's View of Value

To understand what Pzena saw when he looked at bank stocks in 2007, it's essential to delve a bit into his investment philosophy—his view of the role of history in value investing. His own words tell the story best:

"There is enough compelling evidence to suggest that historical trends are meaningful," Richard Pzena told students at Columbia Business School in September 2006. He added: "Whenever you hear the words 'It is different now,' you should hold onto your wallet, because it is not."[1]

This outlook on the world of investing—"Obviously, I am biased due to history," in Pzena's own words—was an informing principle of the investment philosophy that guided what became Pzena Investment Management, which was launched in 1995 in the conference room of a friend's office in Citicorp Center with a staff of four, including Pzena himself. The departure from Bernstein had been somewhat wrenching. Pzena was heavily invested in the firm—both financially and emotionally—so leaving it was costly. Moreover, management had just offered him a major position heading up global research—a vote of confidence that would have meant a major commitment on Pzena's part. But he had long felt the itch to do things his way, and he knew that the window would not stay open forever, so this seemed as good a time as any. Leaving millions of dollars behind in the unrealized value of his Bernstein stock, he traded a secure, well-paying job for the much riskier environment of his own start-up investment management company.

Thanks to the approach Pzena brought to his new firm—an approach founded in his value investing philosophy—the risk paid off in the very substantial subsequent success of Pzena Investment Management. If you were looking for a catchphrase to label the approach, think "deep value." Like any value investor, Pzena looks for companies with stocks priced at less than intrinsic value. And again, for Pzena, that means normalized earnings: not the earnings achieved in a stressed environment nor in a particularly benign environment, but rather the long-term, underlying earnings power. To determine that, Pzena asks three questions: "Is the business any good? Are the problems temporary or permanent? Is it rational to expect that the earnings will return to historic trend?"[2] Answering these questions, says Pzena, is "the hard part." It's how the staff of Pzena Investment Management—now nearly 20 times the size of the original gang of four—spends "all our time."

There's another important variable that features in the Pzena analysis and that also points to history: what he described to the Columbia students as the "cyclical nature of this type of deep value investing." What history has told Richard Pzena about these cycles is that the stocks that make it onto his value investing screen do well in periods of recession—the official definition of which is two successive quarters of a contracting economy. Doing well in such an economy seems counterintuitive, as Pzena admits. "People don't want to own cyclical companies during the recession," he concedes—that is, companies whose performance correlates to the economy, producing strong earnings when the economy expands—"but that is exactly when they perform well." It's *before* a recession that you don't want to own these cyclical stocks, says Pzena, and therefore the trick is "to time the purchases at the start of a recession; that way, you will optimize the valuation." But getting the timing right requires a good deal of slicing and dicing. Looking back as far as the recession of 1969 and tracking 40 years' worth of recessions that followed, Pzena concluded that momentum investing—basically, buying high and selling higher—did well in the period leading up to each recession while his kind of value investing "won in the period following the beginning of the recession."[3]

His explanation? During the latter part of an upturn in the economic cycle, the investment community begins to worry about recession, so, in a sense, a recession begins to take its toll on economic activity before it actually has been defined. Earnings of the most economically sensitive companies begin to slow, and the stock prices of these businesses begin to decline. Activities like construction diminish, and companies that feed or depend on construction—an equipment manufacturer like Caterpillar, for example—suffer from the slowdown. Retailers begin to feel pain as consumers curb their spending habits out of worry over job security. And banks suffer both from customers defaulting on their loan obligations and from their own tightening of lending standards as they worry about borrowers' ability to pay them back. In lockstep with these declines in the earnings and business prospects of these enterprises, the valuation of their stocks also contracts. The reason is obvious: No one is willing to pay as much for a stock when the company's prospects for increased earnings are limited. A snowball effect takes over as the selling momentum increases and as these "cyclical" stocks, reliant on a growing economy, decline.

But markets historically go up more than they go down. And since there are so many mutual funds with a mandate to own equities, investors withdrawing from cyclical stocks will look for what *is* working and will chase that upward momentum. Specifically, they will chase the growth stocks that are less reliant on the economy's ebbs and flows—companies in the healthcare industry, for example. Yes, the growth of these companies may diminish somewhat during a slow economy, but people always will buy medication, regardless of how the economy as a whole is faring. As investors veer from what's not working into what's *working*—the momentum stocks— their price is driven higher and higher.

Again, all this is happening before the recession actually begins. Once it does begin, however, the market, says Pzena, undergoes "a complete reversal in psychology." Investors bail out of what's working, purging those high-priced momentum stocks from their portfolios out of a fear that the prices will decline and they will lose their profits. The worry now is that the contracting economy will take its toll on their investment gains, and the psychology shifts again.

It is at this point that investors turn to valuation. The market, being a discounting mechanism, begins to look ahead to a healing of the economy, and investors swap momentum for perceived value. Caterpillar gets their attention again; it used to trade at $60 a share but is now only $15, Bristol Myers, however, used to trade at $20 and now is trading at $40. Investors sell Bristol and buy Cat. Inherent in this bet is the assumption that the recession won't get much worse or that the stocks have been oversold. Sometimes it's a winning bet, as it was for Pzena in the 1990s. Other times, as in 2008, it is very wrong.

Pzena did well at timing purchases to optimize valuation based on his assessments of normalized earnings. He had put this talent to work with great success at Bernstein, and it would form the basis of the firm he founded when he decided to go out on his own, Pzena

Investment Management. Starting out with backing from a friend and launching the firm with only $5 million under management, Pzena nabbed his first institutional client 30 days after launch, added a number of individual accounts, and by the end of the first year had $100 million under management. At the firm's peak in 2007, Pzena Investment Management had more than $30 billion under management. That was the year Pzena took the firm public. Its stock rose 12 percent on the first day the newly listed company traded, valuing Pzena's ownership at more than $400 million.

2007 was also the year Pzena again decided to invest in financial stocks.

The Year Financials Hit Free Fall

Actually, Pzena had put a toe back into financials in 2006, a year with, in Pzena's term, "not a lot of interesting opportunities." Instead, the firm bought positions in what he dubs "boring" companies—the likes of Microsoft, Pfizer, Wal-Mart, Johnson & Johnson, Kimberly-Clark. Citigroup, says Pzena, fell into "that camp"—not terribly expensive stocks representing strong franchises with powerful earnings capabilities and a history of attractive long-term returns—and Pzena Investment Management took a "modest" position in the giant financial institution.

What Pzena saw in Citigroup was a core set of powerful franchise businesses: credit cards above all, in which Citi was dominant both domestically and globally; regional banking in the New York area and in emerging markets; the non-U.S. private banking capability; Smith Barney's global wealth management franchise; institutional custody services; transaction processing; foreign exchange; interest rate swaps. In all of these businesses, says Pzena, Citi had the scale, the network of relationships, and the recurring revenues that made the institution's competitive position virtually unassailable. If there was a downside, it was that, admittedly, the company had been somewhat mismanaged. But bad management is fixable. Citi was making money in any event, and since it was not heavily involved in a lot of the newer, wilder initiatives—for example, at the time it was not a major player in securitization—it seemed a good bet.

So did other financial stocks, many of which mirrored the kinds of strengths the Pzena team found in Citigroup. So throughout

2007, while the market overall seemed to focus on energy and other commodity-based industries, Pzena increased the relative weighting of financial stocks in his portfolio. In particular, he took large positions in a couple of government-sponsored enterprises (GSEs), Fannie Mae and Freddie Mac. These two behemoths—the Federal National Mortgage Association and the Federal Home Mortgage Corporation—were collectively responsible for nearly half of all mortgages in the United States.

Then, says Pzena, "the collapse in residential mortgages happened," and as financial stocks tanked in late 2007 and early 2008, Pzena believed he was looking at a "once-in-a-generation opportunity to get franchises like Citigroup at five times their normal earnings power."[4] At the same time, the shares of Fannie and Freddie had never been so inexpensive, and with what were thought to be impregnable balance sheets, surely they too represented the buy of a lifetime. In Pzena's view, this all constituted the kind of opportunity possible only when there is panic over the loss of investment value. The last time homebuilding stocks had been under such pressure had been the early 1980s, and that experience suggested to Pzena that this was a crisis that could and would be weathered. As to the financial stocks, they were trading as if there were a 1928-style run on the bank, with valuations that made every value investor salivate.

Mr. Pzena Goes to Washington

Fannie and Freddie and Rich Pzena were in frequent contact. Although the names make it sound like a cabal of text-messaging teenagers, the leaders of the two GSEs and one of their largest shareholders had good reason to share their thoughts, especially as pressure mounted on Fannie and Freddie stock. Fannie's and Freddie's top management would have been remiss not to consult with Pzena on ways to reverse the negative trend—both operationally and in terms of public sentiment, which was souring fast—and in this respect, at least, they were not remiss.

Pzena participated in these discussions thoughtfully and diligently. He probed the leadership about leverage, about their ability to absorb losses from mortgage defaults, and about their strategy for dealing with the housing crisis. History told him that Fannie and Freddie had always been bulletproof. Not only had they survived every economic downturn since they came into existence in 1938 and 1970, respectively; they also had entered the ensuing expansions in great condition. Pzena wanted to make sure the Kevlar vest still had its full repellent capabilities and was still tight across the torso. He saw and heard nothing to persuade him otherwise. The market's reaction, he believed, was a severe overreaction.

In the fall of 2007, Pzena met with Secretary of the Treasury Henry "Hank" Paulson, the former CEO of Goldman Sachs. Paulson had assembled a small group of well-respected investors and economists to offer their views on practical solutions for stemming the now burgeoning financial crisis. "Anybody have any ideas?" Paulson asked to kick off the meeting. Pzena was stunned. This was either a shocking admission that the government had no ideas, or it was a hell of a zinger for getting the conversation going.

Either way, he again participated conscientiously, pleased that the secretary was reaching out to people for whom complex analysis and forecasting were not an abstract exercise but the nuts and bolts of their livelihood. After all, a man like Pzena was not about to buy even severely discounted stocks unless he had assured himself, as best he could through the most diligent due diligence, that the companies had the wherewithal—the planning and execution capabilities—to turn their fortunes around. That's the only way the price of the shares held by Pzena would rise. It made sense, therefore, for the secretary to ask this group what their analyses told them and what underlying realities they saw in looking at the market.

Treasury kept in touch. In fact, in the spring of 2008, Pzena got a call from Robert Steel, another Goldman Sachs alumnus then serving as Paulson's undersecretary for domestic finance. There was talk of Fannie and Freddie collapsing, of the government taking them over or bailing them out, of the potential impact on world financial markets. "What do you think?" Steel asked Pzena.

Pzena told Steel basically the same thing he had told Paulson, the same thing that history and all his analyses of it told him: that the market reaction was an overreaction and that the problem was not capital or liquidity but time. Given time, there would be a return to normal and Fannie and Freddie would recover.

Shortly thereafter, on September 7, 2008, Fannie and Freddie were nationalized.

By then, guided by Pzena's ongoing assessment of their value proposition, financial stocks made up 40 percent of his portfolio.

Assessing the Value Proposition

At the heart of the assessment was the key metric of Pzena's deep-value approach: normalized earnings. Here's how Pzena frames the core question: "Using normal earnings power, what should these franchise businesses earn once you get through the crisis?" To be sure, in the deteriorating credit environment of 2008, it was essential to stress-test each normalized earnings analysis, but "all of our stress tests," says Pzena, "are based on the idea that you have time on your side. That's how banking works: Loan losses happen over time, and banks earn interest over that same period of time. That's what absorbs the loan losses." So Pzena and his team did their analyses, stress-tested their results, and determined that the headlines about collateralized debt obligations and subprime mortgage losses and sinking stock prices were—the by-now standard Pzena term—an "overreaction."

Investors in Pzena's fund, however, had begun redeeming their interest, compounding the hit the fund was already taking from poor stock performance. What Pzena continued to see as market overreaction was also disastrous for the publicly traded shares in Pzena Investment Management, which the 2008 financial crisis had sunk to half their peak price—less than $10 a share.

At the headquarters of Pzena Investment Management, in the very heart of midtown Manhattan, there was vigorous internal debate about the size of the portfolio's weighting in financial stocks: too big, just right, not big enough? In this case as in just about every case, the firm acts when the partners come to a unanimous decision—a hallmark of the firm's strong culture. Ultimately, the focus on financials was unanimously ratified, the thinking being that "there was plenty of capital and future earnings power to absorb the losses." In May 2008, Pzena made Citigroup stock his top pick—a way to take advantage of this once-in-a-generation opportunity.

In his August conference call to clients on the second-quarter results, which Pzena pronounced "awful," he told his listeners that they were "now in territory where rational analysis has been discarded and emotion is driving securities prices." That was no reason, he argued, to depart from the deep-value approach that required riding out the bad times. On the contrary. He was convinced that now was the time to play the timing trick, to position the portfolio for the end of an economic cycle. "If history is a guide," Pzena said during the conference call, "once the recession is under way and the safe haven momentum stocks turn out not to be immune from the normal rules of economics, valuation discipline should return, and value stocks should outperform.

"It's our job," he went on, "to react to market sentiment, to take advantage of it, particularly when it gets irrational. And it's definitely at that irrational point." In his view, nothing about financial stocks had changed fundamentally or permanently. The free fall of these stocks would be a short-term phenomenon; history was on the side of the financials. Experienced value investors had lived through this type of panic before, and each time, the panic had proved to be an incredible buying opportunity. Arguably, this time was no different from that time 16 years earlier when Pzena had had the foresight, again based on diligent analysis, to concentrate 40 percent of his portfolio in financial stocks. In the immortal words of Yogi Berra, surely "it was déjà vu all over again."

"That was our thinking," Pzena says, "and that was the flaw." It was flawed because it did not see the mass psychology that was producing liquidity panic, a run on the banks, a loss of confidence in the financial institutions. All of this defied the logic of history—the logic of what was normal in Pzena's approach. "We never imagined that the liquidity would dry up," he says. He cites the example of what happened later that year with Fannie Mae and Freddie Mac: "Fannie and Freddie were well capitalized the day they were nationalized," he asserts almost plaintively. *"That has never happened before"* (italics mine).

But it happened this time. The banks weren't out of money; they were out of confidence.

There are numerous explanations for why the liquidity panic and loss of confidence occurred. Pzena has rehearsed them all. Blame the mark-to-market accounting technique that focuses on "a moment in time without taking into account normalized earnings value." Or blame the lack of a buyer for the massive leverage built up in the system. Blame the government for stepping in overnight to fundamentally alter the capital markets. Yet Pzena is aware that the underlying cause is that "emotion as well as arithmetic must be taken into account.

"If people lose confidence in Boeing," he explains, "it doesn't matter. There are only Boeing and Airbus, so if you need a plane, this is where you go. It's a different game with financial institutions."

Different and costly: By October 2008, Pzena Investment Management hit a low point, with assets under management dropping by 46 percent and its own stock descending in lockstep, soon to visit the low single digits.

Pzena's Faith in Financial Stocks: A Timeline

2006: Pzena invests in Citigroup as part of a strategy of buying positions in a range of "boring" companies.

2007: Pzena increases relative weighting of financial stocks in the portfolio, takes large positions in Fannie Mae and Freddie Mac.

Fall 2007: Pzena meets with Treasury secretary Paulson and others to discuss the financial crisis, including Fannie and Freddie.

Late 2007–early 2008: As financial stocks tank, Pzena buys big.

August 2008: Pzena tells investors history is on the side of the financial stocks.

September 7, 2008: Fannie Mae and Freddie Mac are nationalized, essentially wiping out their equity value.

October 2008: Pzena's assets under management drop 46 percent.

What Went Wrong

Pzena's superb track record as a deep-value investor rested on a tried-and-true formula. He would choose stocks based on the underlying company's normalized earnings, confident that a temporary disruption in the business causing an interruption in earnings was a short-term phenomenon from which the company would recover over time. Time, in fact, was the only uncertainty in this bet. But for value investors, who seem to be inherently imbued with the personality traits of patience and confidence, waiting it out—even sweating it out—came with the territory.

As it turns out, however—as it turned out for Pzena vis-à-vis financial stocks—**the tried-and-true formula is not always and not necessarily the right one.** Case in point: Richard Pzena found himself with 40 percent of his portfolio invested in financial institutions at a time when financial institutions were being fundamentally restructured—never to be the same again. In other words, there was no going back to the old normal, and nobody had any idea what the new normal was going to look like.

Financial terminology doesn't seem equal to the task of explaining what really went wrong—the true underlying cause of Rich Pzena's billion-dollar mistake. Perhaps it is best expressed by a man not known for his views on finance although renowned in other ways. "All history becomes subjective," wrote Ralph Waldo Emerson in his famous essay on history. "In other words, there is properly no history, only biography. Every mind must know the whole lesson for itself—must go over the whole ground. What it does not see, what it does not live, it will not know."

Precisely because Pzena's investment philosophy relied on history repeating itself, it required him to peel away the emotion the market heaps on a particular stock. That was the methodology for assessing normalized earnings power: Pzena would pore over past financial statements the way he and his classmates had once pored over stock guides, zeroing in on the point in time where the bad news has been fully discounted and an attractive risk/reward ratio comes into view. At that point, when the realities of an economic contraction prompt investors to sell their growth stocks and seek the relative safety of equities that had been sold off earlier, you have reached the inflection at which value is supposed to outperform momentum. Although it was a methodology that had worked well for almost two decades, it eschewed biography—deliberately—and, as Emerson might have put it, what it chose not to see, it therefore did not know.

Another New Englander offers an important take on what Pzena should have seen. "To study the abnormal is the best way of understanding the normal," wrote the nineteenth-century philosopher William James in his classic 1902 work, *The Varieties of Religious Experience*. Or perhaps, combining Emerson and James, there simply is no such thing as normal. Pzena's assumption that sentiment would again become favorable for his portfolio, as it always had—that the fashion would cycle back—turned out to be just plain wrong, certainly for the first time in Pzena's career, maybe for the only time, although that remains to be seen.

Nor did patience work—that other tried-and-true strength of the value investor. Remember that value investors buy stocks at the bottom of their historic trading range so that even if they are early on the timing, the only loss is opportunity cost. Not this time. This time, financial stocks ran out of runway, and sentiment continued to worsen; the bottom of the historic trading range was extended—in the case of Fannie and Freddie, essentially to zero. The switch to value never took place at all.

This time *was* different, but Pzena could not have seen that. No one could.

That doesn't make it any easier. Of course, "we all make mistakes," he says, but it is "disconcerting" when what you saw as a "once-in-a-lifetime opportunity turns out to be a disaster. It makes you question everything you have ever done." Hindsight has given Pzena "a new respect for the things I can't control. I always knew that high leverage is not a value investor's friend, but I always thought financial stocks were different. I no longer think so." Instead, he sees "overall exposure to financial leverage" as the issue. That—and forcing yourself to imagine "a hard-to-imagine scenario," since the hard-to-imagine scenario is what actually took place.

Perhaps the lesson is that history can be a guide to patterns of fact but not to psychology. The emotion of past events is lost within stock charts and data. The effect of sentiment—the power of market psychology—can be weighed only as part of an investment calculation with real-time experience—on-the-spot, live assessment as events are unfolding. In the Pzena portfolio, investor impatience, increasing negative sentiment, and government intervention overcame not just Citigroup's business model but also Richard Pzena's sense of history.

If he were talking to the Columbia students today, says Pzena, he would amend his comments. It's not that the phrase "It is different now" is never true. It's that it is rarely true.

Pzena should know. He got caught in a rare departure from history. But I would bet the store, the farm, and my portfolio that he'll be back.

Lessons Learned

- *Do not assume price declines = opportunity.* Value is not defined solely by stock price and relative performance. Rarely are stocks inefficiently priced. Price moves are usually symptoms of an underlying issue, and it's essential to understand that issue fully before assessing its implications for the value of the stock—and for determining whether those implications will be permanent.

- *Not all great franchises are great stocks.* Companies with historically strong franchises are not necessarily good value. Computer maker Dell is a good example: a very well-known brand with great market share, but in an industry the fundamentals of which reached a plateau—the saturation point for "first" computers, when most households that could afford to buy a computer had done so. That is when Dell stock began to decline in value. The company is unlikely ever to grow as fast as it did in its early years; the stock, therefore, will never receive the valuation that it once did.
- *Normalized earnings are not always pertinent.* Normalized earnings are a pertinent measure *only* if the exact circumstances of the prior recovery can be realized, and, of course, that won't be known until a recovery happens.
- *Practice patience.* Don't catch a falling knife. It may be tempting to buy a beaten up stock, but patience can be a profitable virtue. Often it's better to wait for a recovery to begin: You might forfeit a portion of the upside, but at least the potential downside will be less.
- *Explore why a stock declined.* Carefully review why a declining stock has performed as it has. Is it for the same reasons the stock declined in the past? Is history repeating itself, or is new history being made? Only when you've answered these questions can you forecast the potential for recovery.
- *Historical performance is only one data point.* By all means, consider historical performance in assessing whether to buy a company's stock, but be clear that it is just one data point to be examined. If the circumstances can't be replicated, past performance may not be able to be repeated. Technological innovation, fresh competition, new regulations, and so on all change the circumstances and may affect performance. People used to say of Apple stock that it "always seems to bounce." That may be an interesting observation, but it is a flawed investment strategy—as was proven when both a deteriorating economy and announcements about Steve Jobs's health sank the stock. Or take Citigroup: It had unprecedented growth in each business line because a synchronized global easing of interest rates persisted for a very long time. Once rates reversed, so did Citi's fortunes—and increasing regulation will likely prevent it from regaining prior operating levels.
- *Experience counts.* Before investing in a mutual fund with a value style, make sure the portfolio manager has experienced prior economic cycles and market downturns. This will not ensure that the fund won't lose money in periods of market duress—there is little a mutual fund manager can do when all indices decline—but at least decisions won't be made out of emotion. And when the market recovers, your investment should do well. After all, even Rich Pzena had trouble navigating what has always been a value player's dream—unabashed panic selling—but ultimately, he will outperform other investment managers, as always.

Geoff Grant

STYLE DRIFT: IT'S HOT TILL IT'S NOT

When Geoff Grant got a summer job at Morgan Stanley between his junior and senior years at Columbia University, he admittedly "had no idea what Wall Street was." That's understandable. Although Grant was born in New York, he grew up in what was then Rhodesia—today's troubled Zimbabwe—whose accent and cadence still mark his speech. His parents had divorced when Grant was three; he returned with his mother to her native country to be near her family, and while Grant saw his father only rarely during the years, the two remained in close touch. At the age of 18, Grant was drafted to fight in the bloody civil war that marked the end of white supremacy in Rhodesia and the transition to majority rule in the new Zimbabwe. But just before he was to report for service, his father convinced him to return to New York and enroll in Columbia. Still a U.S. citizen, Grant opted for a pencil instead of a rifle.

By any definition, it was a healthy choice. In due course, however, it would plunge Geoff Grant into another contentious arena, one in which financial instruments, not guns, were the weapon of choice. Still, in the investment combat zone Grant would in time enter—and eventually master—strategy, risk, and performance were as essential as in any war. And the way you addressed all three issues just as emphatically could determine your success or failure.

Investment Style

Investment professionals speak of an *investment style*—the preference for a particular strategy or philosophy for putting money to work. (N.B.: Investment style is not to be confused with investment discipline, which is addressed in Chapter 4 of this book.) An investment style might be defined by the choice of financial instrument—currencies, stocks, bonds—or by the particular characteristics that define the style (i.e., growth versus value investing.) Usually both instrument and characteristics are factors that guide the choices a fund manager makes.

Value and growth investing typically are considered the two core investment styles. The former is defined as investing in companies you believe are priced at less than their intrinsic value—as exemplified by Rich Pzena in Chapter 7. Conversely, growth investing is defined by a focus not necessarily on the underlying valuation of a stock but on a preference for companies whose earnings are growing faster than the overall market average.

To prospective investors, the style embraced by a particular fund manager articulates expectations of both risk and performance. In a very real sense, it is what prospective investors are buying when they invest with a particular fund manager.

And for buyers, it is really a matter of trust—in both the technical and emotional senses of the word. It means investors are confident that they have understood and accepted a particular level of risk and can look forward to a particular level of performance. Based on that confidence, investors will act in certain ways vis-à-vis their overall investment portfolio or financial life. They'll assign a certain place to the investment in this particular fund with this particular style—give it a certain financial weight—and that will influence how they behave with regard to other financial decisions.

That is why investors need to be clear about the investment style of their fund managers, and it is why fund managers carefully define their style when they advertise to prospective investors. Of course, they're not just advertising an abstract concept; investment style is based on the manager's expertise. When you as an investor buy a particular fund manager's investment style, you do so based on the manager's track record of making money with that particular style. And then you trust—not that the risk level is incised in stone or that the performance will exceed your highest hopes—but that the fund manager will stick to his or her knitting and follow the investment style you're paying for, not suddenly drift off in another direction and decide to dabble in another investment style altogether.

The two-billion-dollar mistake that is the subject of this chapter is precisely a mistake of style drift.

The Making of a Macro Trader

Geoff Grant started out wanting to be an electrical engineer. At Columbia, he concentrated on applied mathematics and the squash team, doing very well in the former and rising to number-one player in the latter. Despite the demanding curriculum of one of the country's top universities and the practice regimen of collegiate athletics, Grant found the time to go into business with a friend, selling Columbia-logo polo shirts to their classmates. They had help: Grant's father, who manufactured knit shirts for such high-end labels as Ralph Lauren and Lacoste, was their supplier. As demand increased, the two undergraduates were able to expand the business beyond Columbia and beyond New York. The business continues to thrive today, but without Geoff Grant. He gave it up as an undergraduate when, on the recommendation of a professor, he was offered that summer internship at Morgan Stanley, the venerable Wall Street firm.

Having grown up thousands of miles away from any true financial center and being relatively new to New York, Grant didn't know Morgan Stanley from Joe Morgan or J.P. Morgan. He quickly figured out, however, that he had landed in the world of investment banking and that he quite enjoyed working as an analyst in the financial planning department, where he was assigned to "look at business inefficiencies." For their part, Morgan Stanley managers were equally quick to recognize Grant's potential. Summer employment segued into part-time employment once school was back in session, and it became a full-time position upon graduation.

For recruits with only a bachelor's degree, as opposed to those equipped with a master's in business administration, the typical development route at investment banking firms like Morgan Stanley is to serve in a two-year analyst training program and then attend business school, adding academic credentials to the practical experience. Grant might have pursued the graduate degree, but when he was assigned to a project on the currency desk, he so impressed the head of the department, future Morgan Stanley co-president Zoe Cruz, that she asked him to stay on and work directly for her. The alpha-seeking "Cruz Missile," as she has been dubbed, was a master of foreign exchange (FX), and it was from this master that Geoff Grant learned the business. It was incomparable on-the-job training in the full range of world currency transactions—a more rigorous education, one can posit, than graduate school might have offered. Grant demonstrated unique talent as a trader and a real passion for the business of trading. Despite his lack of an MBA degree—or perhaps because of it?—he enjoyed a fairly spectacular rise in the firm. In 1987, a mere five years after he had joined Morgan Stanley, Cruz asked him to relocate to Tokyo to build and operate the firm's FX options derivatives business in Japan.

It was a heady assignment—a substantive responsibility—and Grant more than rose to the occasion, expanding the Morgan Stanley offering in this key financial center, extending the firm's reach, and burnishing its reputation yet further. It was a notable and noticeable achievement that reverberated globally.

One of the people who felt the reverberations was Lloyd Blankfein, a newly minted partner in Goldman Sachs and its eventual chief executive. Two years after Grant started work in Tokyo, Blankfein managed to recruit him away from Morgan Stanley with the offer of yet another heady assignment. Blankfein wanted Grant to relocate again, this time to the United Kingdom, to run Goldman's European currency options desk headquartered in London. Grant mulled the new offer carefully; he felt an understandable loyalty toward Morgan Stanley and Zoe Cruz, admired the firm, and enjoyed his work. In the end, however, Goldman's strong positioning not just in Europe but around the world made the opportunity too attractive for him to turn down. In 1989, the Grants moved to the British capital.

For the next 14 years, Geoff Grant was a Goldman guy. He went from managing European currency options to heading Goldman's global foreign exchange options, and he eventually became global head of FX. Because proprietary trading was housed in the FX business, Grant was also cohead of that group in London, directly managing the firm's own macro account. The prop desk, as it is familiarly known, was "not capital-intensive," says Grant; instead, "everything is risk." He handled it at a time when other investment bankers—competitors, mostly—credited Goldman's proprietary trading with turning the firm into "a hedge fund on steroids." And it's likely that Grant's record contributed to that characterization, as he became one of the largest and most profitable risk takers in the firm. His 14 years of trading yielded only 2 negative years, 1 flat year, and a pretty sensational 11 years of positive returns.

Grant had been named a partner of the firm in 1996 and was there when it went public in 1999, reaping the substantial rewards of that offering. But by 2004, Grant and his wife were beginning to think about returning to the United States. They had long assumed they wanted their five children to go to college in the United States, and as their oldest child approached high school age, it seemed that the time was ripe for making a go/no go decision about moving back across the Atlantic.

At the same time, Grant, now approaching his mid-40s, had the sense of having "been doing the job for a long time"—even though trading was something he loved. Moreover, it was increasingly clear, as it would be for anyone at that point in a professional career, that Goldman senior management rather expected that Grant's next step up would be to a position that would require "assuming more of a management role," which was not necessarily something Geoff Grant wanted to do.

It was the summer of 2004. The Grants' oldest child was attending tennis camp in California, and the rest of the family was making a vacation of it in the Golden State. The beaches were wide and sun-drenched, an appealing contrast to cloudy and damp London. The family particularly liked the area around Santa Barbara, caught between those sunny beaches and the chaparral-covered Santa Ynez Mountains—and a world away from the frenzied hustle of the global financial centers in which they had been living for years.

Financial traders—especially good ones like Geoff Grant—have a sense about when to follow their gut, the intuition derived from experience and, perhaps, genetics. That summer, intuition seemed to summon all the Grants. They followed their instincts and decided then and there that they would move to California, returning to England only to pack their belongings and tie up loose ends. For Grant and his wife, both born in the United States, it was a homecoming of sorts. For their children, it was a statement about putting down stakes. For Grant himself, moving to Santa Barbara offered both a resolution to and a destination for his nebulous perplexity about his future: The decision to relocate was accompanied by an equally important decision that Geoff would retire at the end of the year and would "take a year off" before embarking on the next stage of his professional life—whatever that might be.

Partners and Profit

Ron Beller was another Goldman Sachs alumnus, a former partner and managing director (and husband of a former managing director), who had headed the fixed income, currency, and commodity sales groups in the London office when Geoff Grant was overseeing global FX and the macro prop trading group. Put simply, Beller's group was responsible for bringing client money into the firm while Grant was charged with the responsibility for investing Goldman's own capital.

Beller also was familiar with the conundrum confronting Geoff Grant in 2004—the question of "What next?" For Beller, however, the question had come earlier; shortly after he left Goldman in 2001, it was discovered that his wife's trusted personal assistant at the firm had fleeced the London-based couple out of millions of dollars. The trial in a London courtroom was something of a sensation for the public—fed lurid details by the notorious British tabloid press—and, no doubt, something of a humiliating experience for the expat couple. It wasn't just the theft that had raised eyebrows; it was also that the Bellers had not discovered it for two years, the implication being that this crass couple was so extraordinarily wealthy that they didn't even notice a loss equivalent to more than a lifetime's wages for most Britons. While the BBC saw the opportunity to memorialize the salacious event in a made-for-television movie, the couple's response to the episode was to "do good." Beller's wife, Jennifer Moses, created an international children's charity while Ron Beller commuted back to New York City as one of several high-powered businesspeople recruited by Mayor Michael Bloomberg to help plan reform of the city's schools.

By 2005, however, Beller hungered to get back once again into the world of finance, and his vehicle of choice was a hedge fund. Beller believed that when hedge funds failed, it was because there was insufficient focus on the business side of the equation: marketing, operations, risk management, growth strategy, public relations. Noted at Goldman for his ability to build and manage a business, he saw the opportunity to put those skills to work. His idea was to create a fund with two equal leaders—one, himself, as the business guy, and a partner who was an expert trader. For that, he turned to Geoff Grant.

"It was a bit premature for me," Grant says of the overture from Beller. He had just left Goldman at the end of 2004, and the family was barely settled in their new home. But he was "attracted," as he puts it, to Beller's idea of an equal partnership combining the two areas of expertise. He believed, with Beller, that such a partnership would indeed make their firm "different." Both men were alert to a measure of concern over the 6,000-mile distance between their two offices—one in London's trendy Soho district, the other in laid-back California a short walk from the beach—but they also felt that in the era of wireless everything, not to mention jet travel, the distance could be bridged technologically and the practicalities likely would work out.

In the end, Grant found the proposition sufficiently compelling, and he decided to partner with Beller in the new hedge fund. A cycling enthusiast, Beller suggested they call the firm Peloton Partners, after the group of riders at the head of the pack in a bicycle race. It is perhaps not coincidental that peloton riders move as a unit, like birds in formation, drafting one another, making minuscule adjustments in response to each other at all times so as to reduce drag overall and conserve each rider's energy.

Peloton Partners LLP was launched in June 2005 as a macro fund, Geoff Grant's specialty. Among the broadest-based of all hedge fund mandates, macro trading specializes in strategies aimed at finding profit in macroeconomic events—shifts in interest rates, impact on currencies, consequences for stocks and bonds. It therefore means participation in all markets—equities, bonds, currencies, commodities—and often makes use of quantitative modeling, an investment selection process that formulaically seeks to take advantage of pricing inefficiencies. With its heavy math component, quantitative modeling was very much Geoff Grant's cup of tea. In Peloton's case, the teabag was the $500 million in capital raised on day one, with another $500 million "softly committed," as Grant puts it, for the first six months. Clearly, investors were eager to put their faith in Grant and Beller; so were elite investment professionals, who lined up to join the firm. It looked like the business expert cum trading expert combination was going to work just fine.

And so it did—at least at first.

"We had a terrific first six to eight months," says Grant. "Of course, this was at the end of 2005, at the height of the hedge fund frenzy." But one must also credit Beller's "very effective efforts as an advocate and marketer" plus Grant's trading savvy. The synergy resulting from that combination seemed to confirm the choice of name for the company, as the partners moved easily in and out of one another's slipstream, generating returns and letting the profits just flow. For the last six months of 2005—the first half year of Peloton's existence—the macro fund was up by "roughly" 10 percent, in Grant's recollection, "annualizing at plus or minus 20 percent."

Then in the early weeks of 2006, says Grant picturesquely, "we were hit by a wall of money," moving "quickly" from $1 billion to $2 billion under management. In the first six months of that year, the macro fund was up by 5 percent; annualized at 12 percent, it looked, in Grant's apt term, "terrific." A gush of excitement accompanied the gush of money, and the mood was decidedly upbeat. Assets under management translated into large fees for the pair and their employees. Plying their trade from the upscale environs of London's Soho district and the beach-cool chic of Santa Barbara, Beller and Grant couldn't help but burnish the super-hero legacies they had built at Goldman.

Yet, market-wise, 2006 was evolving as a tough year for traditional global macro investing. "There was a precipitous decline in volatility across all asset classes," Grant recalls, "so it was a difficult environment for my strategy, the macro strategy." That is because all traders, but particularly macro traders, thrive in volatile markets, where they can leverage their portfolios and find profit in even the small discrepancies that fast-moving change creates in the price of financial instruments. The dip in volatility that year correspondingly dimmed those opportunities for profit.

Given the less accommodating market environment, and equipped with ever more money to put to work, Beller believed that Peloton should broaden its asset base and embrace a multi-strategy fund. To that end, the firm added an equities team, a credit team, a systematic trading team, and a team devoted to ABS—the asset-backed securities that at the time represented the fastest-growing segment of the world's capital markets. As a business decision, this certainly added another layer of challenge even as it augmented the firm's possibilities for gain. Building any new business is demanding enough; managing multiple strategies and risk attributes complicates the demands substantially. The decision also was made to maintain back-office operations in-house, so what had been a small business at its launch—8 portfolio managers and 15 back-office staff—was well on its way to becoming a collection of 30 portfolio managers with a substantial support group. At its peak, the total operation comprised some 85 top-flight professionals in both the front and back offices.

And the peak would rise very high indeed.

To the Summit

Leading the charge up the mountain was the ABS portion of the multistrategy fund. While other strategies struggled month after month through 2006—equities lost a bit, credit gained just a little, macro stayed pretty flat—ABS "kept things going," says Grant, fueling the overall fund to a positive if modest 4 percent return on the year. The reason was simple: Peloton was betting on a meltdown in the subprime mortgage base and would express that view by short selling—betting against—the riskiest mortgage securities, those rated BBB. Peloton strategists also reasoned that if investors suddenly got scared of risky assets, they would abandon those assets for high-rated AAA bonds, so Peloton layered on another trade and acquired those bonds as well.

That is what typically happens in a declining market: Investors flee risky securities for the safe haven of highly rated investments. The term of art for it is "flight to quality." In the case of the subprime mortgage market, however, the flight to quality never quite got off the ground, as funds invested in subprime started selling not just the lower-quality triple-B securities but the investment-grade triple-As as well.

To Beller and the portfolio managers at Peloton, the sell-off looked a lot like throwing out the baby with the bathwater, but it meant that highly rated AAA securities were available at rarely seen bargain prices. The Peloton managers also believed that the sell-off—and thus the bargain prices—would continue for some time before investors started buying again and driving the prices up. On that basis, the firm continued to buy investment-grade AAA mortgage securities at the temporarily depressed prices created by all those other investors liquidating their positions, while at the same time they were still shorting BBB securities. The long position in triple-As also hedged the firm's short position in BBBs, just in case the Peloton strategists were wrong about the continued decline in value of these low-end mortgage securities. If the decline in the BBBs reversed, then surely the AAAs, traditionally the preferred security, would perform even better. That, after all, is what a hedge fund is supposed to do, so this seemed a prudent tactical move.

Such was the reasoning behind Peloton's bet. At the time, as he readily concedes, Geoff Grant saw it as "very, very compelling from a risk/reward perspective," and in December of 2006, Peloton launched a second fund solely for the purpose of investing in asset-backed securities. The new fund was seeded with $500 million from the multistrategy fund, plus additional money raised from outside investors. All of Peloton's ABS activity was concentrated in this single fund, which was placed under the management of Peter Howard and David Watson, two highly experienced experts in the field.

And the fund was, in Grant's phrase, "phenomenally successful." As the subprime lending market in the United States began to weaken, Peloton began winning its bet: The BBB securities absolutely collapsed in value. Using the then-stable AAA securities as collateral with their lenders, the firm kept leveraging the ABS fund, thus multiplying the fund's returns and, in the process, attracting more investors into the fund.

Peloton's ABS fund returned 87 percent in 2007. Its multistrategy fund did well enough, returning 34 percent, a good portion of which was due to its investment in the ABS fund. But ABS was the star, and its ascendancy was stratospheric.

Most investors in the fund—"a small group of very sophisticated investors," according to Grant—were certainly content with these results, and Peloton was careful to serve these clients with constant updates on the state of play and to feed them all the information they could ingest. One investor, it is true—namely, Goldman Sachs itself—bowed out of Peloton in the summer of 2007. The exit was not due to any displeasure over returns; rather, it was a tactical decision: Goldman originally had invested in Peloton's macro fund, and now that the primary strategy—the one that had attracted them to the firm in the first place—had been eclipsed almost totally by something else altogether, namely ABS, Peloton did not fit the firm's overall investing strategy. In other words, it was a case of style drift, and Goldman opted out. A couple of other investors did the same for the same reason. Despite the incredible returns Peloton was generating, ABS wasn't what these investors had signed up for, and the style drift signaled a change in the risk ratio they weren't willing to assume. Despite the lure of incredible returns, Goldman and the others were unwilling to violate their own investment discipline.

For most investors in Peloton, however, the returns said it all—loud and clear. Was that an issue of greed overcoming judgment? Not necessarily. Grant and Beller were extremely capable individuals with strong track records; their firm boasted some of the best investing talent around; and for each new strategy, they had recruited well-trained, experienced, highly motivated portfolio managers. So an investor who saw revelatory truth in the spectacular success of the ABS fund wasn't necessarily deluding herself. The returns were real enough, and they turned Peloton overnight into the megahit of hedge funds.

As the face of the firm in London, Ron Beller seemed to be everywhere. He and his highly accomplished wife were active in philanthropy, the arts, even—their expatriate status notwithstanding—British politics. They sat on boards and hobnobbed with London's power elite and the nation's titled aristocrats. As a couple, they seemed to embody the firm's image—new, bright, a little exotic as far as British sensibilities went, "different." In the same way, both Peloton offices—the upscale headquarters in a glass-walled building in London's Soho district, with its chill-out zones and highest of high tech, its bright North African colors and open spaces; plus the California outlier, with its casual couture and commitment to creativity—seemed to embrace the spirit of innovation and informality, of a new way of seeing the world and a new way of doing business in it.

Geoff Grant and all the Santa Barbara team were as pleased by the ABS success as everyone else. If Grant had any misgiving—and really you couldn't call it that—it was a nagging sense that ABS had begun, in his words, "to overwhelm the rest of the organization.

"Nothing else mattered at that point," says Grant. "There was so much money gushing in as a consequence of the complete meltdown in this market. It was unprecedented. And it started to dwarf all other activities in the fund."

For his part, that fact was both frustrating and a bit disappointing. "One of the reasons I left Goldman Sachs," Grant recalls, "was that I wanted to focus on trading, not on managing large numbers of people." Yet by mid-2007 at Peloton, he was doing just that.

"Trading is not a hobby," says Grant, and the amount of time and effort and energy he expended "staying on top of all the other strategies"—and particularly the ABS strategy—left him precious little time for the work he really loved. "I had ceased to trade my own book," Grant laments—a classic instance of style drift, of getting away from the defined purpose of the fund and certainly from his core expertise. Yet it was hard to argue with returns of 87 percent, especially since, as 2007 rolled into 2008, there was "substantial cash in hand—$1 billion—which should have been comfortable for any margin calls" the firm's financing counterparties might exact.

On January 24, 2008, more than 1,000 leading lights of the world of finance, along with the usual dignitaries and celebrities, gathered at the posh Grosvenor House Hotel in the heart of London's celebrated Mayfair district for the annual EuroHedge Awards dinner. Doubly crowned for 2007—as New Fund of the Year and Hedge Fund of the Year—was Peloton Partners LLP.

In a matter of only a few weeks, it would all come crashing down. Spectacularly.

ABS 101

Start with the assets: from such common receivables as credit card payments, mortgages and home equity loans, car loans, or recreational vehicle loans to complex aircraft leases and, famously, movie revenues. Uneconomical as investments on their own, these loans are pooled together, packaged, and securitized—that is, made to serve as the collateral for securities that are then sold in the market or offered as private placements. It's a way for depository institutions and other corporations to develop new sources of capital as they "liquefy" their balance sheets, raising cash by borrowing against assets. In 2005, the Securities and Exchange Commission (SEC) issued Regulation AB, its "final" rule on ABS. From the overview, here is how the SEC defines and describes ABS:

> Asset-backed securities are securities that are backed by a discrete pool of self-liquidating financial assets. Asset-backed securitization is a financing technique in which financial assets, in many cases themselves less liquid, are pooled and converted into instruments that may be offered and sold in

the capital markets. In a basic securitization structure, an entity, often a financial institution and commonly known as a "sponsor," originates or otherwise acquires a pool of financial assets, such as mortgage loans, either directly or through an affiliate. It then sells the financial assets, again either directly or through an affiliate, to a specially created investment vehicle that issues securities "backed" or supported by those financial assets, which securities are "asset-backed securities." Payment on the asset-backed securities depends primarily on the cash flows generated by the assets in the underlying pool and other rights designed to assure timely payment, such as liquidity facilities, guarantees or other features generally known as credit enhancements. The structure of asset-backed securities is intended, among other things, to insulate ABS investors from the corporate credit risk of the sponsor that originated or acquired the financial assets.

Gobsmacked

All along, the ABS strategy had remained consistent: Short the low-quality BBB mortgage-backed securities in the ABS fund and make leveraged long bets on the high-quality AAAs. That AAA rating made the leverage relatively safe: There was little chance that holders of such mortgage bonds would be unable to make their payments. After all, not one, not two, but three top marks—three As—signaled the market's affirmation that the underlying credit was absolutely secure. Such standing is given only to the best managed, most securely financed, and most liquid companies in the world—bulletproof certification of their bonds and of their obligations in such securitized instruments as ABS funds.

Nor was the amount of leverage inappropriate or inopportune. At the start of 2008, in Grant's recollection, Peloton's ABS fund was "between seven and nine times leveraged, which at the time was not considered particularly aggressive." It just meant that for every dollar Peloton invested, the firm borrowed from seven to nine dollars. To put this into perspective, on the eve of its filing for bankruptcy, Lehman Brothers was 50 times leveraged.

From a somewhat more cosmic viewpoint, however, it was clear that the BBBs, at that point trading at about 10 cents on the dollar, "had nowhere to go," as Grant put it, "but the triple-As did." Priced in the range of 80 to 90 cents, the AAAs had held up well—at least until this point. But now, in early 2008, the valuation floor supporting the AAA-rated asset-backed securities began to sag, then to weaken badly, until in very little time at all, it gave way altogether. The short strategy worked as it was supposed to; the triple-Bs had declined to just cents on the dollar and stayed there, but the AAAs were vulnerable as the spread between the two widened to historic proportions—an untenable relationship. As these top-rated credits began to decline, momentum accelerating their fall, there was nothing left on the short side of the portfolio to offset—to hedge against—their downward spiral.

Elsewhere, as panic seemed to overtake the markets, other ABS investors began to run for the exits. Not at Peloton, however. There, ABS fund manager Howard, who had been so successful for so long, and who had committed his own fortune to the fund, believed the sell-off would hit bottom soon. Peloton stayed put; the firm was even active in the ABX, the index of asset-backed securities, but "on both sides of the market," says Grant, "sometimes using the index to hedge the underlying positions."

But against the background of a worsening global credit crunch, the selling continued, and now Peloton's financing counterparties—the banks and prime brokers that financed the fund—began to do what counterparties always do in such cases. Even as Peloton was being toasted in Mayfair, they tightened their margin lending requirements, demanding more margin payments on the losing positions, more collateral as the value of the investments fell. The tightened margin requirements "effectively sucked 50 to 60 percent of the excess cash out of the fund very quickly," says Grant.

Can it be argued that this was an intentional move by Peloton's lenders, all of them brokerage firms with their own prop trading desks? One would not need to be a complete cynic to make that case. Since the lenders had access to the books of their "client," Peloton, they could quickly spot an opportunity to weaken the fund further, to take advantage of its distress. All they had to do was set new, more aggressive margin requirements, and it would force Peloton into a position of distressed selling. And who would buy the securities sold at these fire-sale prices? The lenders themselves, of course. And that is indeed what happened.

For a while that February, it looked as if Grant, Beller, and the rest of the Peloton staff actually might slip out of the tightening noose as they began a frantic search for other solutions to the growing crisis—including asking rival hedge funds for some kind of bailout. Washington's Birthday was no holiday for Geoff Grant, as he jetted to London to spend a week of sleepless nights working with Beller to forge a rescue operation. Even the extra day provided by the leap year proved to be insufficient, and on that day, February 29, Peloton publicly announced that the ABS fund would be liquidated—at fire-sale prices.

"The market move didn't kill us," says Grant. "It was the financing that killed the fund—the wholesale changes in margin requirement from 3 percent to 25 percent. That's what killed us."

"Gobsmacked" is the very British expression that means to be taken unaware, to be utterly astounded nearly to the point of stupefaction. That's how Geoff Grant felt as, virtually helpless, he watched Peloton lose $2 billion over the first two weeks of February. That's when the spreads on Peloton's portfolio, which had already doubled over the course of January, doubled again—in a mere 14 days—with each widening of the spreads requiring more cash.

Grant's tone is one of sorrow rather than anger when he calls the experience a "tragedy." In retrospect, he wishes there had been some kind of *deus ex machina* intervening from on high with a rescue solution that might have saved them all—"some form of Chapter 11–type situation that we could have invoked to hold creditors at bay during the orderly liquidation of assets." That sort of bankruptcy provision enabling that sort of orderly liquidation "might have recovered 70 to 75 cents on the dollar," Grant believes. But an orderly liquidation was not in the cards; it just isn't the way these things work.

Instead, the way these things work is that the banks—in the case of Peloton, 14 of them—are in control of assessing the value of the bonds being liquidated. Under the standard valuation process—and this is written into the terms of the initial lending agreement—the financing counterparty, an investing bank, chooses three separate dealers and asks each to bid on the assets; the bank then picks the middle price, the compromise position, so to speak. Naturally, it is in the bank's interest to procure the three lowest bids, thus artificially depressing the buying price. That is precisely what happened with Peloton. The banks called in the margined bonds that were the firm's collateral, sold them at distressed prices—in most cases to their own trading desks—and met the margin balance. Six weeks later, most of the bonds had regained significant value, although as the worldwide recession fueled the collapse of virtually all financial instruments, their value again plunged.

Instead of an orderly liquidation, there was a disorderly liquidation and, in the end, disaster. "There was no recourse," says Grant.

Peloton's Three-Year Ride: Timeline

June 2005: Peloton is launched.

December 2005: Macro fund achieves 10 percent rise in its first six months.

June 2006: Macro fund achieves an annualized return of 12 percent; Grant and Beller create a multistrategy fund anchored by asset-backed securities.

December 2006: A fund is created solely for ABS with the strategy of shorting low-grade mortgage securities while keeping long positions in high-grade securities.

Summer 2007: Despite the ABS fund's return of 87 percent, one Peloton investor, Goldman Sachs, bows out.

January 24, 2008: Peloton is named Hedge Fund of the Year by EuroHedge.

February 2008: High-grade ABS securities are in free fall. Peloton loses $2 billion in two weeks as prime brokers call in margin.

February 29, 2008: Peloton announces liquidation of its ABS fund.

Drift, Discomfort, Disaster

No one disputes that an investing mistake was made. The strategy that worked brilliantly in the early days of the subprime crisis became a disaster as the crisis continued and widened. The right bet, shorting the triple-Bs, had run its course while the other right bet, what was intended to be both a hedge and a bet on quality, turned very wrong.

It wasn't that Grant didn't see it. After all, it was the multistrategy fund he directly managed that had seeded the ABS fund with $500 million. When that stake almost doubled in value, Grant felt some stirrings of discomfort over the exposure. He also could not

help but note the disproportionate rise in risk created by the volatility in the mortgage-backed securities market. In the summer of
2007, Grant as chief investment officer directed a rebalancing process, redeeming $250 million from the ABS fund that September
and an identical amount again in December. A third redemption
was scheduled for March 2008, but by then, the game was over.

"In retrospect," says Geoff Grant, "we probably should have gotten
out of triple-As when there was still liquidity in the market—probably
back in the fourth quarter of 2007, when the triple-Bs had lost their
value . . . August or September. We probably could have sold a significant amount of the position at that time. And we all wish we had.

"Nobody," says Grant, "saw the complete drying up of the
financing. Once that happened, we just ran out of time."

Grant also concedes that the long-distance partnership of
equals was not problem-free. The combining of business savvy and
trading expertise that looked so good on paper and seemed to
work so well at first hit some speed bumps along the way. As Grant
puts it: "Did hiring an ABS team constitute a business decision or a
trading decision? The business decision was based on the fact that
ABS was hot at the time," which was true enough, but should the
decision have resided solely in a single domain of the equal partnership? Certainly, building businesses was what Ron Beller did
well, and starting a new fund seems on its face a business-building
move. Yet Grant hints that from a trading and risk point of view, his
domain, the decision might have been a different one. It's a tough
call. And it may partly explain why the relationship between the two
partners had begun to show strain. Grant's hesitancy to dive into
ABS in quite so headlong a fashion translated into Beller assuming
disproportionate credit for the firm's success. It was Beller alone
who attended the EuroHedge dinner and accepted the awards for
Peloton while Grant stayed in Santa Barbara.

In fact, the two had already begun talking about changing the
shape of the relationship. As Grant interprets it, Beller saw himself
as the architect of ABS and Peter Howard as the driver. In that way,
the two of them were responsible for Peloton's big success, while
Grant and his macro fund were not doing all that well. Beller's idea
was to reorganize the firm's ownership "in a way that would not
have interested me," Grant says. In a sense, he was back where he
was before Peloton was formed—wondering "What next?" for his
career. "Peter's profile was very high, Ron was the front guy, and

I wanted to get back to trading macro," Grant says, referring to ABS fund manager Howard, partner Beller, and himself. "My life had been consumed by the ABS portfolio," and he wasn't happy with what that meant. "When ABS was doing well, it wasn't my trade or my success, although I certainly basked in the referred glow." But when ABS went down, says Grant, "I became much more front and center." He doesn't exactly complain about that: "It was my responsibility ultimately," he concedes, but he also knew that when the disaster struck, "it's going to be my name in the *Wall Street Journal*"—which indeed it was.

Still, the two-billion-dollar mistake from the Peloton experience is not so much betting wrong or having a blurry tie-breaking procedure in the management ranks. It's something more fundamental.

What Went Wrong

The underlying mistake at Peloton—the error that led to the actions that brought the firm down—was style drift. We've already said that style is what a fund manager markets to potential investors. It represents his or her expertise—demonstrated by a track record of experience and achievement—and defines the strategy he or she will follow.

Style drift undermines both the expertise and the strategy.

On the simplest level, a value fund manager drifting into growth investing actually is entering a whole new territory—uncharted territory, an unfamiliar topography. For even on the simplest level, very, very few investors—if any—can be proficient in multiple financial instruments or strategies. The reason? The world of finance is complex, and it is complicated. The knowledge, perception, experience, and judgment required to find underpriced assets—value investments—are way different in both kind and character from the knowledge, perception, experience, and judgment required to spot assets with growth potential.

Similarly, the analysis you need to do to invest in stocks is totally different from the kind of analysis you need to perform when you are investing in bonds. The former demands the ability to gain comprehensive knowledge of the company issuing the stock, its management, its competition, its products and operations, *plus* the ability to determine whether the market is asking a stock price that fairly reflects both the opportunity and the risk. Bond analysis, by contrast, focuses primarily on balance sheet; even if the company's brand-new product is a dud, as long as there is enough cash being generated to pay the yield and principal, it's a good investment, and the bond investor, who seeks lower risk at the cost of lower yield, will be happy.

Drift from the investment style you know and you also are entering uncharted risk territory, for certainly, each asset class and investment strategy exhibits its own specific risk attributes. And as everyone can appreciate, being in any way ignorant of the risks associated with a particular style of investing can be a fatal flaw—one that unfortunately may not be evident until the risks are realized.

Style drift is precisely what dragged down Peloton. This was a firm that had been created around the multistrategy expertise of its chief investment officer, Geoff Grant, to carry out precisely the kind of macro trading at which he excelled. When the "business decision" was made to go into ABS, an area with which Grant was familiar but in which he claimed no particular expertise, that part of the business effectively slid away from the chief investment officer's purview—or was taken out of his hands. Grant was left to focus on the multistrategy fund, while the business guy, Ron Beller, and asset-backed securities expert Peter Howard effectively oversaw the management and risk of the ABS fund.

When the EuroHedge dinner rolled around in late January, starring only one of two equal partners, it provided visual confirmation of trouble that had been brewing for a while. As the architect of the ABS fund, Beller believed he was solely responsible for the superlative returns Peloton generated in 2007; going forward, therefore, he believed he should take the lion's share of the firm's profits, or at least that Grant should not enjoy an equal share. Grant had little appetite for the debate this provoked and began to consider striking out on his own. Perhaps he should have.

But the truth is that Grant was not blameless either. By his own admission, he enjoyed the returns the ABS fund was generating—to the point of not attending too closely to how they were being generated. Although he does not think that financial results paint the full picture, "I got sucked into that," he says, adding that "it's hard not to." Yes, it is, and it's all too easy, as Grant affirms, to therefore "get sucked into turning a blind eye to potential warning signs." Which is what he did. "The big thing," he says, "was to sense that we lost perspective as it became as successful as it was." For Grant, this became a lesson in the importance of objectivity and in the need to apply objectivity to the process and not just be seduced by the results.

My bet about Peloton? Had it stuck to its knitting and not deviated from the investment style it had marketed originally to investors, it would still be in business today. Grant's pre-Peloton track record of 14 years as a macro trader supports this conclusion. So does his time at Peloton, where, after all, his segment of the business performed well.

At least one investor understood this. Goldman Sachs, for which both Beller and Grant had worked, bought into the multistrategy style the two advertised—and into the track record Geoff Grant had racked up as a Goldman Sachs partner. And as related earlier, Goldman got out when its management saw Peloton Partners move away from what the Wall Street giant had originally invested in.

One other investor was wary of the move into ABS. Geoff Grant had—and lost—an investment in the multistrategy fund, the value of which declined by 45 percent when Peloton's ABS fund went down. But he had never personally invested directly in the ABS fund as had Ron Beller and Peter Howard. It wasn't his style.

Unwinding to a Fresh Start

"Wheels Come Off."[1]"Peloton Runs Out of Road."[2] "Pile-up."[3] The headlines that followed the disaster offered bad cycling metaphors and a hint of self-satisfied gloating. The word "failure" was used a lot, and the glee over the two Goldman Sachs "stars" who had proved to be not nearly as shrewd as they thought they were was barely disguised.

Geoff Grant got to read about it even as he dedicated himself for three solid months to unwinding Peloton—and perhaps to reflecting with greater clarity on how to answer his "What next?" career question. Then he picked himself up and launched a new hedge fund, Liquid Macro, in September 2008. The name says it all: A single and specific investment style will be at work in this fund, and "we are focused on sticking to our core strategy," says Grant.

It is instructive—and proved persuasive to investors in Liquid Macro—that the Santa Barbara–based staff of Peloton, all with 20-plus years of trading experience apiece, decided en masse to stick with Geoff Grant and go to work for Liquid Macro. And it is equally instructive that Grant built into the structure of the new company a "mechanism for the partners to overwhelm me, to veto my super-vote."

It's Grant's company—"I'm the main guy," as he says—but if the main guy deviates from the liquid macro investment style, the partners can overrule it. "They can collectively tell me I'm crazy," says Grant—a fitting adjective to describe style drift and its dangers.

Lessons Learned

- *Verify investment style continually.* Check routinely for consistency of investment style. If and when you see a glitch in consistency or a deviation from what you bought into—when you see any kind of style drift—get out. Here's how to monitor your investments for style drift:
  - Study the fund or stock statements sent each quarter and annually, the fund or stock prospectus, and marketing literature.
  - Check with Morningstar, the independent research organization specializing in evaluating mutual funds. If the manager overseeing the portfolio you are interested in is prone to style drift, Morningstar will likely tag it with a low rating. Online membership is free: www.morningstar.com.
  - Call your fund manager or broker and ask questions.
- *Diversify investment styles.* A well balanced portfolio of investments should include a diversity of investment styles just as it includes a diversity of instruments or asset classes. A growth style typically will outperform value in an expanding economy. High-yield bonds may do better than a growth style when interest rates go down. Diverse investment styles distribute volatility risks.
- *Know who is managing your money.* Fund managers often are rotated; know the track record of your current manager, and assess the ongoing strength of the management culture. Make sure you know what your fund manager knows—his or her area of expertise. If your portfolio is half value and half growth, and your bond fund manager starts buying stocks, more than balance is at stake. The real question is whether the bond manager knows *how* to invest in stocks. If not, you could end up like Peloton's investors.
- *Don't be blinded by hyperreturns.* In fact, be wary of them: They're a hint to look under the hood. Remember that high return means higher risk, and higher risk can wipe out your principal.
- *Make sure your own investment style doesn't drift.* If you often visit McDonald's and notice that a new menu is attracting more diners, it's easy enough to draw the conclusion that business is getting better and that stock in the fast-food chain may be worth buying. But if you overhear two chemists talking about synthesizing aluminum clusters to produce hydrogen, unless it is your personal area of expertise, do not invest in it. Do as you want your fund manager to do: Stick to your knitting.

CHAPTER

Volkswagen and Porsche

THE HARE FINALLY WINS AND THE SHORTS GET SQUEEZED

All of the profiles in this book thus far have been of single investors. In this chapter, we depart from that practice to profile an investing strategy—short selling. It's a strategy that even professional investors are careful about implementing, and it's a strategy they typically are hesitant to discuss. The short-selling incident related here, one of the most famous in recent history, involved some of the savviest hedge fund investors in the world and one of Europe's best-known billionaires. His story, apart from its tragic aspect, exemplifies the dangers at the heart of the short-selling strategy, but it is the strategy itself that is the real subject of this chapter.

A Short Story

There isn't much to say about the town of Blaubeuren, in southern Germany, some 12 miles from Ulm. Sitting prettily in a valley of the Swabian Alps, the town has fewer than 12,000 inhabitants, some lovely timbered buildings, and deep religious roots—as evidenced in a late Gothic church, a Benedictine abbey, and a monastery that dates back to the eleventh century. It is a stop on the Freiburg-Ulm railroad line, and connections are frequent, the train track running past fields and lush forests. It was on the track winding through this bucolic town, with its intense medieval charm, that Adolf Merckle, one of Germany's richest men and a prominent

171

citizen of Blaubeuren, hurled himself in front of an oncoming train at a point on the line not far from his villa.

At age 74, Merckle was "broken," as his family's statement put it, by the struggle to save his business empire. That empire, a portfolio of companies employing some 100,000 people and anchored by pharmaceutical giant Ratiopharm and construction products conglomerate Heidelberg Cement, had earned Merckle a fortune estimated at $9.2 billion in 2008, making him one of the wealthiest individuals in Germany. When the empire was threatened, Merckle went all out to save it, looking for buyers for his assets and spending weeks negotiating with banks for bridge loans. But the pressure must have been too great—to the point where it was simply easier to walk to the railroad track and stand in the way of the engine.

The threat to the empire had come at Merckle's own hand. Months before, back in 2008, he had shorted the stock of Volkswagen (VW), a speculative bet that went horribly wrong when Porsche began buying up a controlling interest in its sister auto company. Volkswagen's products were plebeian compared to Porsche's patrician luxury autos—deliberately, of course; Volkswagen means "the people's car"—but VWs were among the world's biggest sellers, and Porsche had been acquiring VW stock since 2005. In March 2008, however, with no fanfare, the company announced its intention to increase its VW holding. It did so primarily in cash-settled options, ownership of which, by German law, need not be disclosed. By the time the full measure of Porsche's intention became clear—nothing less than a takeover—it was too late; there weren't enough VW shares to go around to unwind bets like Merckle's. As Volkswagen's stock price soared, Merckle's short position equated to as much as a "three-digit million euro loss"[1]—some have guessed as much as €400 million to €500 million. Given the currency conversion rate at that time (1 €=$1.52), that would have translated into a loss of well over half a billion U.S. dollars—a significant sum, even for a billionaire.

The short squeeze Merckle faced was not the only challenge to his wealth; the German economy was in the grip of a worldwide recession, and the consortium of lenders to his debt-laden holdings were asking for repayment. His request for a government loan was rebuffed, but there seemed still a chance that the commercial and investment banks owning the debt would renegotiate the terms. Then, for reasons he divulged only in a private note to his family, Merckle simply gave up.

He was not alone in manifesting his negative assessment of VW's prospects by shorting the equity. Nor was he alone in suffering significant losses. Among the hedge funds caught in the same squeeze were Greenlight Capital, SAC Capital, Glenview Capital, Marshall Wace, Tiger Asia, Odey Capital, Perry Capital, and Highside Capital[2]—funds managed by some of the industry's savviest investors. Hedge funds, in fact, are—supposedly—past masters at going short as well as long; that's the hedging for which they're named.

It's an interesting paradox: When you short a stock, you win by picking a loser. It's not unlike a day at the racetrack: You win if the horse you bet on comes in first, but you can also win if your horse loses—if you have bet on him to place and he comes in second, or if you have bet on the horse to show and he comes in third. Of course, if you hedge your bets right and put money on the three horses that come in win, place, and show, you really profit—on both the winner and the losers.

Lose a bet at the racetrack, and it's bad news; you tear up your ticket and head for the bar. Short selling in the professional investing game, however, can be very dangerous indeed. Simply put, you can lose more than you have invested; in theory anyway, your loss can be infinite. Bottom line? A wrong bet on a shorted stock becomes a disproportionately large portion of your portfolio.

If a short selling bet succeeds, however, the profits can be enormous. In 2008, for example, the year the financial markets plunged in the face of the global economic crisis, investors holding long positions lost some 45 percent of their money; those who held both long and short positions may have come out ahead at year-end—depending on the stocks they bet on; and those who were "net" short—that is, the amount of money they had invested in short positions exceeded the value invested in long positions—made a fortune. That is why, despite the danger, professional investors keep on short selling.

Here's one spectacular example of the kind of profits shorting can provide: In 2007, when market indices had fairly benign performance, hedge fund manager John Paulson's firm, Paulson & Co., achieved a gain of almost 600 percent by taking short positions on the housing cycle. Paulson's personal reward for correctly predicting the carnage in the subprime market was a paycheck estimated at $3.7 billion.[3]

But shorting is speculative, it can be tricky, and while the transaction itself is fairly simple, it takes a bit of nerve to see it through.

Like the hedge funds and other investors who shorted Volkswagen in 2008, Adolf Merckle had the nerve to see it through. Living with the consequences, however, was apparently something he was not willing to do.

Not for the Faint of Heart

Shorting a stock simply means you anticipate that the stock will lose value. To take advantage of that belief, you borrow the stock from your broker—who either has it on hand in inventory or gets it from another customer or another brokerage—and you sell it, pocketing the proceeds into your margin account at the brokerage. In other words, you have sold a stock you don't own. In time, therefore, you will need to cover that transaction; that is, you'll have to buy back the stock—in the same number of shares—and return the stock to your broker.

If, as you anticipated, the price of the stock has gone down, you will make money on the deal. Take a look:

> Suppose you decide to short ABC Corporation. You borrow 100 shares of ABC stock at $50 per share and sell them, reaping income of $5,000. You've just borrowed the shares; you haven't yet spent a penny, and you have $5,000 in your account.
>
> Now the stock price sinks, just as you had guessed, and you buy the shares back at $40 per share for a total price of $4,000.
>
> You made $5,000 and you spent $4,000, so your profit is $1,000. Not bad.
>
> Of course, if the stock price goes up, and you have to buy back the shares at $60 per share, you lose $1,000. Not good.

That's the bare bones of short selling.

The issue, therefore, is to be very careful when you are choosing a stock to short. It isn't easy; it is definitely tougher to deliberately pick a loser than a winner. One reason is that, despite the global financial crisis that began in 2008, markets trend higher much more often than they decline. That's why most professional investment managers ply their trade as long-only stock pickers—that is, they only buy stocks and do not short them—even though hedge fund managers who go both long *and* short have much greater earnings potential. It's also why professional investors who do practice shorting go to great lengths using a range of metrics to identify candidates for shorting.

One metric is valuation. Say a stock is selling at 50 times earnings while the shares of other companies in the same sector are priced at only 20 times earnings. The company's revenues are most likely growing faster than the industry average—possibly because it is better managed than its peers or has a sexier product or is better at marketing. Whatever the reason, it's a tempting stock to short. Why? Certainly, the better earnings—and better management, product, marketing— warrant a higher valuation than the shares of other companies in the industry, but in this case, the difference in valuation is too great. And that valuation variance could signal that the earnings performance is but a temporary glitch; it is anomalous—irrational. The stock is therefore a candidate for a *valuation short*, as it is called.

But there's a particular danger about valuation shorting, and it's this: The market can afford to stay irrational for longer than most investors can stay solvent. That means that shorting a stock based only on a perceived irrational valuation is often a losing trade, unless it is timed somewhat perfectly. In any event, it's a gamble.

Then there is the *crowded short*, and Volkswagen was a perfect example of that. It's based on the metric of short interest—that is, the number of outstanding shares, called the *float*, that have already been sold short. Short interest data are reported once a month by the stock exchanges and published in the stock tables of most newspapers and on the financial Web sites of the Internet. If more than about 10 percent and certainly more than 20 percent of the float is held short, that is considered crowded.

There are three ways to look at a crowded short. One way is to see it as a *sell signal*—a reflection of negative sentiment toward the stock or an indication that something is about to go wrong at the company. Another way to look at it is as a sign of a potential short squeeze that will make the stock trade a lot higher. A *short squeeze* occurs when too many traders who are short the same stock try to buy it back—to cover their short—at the same time. As with any item in high demand, the price goes up. This is precisely what happened to Adolph Merckle. Finally, a high short interest also may indicate that the bad news is already public and has been discounted in the share price.

There is no shortage of kinds of short; thematic shorts, catalyst shorts, and accounting shorts are some other useful shorting targets—useful to know about, in any case.

In 2007, Paulson made his $3.7 billion in a *thematic short*; he simply was convinced that the housing bubble was about to burst, so he presciently sold short everything in his portfolio with a real estate theme—everything having to do with real estate at all.

Shorting a stock in expectation that a company will report lower earnings than forecast, causing the stock to trade down, is a *catalyst short*. The gap between forecast and actual catalyzes the downward movement.

Accounting shorts are perhaps the most esoteric; in any event, they probably require the most work. First of all, an accounting short requires comprehensive knowledge of accounting laws. Based on such knowledge, the investor performs a forensic analysis of a company's books and/or procedures to ascertain if any rules were broken. For example, suppose a company has inflated its sales figures by transferring products between subsidiaries and booking the transfers as sales. If you could find that out and short the stock, you probably could do very well indeed. Accounting shorts usually are devastating to stock prices, because they directly undermine the relationship of trust so critical to shareholders and managements.

Short sellers—that is, investors who short stocks—are actually known in the trade as "shorts." Are shorts villains? Ogres looking to prey on the investing mistakes of others? Cynical pessimists about human behavior and how markets work? Not really. Shorts don't make the news; they only position their portfolios to take advantage of what they believe the news will be. It's true that a short seller wins only if another fails, but isn't that what business is about? When one company gains market share, another loses it. Most knowledgeable market observers believe that shorting is a necessary part of market dynamics. In September 2008, in fact, in the darkest days of the bank stock sell-off in the United States, when the Securities and Exchange Commission (SEC) imposed its prohibition on the short selling of financial stocks, it was only "temporary in nature," as the emergency order proclaimed. The order went on to say that such a prohibition "would not be necessary in a well-functioning market," another way of saying that short selling is an integral component of markets that are working the way markets should.

But it isn't for the faint of heart, and it does take some nerve.

The 2008 Ban on Short Selling

Bear Stearns was gone. Countrywide Financial was gone. Interest rates had plummeted. Fannie Mae and Freddie Mac were in peril, and the broader market indices remained under severe pressure. A scapegoat was needed, and short sellers were easy targets—not solely because they were the only ones making money but also because the core of their strategy, profiting from another's misfortune, was a practice that had few supporters. The government decided to act.

July 15: The Securities and Exchange Commission issued an emergency order banning short selling in Fannie Mae, Freddie Mac, and 17 other financial firms—among them some of the nation's signature banks and investment banking firms, all of them seemingly in trouble.

The emergency order was aimed specifically at "naked" short selling—that is, ordering a sale without having arranged to borrow actual shares. Considered an abuse of the process at best, possibly illegal at worst, naked shorting was banned altogether by the order for the period July 21 through July 29; the ban was extended July 30.

September 19: Two months later, the SEC went a step further and halted all short selling of financial stocks. In its statement, the commission called the ban "temporary" and "a time-out." The order, which followed by a day a similar ban in the United Kingdom, affected 799 financial stocks.

The ban was lifted October 9, 2008, but new rules for restrictions on short selling were promulgated in 2009 and are under review as this book goes to press. Many will debate the restrictions, believing that short selling is a necessary part of market dynamics, whether serving to temper irrational exuberance or to keep supply and demand for stocks in greater balance.

Porsche and VW

Adolf Merckle was the ninety-fourth richest human being on Earth, and chances are good he didn't achieve that wealth by being faint of heart or because of a lack of nerve. Ditto for some of the most astute and successful hedge fund managers on Earth—Larry Robbins of Glenview Capital, Steve Cohen of SAC Capital, Crispin

Odey of Odey Asset Management, Paul Marshall and Ian Wace of Marshall Wace, and David Einhorn of Greenlight Capital. In fact, earlier in 2008, Einhorn had made a spectacular killing by shorting Lehman Brothers—an act of nerve if ever there was one.[4]

For all of them, shorting Volkswagen in 2008 must have seemed like a no-brainer. Virtually every other automobile company on the planet—including the Japanese manufacturers—was at best declining, at worst falling apart. The German economy was hurting; the U.S. economy, a major market for Volkswagen cars, was hurting just as badly if not worse. It was natural to assume that the stock price of Volkswagen would start to go downhill as well. Porsche's March announcement that it would increase its stake in Volkswagen was deemed a footnote to the main narrative, not a scene stealer, if analysts noted it at all. After all, Porsche had been slowly adding shares of Volkswagen since 2005. Instead, the word was out that shorting VW was the safest play in town. So these hedge fund managers— and Herr Merckle—instructed their brokers to short Volkswagen, which eventually became the most shorted stock in Germany's benchmark Deutscher Aktien IndeX (DAX)—the blue-chip index of the 30 major German companies.

In September 2008, Porsche quietly announced that it now had 35 percent of VW stock. The Porsche family denied that it would seek a controlling stake in Volkswagen because to do so would activate Germany's so-called Volkswagen law, which gave VW workers and the German state of Lower Saxony (which controls 20.1 percent of the company) effective veto power and authority over certain key managerial decisions (i.e., factory closures). The Volkswagen law was declared invalid by a European Union court, but the German government led by Angela Merkel was continuing to fight the law even as Porsche was building up its stake. Thus, Porsche's insistence that it didn't want to tempt the activation of the still-valid Volkswagen law sounded reasonable, even though later it would prove to be a coy disclaimer.

There was another German law at work during this time—a law stating that Porsche did not have to disclose its purchases if those purchases were in the form of cash-settled options. Porsche was eager to put this law, unlike the Volkswagen law, into effect, and that is precisely what it did, slowly and in a sense stealthily adding to its stake in VW. There was no way to know that what the company really was doing was quite simply buying up Volkswagen in order to take it over.

But then Porsche finally showed its hand.

On Sunday, October 26, 2008, Porsche announced that it held 42.6 percent of Volkswagen stock and had options for 31.5 percent more—for a total of 74.1 percent. The weekend was an unusual time for such an announcement, and this one caused a frenzy of consternation on several continents. Here's why: In addition to Porsche's 74.1 percent ownership or option for ownership of VW, Lower Saxony still held its mandated 20.1 percent. It meant that a grand total of 94.2 percent of Volkswagen shares were locked up and that a mere 5.8 percent of its stock—some 18 million shares— were available to buy. But the hedge funds had shorted 12 percent of VW's shares. There were thus about twice as many shares short as there were shares trading freely in the market.

Compounding the problem was Porsche's announcement that it wanted to recall the shares that the short sellers had borrowed and shorted before the company acquired the last part of its stake in VW. Now remember: Shorting a stock means borrowing it from another, selling it, then—one hopes—buying it back later at a lower price and pocketing the difference as a gain. So when Porsche decided it didn't feel like lending the short sellers any more of its stash of VW stock, the automaker instructed its banks to recall the shares, and the hedge funds were contractually liable to return them.

Put it all together and it was crystal clear that when the German market opened at 8:00 the next morning, Monday, October 27, 2008, there were going to be too many short-betting hedge fund investors chasing way too few available Volkswagen shares.

Sunday afternoon is normally a lazy time in European financial capitals. It is fair to say that this particular Sunday afternoon was anything but lazy for the hedge fund managers scrambling to call their brokers—and for the brokers taking the panicked calls. Thanks to the time difference, American investors and brokers had more hours available to worry about the issue, but only because they were most likely still asleep when the news broke. Global markets being what they are, one usually is open in some part of the world at just about every hour of the 24, and markets wait for no one. But time was not the key factor here. The key factor was that there simply weren't enough VW shares to go around, and when the markets opened Monday morning and the scramble for VW shares began, those people holding the shares could name their price. Which is exactly what they did.

It was effectively a short squeeze, although it did not precisely fit the classic definition. In a classic short squeeze, there are enough shares available, but the trading volume is too thin to accommodate a large number of shorts trying to cover at once.

No matter. To those caught in it, it felt sufficiently constricting, classic squeeze or not.

Volkswagen opened Monday morning at $273 a share and by the end of Tuesday was selling at $1,303.60 per share. Indeed, at one moment on Tuesday, VW became the world's most highly valued company—with a total market capitalization of $456 billion. According to Larry Robbins of Glenview Capital, one of the short sellers, that sum was equivalent to "five percent of the current value of the entire U.S. equity market."[5] Clearly, the manufacturer of Herbie the Love Bug wasn't being valued on fundamentals.

The losses for the hedge funds that had shorted Volkswagen were stratospheric—estimated at as much as $5 billion to $6 billion in the case of some of the larger funds.[6] Hedge fund managers and traders around the world demanded an investigation of the regulations that safeguarded Porsche's failure to disclose its buildup of VW stock—they charged market manipulation, and one wag dubbed the episode a "sting operation."

Some hedge fund managers blamed their prime brokers too. Larry Robbins told Glenview's investors that "we did not anticipate the prime brokerage community could view an automotive company at 1 to 300 times earnings—and greater in value than Exxon Mobil—to be the riskiest short in the marketplace, necessitating multiples of capital posted as margin." Added Robbins dryly: "Our imaginations were not large enough."[7]

Robbins contended in fact that there was no shortage of available shares. He believed that if other short sellers had been more patient and knowledgeable about the fundamentals of the trade and had not rushed to cover their positions, the stock would never have risen so high. In his analysis, Porsche never had the wherewithal to acquire all of Volkswagen; the cash-settled options Porsche had bought obviously cost less than purchasing the shares outright. Robbins stuck persistently to his view that VW was overvalued, and Glenview continued to hold its short position in VW stock.

Porsche profited far more from the short squeeze than it ever had from selling cars. At one point during the frenzied trading of October 27–28, its paper profit exceeded $120 billion. In January

2009, it announced it had increased its VW stake to 50.76 percent plus options to buy more. And it reported a windfall profit for its fiscal first half—$7.49 billion versus $1.64 billion for the same period the previous year.

Anatomy of a Short Squeeze: Porsche's VW Timeline

March 2008: As major investors go on a shorting spree on VW stock, Porsche quietly announces plans to increase its stake in the carmaker.

September 2008: Just as quietly, Porsche announces it has 35 percent of VW stock.

October 26, 2008: Porsche reveals it owns 42.6 percent of VW stock with options for 31.5 percent more for a grand total of 74.1 percent of VW stock.

October 27-28, 2008: VW stock goes from $273 per share to $1,303.60 as short-betting hedge fund investors chase too few available VW shares.

January 2009: Porsche announces it holds 50.76 percent of VW stock plus options and releases a profit figure of $7.49 billion versus $1.64 billion for the same period the previous year.

They May Be Called Shorts, but if You're Wrong, They Can Get Pretty Big

Let's say you have $100 invested in the market—one share of ABC Corporation and one of XYZ Corporation, each share priced at $50. Time passes, and XYZ trades up to $100 a share while ABC stays flat at $50. In the world of long only, XYZ stock is now twice as big a position as ABC; it is equal to two-thirds—67 percent—of the value of your portfolio ($100 invested in XYZ + $50 in ABC = $150). If XYZ declines by half to $25, however, then the size of the XYZ position would equal only one-third—33 percent—of the portfolio ($25 in XYZ + $50 in ABC = $75).

With short positions, the reverse is true. That is, when you lose money on shorts, they become bigger issues within a portfolio. Suppose you sell short one share of ABC at $50 because you're convinced the company will have to lower its earnings forecast. Instead, management raises its estimates, and there is a race to acquire the shares by new buyers as well as by short sellers trying to cover—that is, to buy back the stock because they have to return it. ABC stock trades to $100 a share while XYZ remains flat at $50. ABC stock has now become your biggest position because its market price is $100 per share. Unfortunately, however, you have wiped out your entire account in terms of net value because you have a liability of $100. What's more, your broker is nervous because you don't have enough value in your account to meet the margin requirements. You have no choice but to cover the short and return the stock to the lender.

Here's how the math works. You borrowed a stock at $50 and sold it short, receiving proceeds of $50 in cash that went into your margin account. You had hoped to be able to buy the stock back at $25 and return it to the broker, keeping the $25 cash in your account. Instead, you now have to buy the stock at $100. In order to do that, you will use the $50 that went into the margin account from your initial short sale of ABC, *and* you will have to sell your single share of XYZ for $50 in order to come up with the $100 to repurchase the borrowed shares that you sold short.

Merckle's problem was that he didn't own enough unencumbered assets that he could sell to meet the margin call when the VW liability became such a big part of his account.

The shorts simply got too big.

What Went Wrong

Short selling is a dangerous strategy, and the Porsche-Volkswagen incident is an example of its dangers writ large. Granted that one component of the incident was unique to Germany—the rather elastic financial disclosure regulations—it nevertheless shows the many ways an investor can lose when shorting a stock—and how very much can be lost.

Of course, any investor can lose on any investment. Risk is inherent to the investing proposition. But short selling is a gamble unlike any other when it comes to investing in stocks. After all, for centuries, despite wars, natural disasters, and economic volatility, stocks have tended upward in value. Even if only because of inflationary pressures, stocks ride a rising tide. **To short stocks is thus to go against the tide. That is precisely why it can be so profitable, but** it makes for a very risky venture—often with risks the investor does not or cannot see.

Shorting VW seemed safe precisely because it did not so much buck the tide as catch the last downward wave in a sea of waves that had already crashed to shore. **All the signs were clear that the VW wave soon would have to head down, except the one sign not available to be read:** the Porsche family's intentions. Investors thought the facts were clear—the global economy was in recession, Germany was particularly hard hit, and auto companies everywhere were reporting much lower sales—and the gamble seemed safe. It turned out, however, that investors didn't have all the facts, and the gamble was a disaster.

From a practical standpoint, the most painful short positions are in those stocks that keep going higher. Every tick every day is a constant reminder that you are wrong, are losing money, and getting farther away from your break-even point. Some investors think the acquisition of the company whose stock you shorted is worse; after all, acquisition means there is no chance you'll recover your losses. In my view, however, while both eventualities are equally agonizing, losing out to an acquisition at least affords certainty: You know what your ultimate loss will be. It's almost like a mercy killing, like the lame horse that has to be put down. The only possible reprieve—for the short seller, not for a lame horse—is if the company were acquired for stock instead of cash. In that case, the value of the purchase price may be tied to the stock price of the acquiring company. Since not all acquisitions are uniformly appreciated, there's a chance it could lead to pressure on the buyer's share price, which in turn could mean pressure on the shares of the acquired company—the shares that are being shorted. It's far-fetched, but at least you can hope.

Another danger of shorting is that it is done on margin. In the case of Porsche and Volkswagen, when brokers increased the amount of collateral or cash that had to be placed in the margin account to cover their risk on loaning VW shares to short sellers, some short sellers were unable to provide the increase. Instead, they had to return the stock, and the only way to do that was to buy it back. That is why Adolf Merckle sold off assets, asked his government for a loan, and was begging the banks to help him bridge his losses when he finally gave up.

The short squeeze makes all this happen very fast and can drain all the profit out of the investment, turning it into a considerable, devastating loss. The Monday morning rush for shares that sent VW stock soaring and briefly made the company the world's most valuable business left almost every player in VW shares, except Porsche and Lower Saxony, considerably poorer—in the space of 48 hours.

In shorting, even if you are right, you could be right at the wrong time. In a bubble—the prime example is the dot-com bubble of the 1990s—you've got to guess absolutely right about when the top will be reached, as far too many dot-com investors did not. Many shorted the Nasdaq in 1999 when it was up 86 percent—and lost badly. They believed that the valuations on technology stocks—more specifically, on Internet stocks—were ridiculously high. They were right, but remember: The market can stay irrational much longer than anyone can stay solvent. As the ultimate deep-pockets adversary, the market won on timing, and those shorting the Nasdaq in 1999 lost.

Other short sellers thought they would wait for the first cracks to occur, and when they heard the first hissing sound of the Internet bubble beginning to deflate, they would lay out their short bets. They might miss a 10 percent or even 20 percent downward move, but by waiting, they would significantly limit their risk that those stocks would keep rising. Many of these Nasdaq short sellers also lost out. It is very, very tough to pick tops and bottoms in stocks and markets.

The short story on VW ultimately would play out as Glenview's Robbins had forecast. Although Volkswagen was the strongest of European auto companies, the slowing global economy would take its toll. The hunted would become the hunter as the heavy debt load assumed by Porsche for the purpose of acquiring VW options would drive the company to seek emergency financing. The financier? None other than VW in the role of acquirer: The two companies agreed to merge, and Porsche CEO Wendelin Wiedeking was out. But this was not a trade that would make Glenview or any other short seller rich. While the stock price sank from its highs, it never declined to a point where the early short sellers could make much, if any, profit.

One of the key aspects of short selling—and one of its core risks—is timing. If the trade goes against you—that is, if the stock continues to trade higher—you will be forced to cover; as noted earlier, in shorting, the risk is unlimited. Even in the case of VW, the macro fundamentals proved correct, but new factors came into play and put a floor under the stock price. Result? The company was able to gain control of a premier brand, Porsche, for a significant discount.

So where does this leave the individual retail investor like you? Do you just vow to stay away from shorting and abandon all chance for the kinds of returns it can yield?

Not necessarily.

I'll Take the Guy Wearing the Green Eyeshade with Plastic Pocket Protector

Pretend you are playing a game against an opposing team. Not pickup basketball or baseball, but trading. And not trading stocks, but an even bigger game, with more on the line: trading companies, big billion-dollar companies. You win the coin toss and have the first pick—whomever you want on your team.

Do you pick the $6 billion man, Stevie Cohen, who is perhaps the world's best trader? . . . David Einhorn, who blew the whistle on Lehman Brothers, shorting the stock into the biggest bankruptcy in history? . . . Billionaire private equity investor Steven Feinberg of Cerberus Capital? . . . Dieter Zetsche, chief executive of German auto company Daimler, whose prominent white mustache is the size of a whisk broom? . . . Or another German auto executive, Holger Haerter, bespectacled chief financial officer (CFO) of Porsche—at least till the merger with VW sent him packing? If you selected Cohen, Einhorn, or Feinberg, you lost the game and lost big.

Big-ticket items like automobiles were among the first casualties of the global economic crisis that began in 2007 and extended into 2009. But two German automakers found a bit of solace through their trading acumen.

Daimler had purchased Chrysler for $37 billion in 1998 and never realized enough synergies to make the merger a success. So its management looked to sell, but no strategic buyer stepped to the plate. Instead, Steve Feinberg decided to make a bold move and purchased the company for $7.4 billion, most of which immediately went toward liabilities that Chrysler had incurred in the day-to-day running of the business. Had Zetsche not found a buyer for its American subsidiary—which of course went into U.S. federal bankruptcy protection in 2009—Daimler would have had to inject the capital.

Haerter, the well-paid CFO of Porsche, orchestrated a trade of similar magnitude, although at one point his profits were in excess of $100 billion, all at the expense of the other team.

Cohen's SAC Capital, Einhorn's Greenlight Capital, and a multitude of other hedge funds shorted shares of Volkswagen, the thesis being that auto sales were contracting. They saw VW's shares holding up much better than the stocks of other auto companies, thought that presented an opportunity, and didn't believe Porsche had the financial wherewithal to complete an acquisition. They were right— sort of. Haerter was looking to make money, and make money he did—between $7 billion and $12 billion—more than Porsche would earn from its car business. Instead of wealthy hedge fund managers exchanging their money for the right to squeeze into one of those nifty little sports cars, they got squeezed out of their shares of VW stock.

Final score: German auto companies: +$14 billion; hedge fund industry: –$14 billion.

To Short or Not to Short

As evidenced by the Porsche-Volkswagen incident, it is safe to concede that shorting stocks is a risky strategy. Yet it's also essential to note that shorting can be effective as a hedge against long exposure and as a moneymaking strategy. Is there a way then for the average retail investor to enjoy the potential gains of shorts while avoiding the equivalent of a billion-dollar mistake? Yes, so long as you keep in mind that every investment represents a compromise: You get something, you give something. Specifically, if you are going to limit the attendant risk of shorting, you need to be willing to cede a portion of the potential return.

There are three ways the average investor can get in on the benefits of shorting while mitigating its risks as much as possible: buying put options, investing in exchange-traded funds (ETFs), and outright shorting of a stock but doing it very, very carefully.

In a put option, if the underlying equity—the stock that the option is derived from—trades down to a predetermined price within a predetermined time, the option holder has the right to "put" the shares back to the firm that sold them—that is, to sell them back at that predetermined "strike price," as it's called. (See more about options in Chapter 4.) The good news about buying a put option is that the risk is limited to the premium you pay for the option, which is a right but not an obligation to sell the stock. The risk is therefore limited, not infinite as it would be if you just shorted the stock.

But there are trade-offs. For example, options become worthless on their expiration dates; for that reason, the investor needs to be as certain as possible that the stock will decline within the stated period. Moreover, the farther out the expiration date occurs, the more expensive the premium for the option will be; you're paying extra for what's called the time value. Also, the closer the option is to being in the money, the more it will cost. And of course, not all stocks have options, particularly the smaller-capitalization companies.

Another way to get in on shorting is the exchange-traded fund the sidebar. ETFs are essentially packages of individual securities that replicate the movement in an industry. For example, suppose you conclude that economic times are tough for the consumer and that it therefore makes sense to short Wal-Mart. Instead of shorting the single stock, consider an ETF of consumer equities. In fact, there is such a thing—the ProShares UltraShort Consumer Services ETF. It will provide you with short exposure to Wal-Mart, McDonald's, Disney, and other brand-name consumer companies in the Dow Jones consumer services index. Because no one company in the ETF has more than a 17 percent representation in the ETF—thus evening out the weighting a little—this will mitigate your risk of one of the companies being acquired. What's more, this ETF is levered to a 2:1 correlation with the underlying stocks—that is, it tracks twice the inverse of the daily performance of the underlying index. If the index of consumer companies goes down, your investment goes up by a factor of 2. And vice versa: If the index goes up, your investment goes down twice as much. This allows you to realize greater profits if your original investment thesis is correct, but if it's wrong, it will be twice as expensive. After all, Ultra ETF's are leveraged securities and we have visited the downside of leverage in previous chapters.

A Longer View of Shorting

One handy way to reap the potential benefit of shorting without taking the kinds of lumps suffered by the pros is the ETF—the exchange-traded fund.

What's an ETF? Think of it as a mutual fund that trades like a stock. That means you get the diversification of the former and the flexibility of the latter—including the ability to short sell. Every ETF has a ticker symbol and is traded on one of the stock exchanges like the New York Stock Exchange (NYSE). Just as with any security on a public exchange, an ETF will trade throughout the day, its price fluctuating in line with buy and sell transactions. The beauty part of ETFs is that they possess incredible liquidity that protects against short squeezes. While shorting individual stocks requires the use of margin, ETFs are purchased in cash accounts.

There are many different types of ETFs. Some are proxies for indices like the Dow Jones Industrial Average (DJIA), the Standard & Poor's 500, or the Nasdaq 100. These ETFs will mimic the moves in those indices. The DOG ETF, for example, comprises the 30 stocks that make up the Dow sold short and packaged into a fund that is traded on the stock exchange. Invest in DOG if you want to short the DJIA.

An ETF that is a short play has an inverse correlation to the index it is based on—that is, it trades in the opposite direction. If the DJIA trades down, the DOG will trade higher.

If a trader is really bearish, DXD is the fund to buy since it is leveraged to multiply the downward move on the DOW twofold. That means that for every dollar that the DJIA trades lower, DXD will trade higher by $2.

Other ETFs are constructed to provide exposure to a specific sector or country. For example, if you believe that financial stocks are poised to move higher, you might purchase the XLF, the financial ETF. The XLF is composed of 80 different bank and insurance company stocks. They are not equally weighted—that is, some stocks are more important to the index than others. J.P. Morgan Chase & Co. (JPM) makes up almost 14 percent of the ETF, while Allstate Corporation has a 1.3 percent weighting, and MBIA Inc., the municipal bond insurer, has only a 0.9 percent weighting. Clearly, JPM will have an influence on how the XLF trades, while MBIA's impact will be negligible at best.

ETFs can be effective hedging tools. For example, suppose a trader really likes a particular stock but hates the sector. A reasonable way to play that dichotomy is to buy the stock and short the ETF. That way, the trader is effectively eliminating the sector risk and isolating the fundamentals of the company. Traders also can hedge market risk against a portfolio of stocks by shorting the index funds for the stocks.

Leveraged ETFs like DXD are very volatile and generally should be avoided by individual investors—as should most leveraged instruments. They move as if powered by rocket fuel, and it is difficult to get a good grip on the risk involved.

But hundreds of ETFs allow investors to bet on almost anything—including the price of oil, gold, or which way the emerging markets will trade. As with mutual funds, a number of companies—ProShares is one—sponsor ETFs. Check out the ProShares Website for a listing: www.proshares.com.

Some single stock shorts do make sense—that is, the risk that the stock will go up is more or less equivalent to the downside risk of owning a particular stock. When and how should the average investor call his or her broker and say "Short that stock!"? Only when a few specific conditions are met, and only very, very carefully.

Basically, you want to bet on the fundamentals. That means you want to focus on big, liquid names—any company whose stock trades like water—and you want to wait till the bad news about the company has just started to come out.

There's no bigger or more liquid name than McDonald's, so let's use it as an example. Suppose you stop in to your local Mickey D's one day and are surprised to note that its menu has gone completely vegetarian and its prices have been raised significantly. At the same time, Burger King across the street has lowered its prices and maintained its traditional offering. Your culinary and environmental preferences aside, you're pretty convinced that McDonald's has made a dumb decision and will lose a lot of business, so you begin to assess the risk of shorting its shares.

Given McDonald's size and liquidity, you already know that the technical risk is exceedingly low. A short squeeze is highly unlikely. McDonald's short interest is usually around 1 percent and, with the company's daily share volume in the tens of millions, can be covered in less than two trading days. You also know that the fundamental risk is exceedingly low: Given McDonald's market value—more than $60 billion as of this writing—the likelihood of it being acquired by another company is close to nil.

But is that all you need to look at? No. In shorting a stock—perhaps more than in any other equity transaction—due diligence is the name of the game. How do you do it? Head for the Internet. Plenty of financial sites track company data—Bloomberg (www.bloomberg.com), MSN Money (http://moneycentral.msn .com/home.asp), Yahoo (www.finance.yahoo.com). In Yahoo, for example, find the investing tab, then enter the ticker symbol for the stock—in this case, MCD—to start your research. You can track all the current and historical data on the stock's performance. You can note short interest data. You can find out what analysts say about the stock and whether they recommend it as a buy, sell, or hold. You can explore insider transactions—that is, which officers of the company are buying stock, selling it, exercising their options, and the like. And you can of course find out all the company's financial data: balance sheet, cash flow, income statement. In just about all of these cases, you can see trend data as well as current situations. Do your due diligence, remember that what counts are the fundamentals, decide if you really believe McDonald's stock value will go down, then make your bet.

But care and caution are required in interpreting the data—in reading the tea leaves. For one thing, bad news is not always a hint that the stock will go down. Why? Because the bad news may already be built into the stock price. Take the example of another restaurant chain—P.F. Chang's China Bistro—and go back to 2008, when the recession had a lot of people deciding they were going to eat home more often. It would have been natural to think that the earnings of a company like P.F. Chang's would decline. And indeed if you had looked at analyst recommendations at the time, they would have been almost unanimous against buying the stock for just that reason.

Here's a tip: When everybody is bearish, that's a bullish sign. Expectations are low; the downside is likely already a part of the stock price. Indeed, at China Bistro in 2008, the business fundamentals were under pressure, and the valuation of the company's worth—24 times earnings—was high for a business whose earnings had not grown appreciably for some years. But the short interest was 34 percent—extremely high, well above the 10 percent to 20 percent do-not-short rule of thumb. And indeed, it would have been a mistake to do so. For while earnings declined, the stock price rose from some $14 per share to $33 per share. Why? Part short squeeze, part investor psychology: There was too much negativity already reflected in the stock at $14 and too many short sellers chasing the stock.

Timing is also essential in shorting a stock. A few years ago, I noticed that my kids and all their friends were wearing those odd, colorful rubber clogs all summer long. Crocs had entered our life and our house in a big way, so I took a look at the stock and gave some consideration to shorting it. My thinking was that the shoes were a hot fad and therefore a ripe candidate for knock-offs. Moreover, the fad had exploded into success so suddenly that I didn't think it could possibly be sustained. Back in 2006, however, when I first took a look at Crocs, the short interest was 29 percent of the float. That seemed crowded, so I decided to wait.

What I was waiting for was some indication that the fundamentals were beginning to crack. I was waiting for the day when I would see Crocs on sale in a discount store, or notice that my kids were wearing the knock-offs or had moved on to some new fad altogether, or register an uptick in insider selling, or read a report that sales were slowing. I was right to wait: Crocs stock rose throughout 2006 and into most of 2007 before plunging badly in 2008. The right time to short the stock would have been in 2007, but as has been said before in this book, picking the right bottom and top of a market is difficult at best; it's particularly tough with momentum stocks, and Crocs was certainly a momentum stock at the time. The right time to short it would have been when the weakening fundamentals were accompanied by a weakening stock price, a sign that the momentum and growth players were giving up. Growth stock investors usually hold a grudge so it takes a while before they are willing to jump back in the pool. I missed the moment and shorted the stock too early; only good risk control kept me from getting killed.

Shorting a stock has a place and purpose in a portfolio. But it takes due diligence, a good reading of the tea leaves, and the right timing if you're going to avoid being carried out feet first. If you get it all right—the research, the interpretation, and the exact moment to call your broker—the rewards can be substantial.

Lessons Learned

- *Short selling: proceed with caution.* Short selling single stocks is risky; even professional investors often have difficulty with the tactic. A short trade should be entered into only with the utmost care and caution. There is unlimited loss potential on short positions. Stocks can go higher forever, while the potential loss on a stock owned is limited to the amount you invested.
- *Stay away from crowded shorts.* Short interest is reported monthly and can be found in the stock tables of numerous newspapers, including the *Wall Street Journal* and *Barron's*. Generally, if more than 10 percent to 20 percent of the outstanding float is short, there is significant potential for a short squeeze. Whether the caution level is 10 percent or 20 percent depends on how many shares are outstanding and on the level of the daily volume. For example, General Electric has 10 billion shares outstanding and trades an average of almost 200 million shares a day. A squeeze would be unlikely in the stock even if 20 percent of the float were held short.

- *Don't neglect short interest ratio.* Also important, short interest ratio tells you how many days are required for all the short positions to be covered. The ratio is computed by dividing the number of shares held short by the average daily trading volume over a 30-day period. For example, if the there are 2 million shares short and the stock trades 200,000 shares a day, the short ratio dictates that it will take 10 days to cover the entire short interest. Stocks with a ratio of 5 or higher are likely to be involved in a squeeze. In fact, technical traders regard this as a bullish sign owing to the high level of pessimism. Short interest ratios of 3 or less are bearish—not enough pessimism.

- *High short interest is not conclusive.* Just because high short interest exists doesn't mean that the trade will not work out. But there is likely to be huge volatility in the shares and the real likelihood of a margin call forcing the investor to cover the position if there is a significant squeeze. Crocs, the manufacturer of the ubiquitous rubber shoes, at one point had a short interest equivalent to 40 percent of the float. There were many short squeezes along the way forcing traders to cover, but short sellers who were able to stay with the trade made out well, as the stock eventually traded to less than $2 per share from an all-time high of $70.

- *Keep short positions smaller than long positions.* If short positions go against you, they become much bigger positions very quickly. That's why it is a lot more difficult to have staying power in a short than in a long position; if a long goes against you, it decreases in value, becoming a smaller portion of your portfolio. (Yes, poorly performing longs can also result in margin calls.)

- *Believe trouble signs.* Just because things are obvious doesn't mean they're not real. Porsche had made clear its intention to acquire Volkswagen, yet Merckle and others apparently didn't believe it. It made strategic sense for the companies to merge; they shared technology, manufacturing, and even a common legacy dating back 60 years.

- *Look for the catalyst.* Before shorting a stock, identify a specific catalyst that will cause the shares to go lower and a specific time frame when you believe this will happen. Entering into a short position solely because a stock is perceived to be overvalued is often a bad idea. The momentum in the stock price can propel the shares higher, as we witnessed in the technology bubble in 1999. A lot of short sellers got carried out on stretchers before the bubble popped. There must be an identifiable catalyst that will rationalize valuation.

- *Hesitate before shorting.* Particularly for individual investors with a limited portfolio, it is often better to wait until there is some legitimate sign of a company's flaws before initiating a short position. Occasionally there won't be time to get in on the bust, but on balance it's a good risk strategy.

- *Lessen the chance of loss.* Here's a checklist for lessening the chance of significant loss on a short position:
  - ❑ Check the current short position. Ideally it should be as low as possible, preferably below 10 percent.
  - ❑ Short only large market capitalization companies that are unlikely to be acquired and where the trading of the shares is very liquid—for example, Wal-Mart, the largest retailer in the world.
  - ❑ Identify a specific catalyst that might entice current shareholders to sell what they own.
  - ❑ Assess what the current sentiment is on the company. If everything written about the stock is negative and the shares have sold off substantially, all the bad news already may be priced in. Such a bearish torrent of opinion actually may be a bullish sign. Remember, it's always darkest before the dawn.
- *Use the stop-loss mechanism.* Stop loss automatically closes out the position when it trades to a certain price. This removes the emotion from your decision-making process so as to limit your loss. Merckle was clearly too emotional. It's worth repeating: The market can stay irrational much longer than you can stay solvent.
- *You're short; who is long?* When shorting a stock, be aware of who is long—that is, the competition on the other side of the trade. Understand what they are thinking—and therefore where your investment thesis might go wrong—even if you have to translate from the German.

10

Chris Davis

IT WAS DRESSED LIKE AN INSURANCE COMPANY, BUT IT DIDN'T QUACK LIKE ONE . . .

Say the word "insurance" and most people, once they've stopped yawning, picture a buttoned-down, gray-suited, gray-haired, probably gray-thinking guy droning on about term life, whole life, and home-owner policies. The very word historically has been a metaphor for dullness, evoking Dickensian images of clerks poring over actuarial tables in musty offices. There are people who remember Wallace Stevens less for his poetry than for the fact that he was the vice president of an insurance company; the idea that poetry and insurance can coexist in a single individual seems stunning in its incongruity.

Chris Davis, chairman of Davis Selected Advisers, the family-owned investment counseling firm overseeing some $60 billion in client assets, seems to share that view of the insurance business— good, gray, solid, and boring. At least, that's the impression one gets from Davis's affectionate comment about the fact that his grandfa-ther was appointed superintendent of insurance for New York State way back in 1948. The superintendent's office is charged with over-seeing all the insurance business in the state, and, said Chris Davis about the position in which his grandfather had served, "It just doesn't sound like a plum job."[1]

Grandpa was legendary investor Shelby Cullom Davis, who famously turned a $100,000 stake into an $800 million fortune by seeing investment opportunity in all those good, gray, solid, boring insurance company stocks. Perhaps Shelby was able to see the opportunity because he brought a fresh eye to the insurance landscape. Trained in international relations and public policy, he worked as a speechwriter for Thomas Dewey during the 1948 election and was given the insurance superintendent's job as a consolation prize after Dewey lost to Truman. Wall Street had always dismissed insurance stocks because the accounting focused on the losses typical in the first year a policy was written—thanks mostly to sales costs and commissions. Shelby, however, took the longer view and saw the solid, steady, lifetime earnings that insurance could realize. He started a brokerage house specializing in insurance stocks, invested his own capital in such stocks, and became immensely wealthy. Shelby Cullom Davis's insight about insurance stocks, and the discipline he developed around it—eventually expressed in the mantra "Boring is beautiful"—became part and parcel of the Davis family tradition, which has graced Wall Street for three generations.

But even the sharpest insight can grow blurry after 60 years. So it is perhaps not surprising that Christopher C. Davis, the current scion of the family—and one of the ablest and most successful value investors on Wall Street—may have forgotten just what it was about boring old insurance that his grandfather found so beautiful.

In Davis's case, the line that American International Group, Inc.—AIG, as it is more commonly and conveniently known—"is not your grandfather's insurance company" was literally true; it bore little resemblance to the kinds of insurance companies Shelby Cullom Davis had purchased when he managed the portfolio. By the time Chris Davis began investing in AIG in a big way, it was the twenty-first century, and AIG had become the biggest, most expansive, most unboring, uninsurance insurance enterprise the world had ever seen. It was so big, in fact, and so sprawling that neither Chris Davis nor just about anyone else actually could see the whole enterprise end to end. And no one really was sure what all the moving parts of the enterprise actually did. It was a black box: Its performance characteristics were specified and documented, but its internal structure—how it achieved its performance—was unknown, a mystery. Later on, it would cost the U.S. government almost $200 billion to try to figure out the mystery.

That was Davis's billion-dollar mistake—not that AIG was different from the insurance stocks his family knew and loved, but that he didn't see how the difference worked. He couldn't see inside the black box, but he put his money there anyway.

And it cost him.

"Old School"

Tradition clearly counts in the Davis family. So does principle. "Old school" is the phrase that comes to mind. As an investment manager, you're responsible to the people who place their trust in you; their wealth is in your keeping. Therefore, you measure a company not by its stock price but by its management's ability to create value—or destroy it. You invest for the long term, and you invest in quality companies. Where financial companies are concerned, don't look for discounts; instead, remember that everybody is a customer, that good management stands out, and that financial firms generate a lot of cash they can return to those shareholders who have invested with you.

Shelby M.C. Davis, son of Shelby Cullom and father of Chris, honed and formalized those principles in starting and shaping the Davis family business. Shelby M.C. began his career by going to work for the Bank of New York, where he became its youngest vice president since Alexander Hamilton. In 1966, he founded his own fee-based investment management firm, expanding the offering to noninstitutional clients in 1969 as the Davis New York Venture Fund, still the flagship among the funds Shelby M.C.'s son manages today.

Yet Christopher almost didn't go into the family business. Perhaps it was a case of familiarity breeding a desire to try new things. The Davis children were schooled in investing the way builders' kids know about joists and insulation and lawyers' kids absorb the language of contracts and procedures. Shelby M.C. assigned his kids to write research reports on the companies that loomed large in their lives—Nike, Apple, and the like—and paid them $50 per paper. It was a good grounding in how companies operate—and an even better grounding in how to do research, a lesson in going beyond the annual report and the statements by the investor relations department to dig deeper. Later, when Chris Davis finally did return to the family profession, he would find his first real home in research. But first, he needed to spread his wings.

The young Davis attended the venerable St. Andrew's University, founded in 1413, the third oldest university in the English-speaking world and the oldest in Scotland. He studied theology and philosophy, gave some thought to joining the Episcopal priesthood, became a seminarian, and moved to Paris. Ironically enough, it was in Paris, an explosion of Technicolor after the bleak winters of

Scotland's east coast, where Chris reconnected with the world of business, seeing it not as something divorced from his spiritual life but rather as a set of practices his religious beliefs could guide.

He returned to the United States and got a job at State Street Bank in Boston as an entry-level accounting trainee, boning up on his numbers expertise before joining Tanaka Capital Management in New York. At this private and prestigious firm, Davis specialized in research—specifically, on financial companies. It must have felt a little bit like the grown-up version of those research papers his father had assigned—only this time, instead of being compensated based on effort, he would be judged by the impact of his work on Tanaka's portfolio.

In 1989, Chris Davis left Tanaka and formally went home to the family tradition and the family business, working with his father at Davis Advisors. As his father did, Chris Davis learned the investment business on someone else's dime and with another's capital. This was a shrewd tactic—and not just for the obvious reason. Rather, it meant that when the younger Davis arrived at the family firm, he was not coming in as the fresh-faced, inexperienced son of the owner but as someone who had earned his stripes in the business. His first assignment: figuring out how to move the fortune of the elder Davis, Shelby Cullom, into family-managed funds and, eventually, a foundation structure. In 1991, Shelby M.C. created the Davis Financial Fund for Chris to manage—a way to show he had the stuff for a major role in the company, if indeed he did.

He had the stuff and then some: Davis Financial outperformed all the other Davis Advisors funds. As a result, Chris continued to move up in the company hierarchy. Today, he and Kenneth Feinberg, who joined the firm in 1994, lead the portfolio management team for the Davis Funds and are co–portfolio managers of the Davis New York Venture Fund and the Selected American Shares Fund.

The Simple Business of Insurance

The definition of insurance is pretty simple, and so is the business model of an insurance company. *The American Heritage Dictionary of the English Language* puts it succinctly, defining insurance as "coverage by a contract binding a party to indemnify another against specified loss in return for premiums paid."

As the definition indicates, insurance companies operate under incredibly simple business models: Calculate a premium—a payment—in return for accepting another's risk. The people who do the calculating are actuaries; they assess the probability and amount of potential losses from the company's line of underwriting policies—whether property and casualty, life insurance, or such esoteric business lines as the policy Lloyd's of London underwrote to insure "cinema-goers against death from excessive laughter while at the cinema."[*] Actuaries base their forecasts on extremely large data samples, thus limiting the probability of a mistake. Few professionals live up to their stereotype, but actuaries, often pictured wearing a green visor, pocket protector, thick glasses, and the redundant safety of a belt and suspenders, don't disappoint.

After the actuaries have done their calculations, the insurance company invests the premium the customer paid for the insurance policy. Typically, these funds are invested in what are considered safe instruments—for example, government bonds and highly rated corporate bonds—to generate profits in excess of any losses forecasted by the actuary.

Despite rigorous regulation of insurance companies and their own risk management systems, failure is not uncommon. According to A.M. Best, the well-regarded company that rates insurance company creditworthiness, 1,023 property casualty insurance companies failed between 1969 and 2007. The largest insolvency was Reliance Insurance, which went down in 2001 to the tune of $2.27 billion.[†] Most failures, however, are fairly insignificant, and the policies typically are absorbed by other insurance companies or paid out of state funds.

AIG, featured in this chapter, did not fail. But that is because the government wouldn't let it—"It was too big to fail," and its business interests were much more far-reaching than insurance. This was the problem; an argument could easily be made that insurance was a sideline, not a focus, and that AIG departed from the simple model that is the core of the insurance business. AIG invested the premiums it received in subprime mortgages and insured such mortgages, on behalf of others, against default. The company also invested in derivatives, the riskiest of all financial instruments because of their inherent leverage.

All these investments served to complicate what is basically a simple business and a simple business model.

---

[*] NewsCentre post, Lloyds.com, Mary 4, 2007, www.lloyds.com/News_Centre/Features_from_Lloyds/Its_not_unusual.htm.

[†] Robert P. Hartwig, "Financial Crisis and the Future of P/C Insurance," Insurance Information Institute presentation, November 20, 2008.

A Sense of Stewardship

Managing a fund, as this book makes clear over and over and over, is about more than just choosing stocks and monitoring their performance. It is about an investment philosophy or style, about the discipline for executing the style, and about the values that shape the style and drive the discipline. In style and discipline, the Davis family's funds are a classic exemplar of value investing: The firm invests at least 80 percent of its net assets to buy the securities of solid, well-managed, large-capitalization companies, principally in the financial sector, at value prices—often when the companies are out of favor—and holds them for the long term. In the Davis New York Venture Fund, for example, that means four to seven years on average. The values that guide the way those activities are carried out, however, derive directly from Chris Davis's conviction that when it comes to managing people's money, the money manager's role is one of stewardship. That conviction affects everything the firm does and everything Chris Davis does.

You can see the sense of stewardship in Davis's nonbusiness, extracurricular interests as well. He is deeply involved in protecting the land and environment of a region precious to him, the Hudson River Valley just north of the New York metropolitan area: Davis is president of the Hudson Highland Land Trust and is a trustee of the Scenic Hudson Land Trust. He also sits on the board of the American Museum of Natural History. In addition to serving a number of other nonprofit and advocacy organizations, Davis was named to the board of directors of the Washington Post Company in 2006—an appointment you probably don't get unless you have a well-earned reputation for probity and for taking great care with money.

In business, where the stewardship value is equally evident, it often has made Davis and his firm stand out. For example, by design, Davis directors align their own investing with the interests of clients. As the company Web site puts it, "The Davis family, employees, and directors are among the largest shareholders in the Davis Funds," with "almost $1.5 billion of their own money invested side by side with fellow shareholders." What gives that alignment of interests particular meaning is the Davis dictum that boards of directors should consist predominantly of independent directors—perhaps particularly important in a family-owned firm. In fact, the directors of the company's Selected American fund—more than three-quarters of them independent—proactively, voluntarily, and summarily fired the fund's manager (Kemper Financial Services Inc.) in 1994; it's the only large fund ever to have done so.

Ten years later, the Davis board made another surprise move, taking a stand against an unpopular rule at Charles Schwab & Co. Inc. that effectively charged shareholders who bought Selected American shares through Schwab an extra expense. By creating a share class with lower expenses than those offered through Schwab's transaction platform, Davis made good on his belief, as he expressesd it in a letter to investors, that "it was inappropriate for us to charge for those services if we weren't providing them." It was another case of taking care of other people's money entrusted to the Davis name.

It isn't as if fund performance has suffered because of Chris Davis's refusal to compromise his values. Davis Advisors as a whole beat the Standard & Poor's (S&P) 500 every 10-year rolling period since its founding in 1969. The Financial Fund, which Chris Davis directly manages, enjoyed an annual average return of 16.4 percent from its inception in 1991 through 2007, a time when the S&P 500 averaged only 11 percent.

Investing in AIG

Records are difficult to come by, and there is some uncertainty as to when the Davis Family of Funds first positioned AIG in its portfolios. Ask the company's shareholder services department, and you will be told that the Davis Funds have owned AIG since its initial public offering in 1972. The statement is a bit inexact. AIG actually went public in 1969, the year, coincidentally, when Shelby M.C. Davis launched the venture fund. But whether the funds first owned the stock in 1969 or 1972, the company basically had two decades of affiliation and institutional knowledge of AIG before Chris showed up for work at the family business. He apparently liked what he saw because he maintained the connection, ultimately and significantly increasing New York Venture Fund's ownership to levels that would make its AIG position one of the firm's largest.

The word "insurance"—that good, gray, boring word—doesn't appear in the name of AIG, which stands for American International Group. Yet it has always presented itself as an insurance company— "the leading international insurance organization," as its Web site boilerplate puts it. Still, it isn't as if Davis Advisors, with all its research expertise, did not know that AIG had moved into many other kinds of business activity. In fact, there is no way that Davis could not have known. AIG's 1990 purchase of International Lease Finance was a major event at the time it occurred, costing the company $1.3 billion. That should have been a tip-off that AIG was departing from the simple old insurance business model. After all, buying big commercial airplanes and leasing them to the likes of American and Continental Airlines may provide a steady stream of income, but it is far riskier than investing policyholder's premiums in government bonds.

Maybe Chris Davis told himself he was following in his grandfather's footsteps when he invested in the insurance giant—international or not, bigger than most or not, it was still insurance. Maybe he was motivated by the speed and power of AIG's growth under its legendary chairman and chief executive officer (CEO), Maurice "Hank" Greenberg. Or perhaps he was impressed by Greenberg's rapid-fire expansion into non-U.S. businesses—particularly in Asia, where Davis saw potential. He was not alone in his eagerness to participate in the burgeoning economy of China; lots of money managers were doing so. As an investor in financial stocks, Davis was more limited than many of his colleagues; they could populate their portfolios with consumer and industrial companies, but the palette of financial stocks available was smaller and less colorful. Yet he needed to keep pace with the broader market average and with the competition that was counting on Coke to sell more soda and Nike more running shoes into a country like China with its 2 billion new consumers. So Asia, and AIG's penetration there, must have looked to Davis like an appealingly speedy route to growth.

And maybe Davis thought AIG was just faster out of the gate than anything his grandfather or father had ever invested in—an exotic thoroughbred among all those good, gray insurance companies.

Whatever the particular motivation, Davis's timing was less than fortunate. Up until 2005, AIG was a steady contributor to the positive, industry-leading performance of multiple portfolios at Davis Funds. Yet 2005 was when Davis chose to go "all in" on the stock, meaningfully increasing ownership across all funds—reaching a peak in 2008—betting on his racehorse to win, place, and show across the board.

It turned out, however, that in investing in AIG, Davis was betting on a horse of a different color, with the wrong jockey aboard, on a racecourse whose twists and turns he did not see. In its performance from 2005 to 2009, AIG would prove to be a bad bet.

And everything Chris Davis knew about investing—deep research, boring is beautiful, the principle of stewardship—should have told him that.

Boring Is Beautiful

Morefar Back O'Beyond is a private golf course on 500 acres of wooded land in Brewster, New York. You cannot see the 18-hole course from any of the winding roads around it, and you cannot play the course—even if you have the wherewithal for the membership and green fees—unless you are an employee or the guest of an employee of what the Professional Golf Association (PGA) Web site refers to only as "a private corporation."

The PGA is being unnecessarily discreet, as it is by now well known that the private corporation was once AIG—back when Hank Greenberg ran the show and used Morefar as his private playground. Greenberg was of course deposed in 2005, although he is still embroiled in lawsuits against his former company—lawsuits that play out more like dynastic warfare than civil litigation. One of the trophies of that warfare is Morefar, which Greenberg still controls as chairman of private insurance firm C.V. Starr and Company.

The golf course is exotic in many respects. It is sprinkled with some 25 sculptures—one of them actually located in a sand trap; it runs on rigid rules based on corporate hierarchy rather than on golf; and it holds, between the fourteenth green and the fifteenth tee, the ashes of AIG's founder, Cornelius Vander Starr, the man who hand-picked Hank Greenberg to be his successor.

Golf is not Greenberg's game, but that doesn't much matter. Morefar—so named, it is said, because a Chinese worker on Starr's estate told a would-be visitor seeking directions that the place was "more far"—was never so much about the game of golf as it was about the sport at which Greenberg excelled, which was building AIG into the biggest financial services company in the world, to some extent by demoting insurance and promoting other businesses. In his salad days as CEO, in a simpler time when he could enjoy the perks of his station, Greenberg would swoop down onto Morefar by helicopter—unannounced and unscheduled. Play would come to a standstill. And whichever foursome was getting ready to tee off would defer to the chairman, who controlled access to the place in any event.

Colorful, blunt, a World War II Bronze Star recipient who was with the troops who liberated Dachau, a covert operative for the Central Intelligence Agency or the Israeli Mossad, friend to such luminaries as David Rockefeller and Henry Kissinger, mover and shaker in the worlds of art and philanthropy, and a man who once took the Fifth rather than give legal testimony, Hank Greenberg is about as far away as you can get, in style and sensibilities, from Chris Davis. Forced out of AIG after the then-Attorney General of New York, Eliot Spitzer— the so-called sheriff of Wall Street—targeted him in a fraud investigation, Greenberg would see all criminal charges against him dropped, but civil actions against him proceed as of this writing. Meanwhile, as head of C.V. Starr, Greenberg continues his own battle against his successors at AIG—first Martin Sullivan, who is married to the daughter of Morefar's manager, then Edward Liddy, virtually a government appointee to oversee the taxpayer bailout of the failed company.

Greenberg blames his successors and their directors for that failure. AIG's Financial Products group (AIGFP), he told the House Committee on Oversight and Government Reform in October 2008:

> reportedly wrote as many credit default swaps on collateralized debt obligations, or CDOs, in the nine months following my departure [in 2005] as it had written in the entire previous seven years combined. Moreover, unlike what had been true during my tenure, the majority of the credit default swaps that AIGFP wrote in the nine months after I retired were reportedly exposed to sub-prime mortgages. By contrast, only a handful of the credit default swaps written over the entire prior seven years had any sub-prime exposure at all.[2]

He put it a bit more bluntly to a television interviewer just prior to the House testimony: "After I left the company," Greenberg said on *Good Morning America*, "all the risk management procedures that we had in place were obviously dismantled. I can't explain that."[3] Disingenuous? Perhaps. But Greenberg had just seen two-thirds of his $3 billion net worth dissolve and had been kicked off the *Forbes* 400 list of richest billionaires, so his bitterness is perhaps understandable.

What Greenberg always has been happy to take credit for, even as he points the finger of blame elsewhere, is expanding AIG and transforming it into a global behemoth. He did it by diversifying the company into activities and sectors well beyond insurance and in addition to it—airplane leasing, most notably, and, in the London-based Financial Products group, those esoteric instruments, such as credit derivative swaps, he talked to the House Committee about.

There was absolutely nothing boring about the AIG that Greenberg built. It was exciting, colorful, good copy for journalists trying to ferret out what he would do next. Granted, a lot of what was colorful was Greenberg's management style, which was uncompromising at best and downright punitive at worst. During his reign—an apt term since he ruled over the company with the absolutism of a despot—any criticism by a Wall Street analyst was met head-on. Greenberg would place a call to the CEO of the offending firm and/or beckon the analyst to his office for a famed "fireside chat," during which the error in the analyst's research report would be discussed and rectified. The penalty for violating the unwritten rule not to cross Hank would be the withdrawal of access and, possibly, the termination of any future underwriting business, including the sale of bonds or commercial paper, both yielding sizable fees for the investment banks. The tendency to exact retribution may even have extended to his sons, whom Greenberg reputedly drove from the company[4]—although whether he did so intentionally or as a by-product of his unyielding personality is not clear.

Still, it was all very exciting—very un-insurance-like. There was an exuberance about the expansion into esoteric financial instruments, even if the press—or anybody else, for that matter—didn't quite understand what the instruments did or how they worked. It was kind of thrilling to see an insurance company turn itself into the biggest airplane leasing organization on Earth. If AIG could do that, it was thought, there probably wasn't anything it couldn't do.

All of this was certainly a far cry from the solid insurance business that had so attracted Shelby Cullum Davis in the late 1940s. What he had found beautiful from an investment point of view was a business that, when it invested the premiums it collected, did so in such interest-bearing instruments as government or corporate bonds rated triple-A. The reason "Boring is beautiful" had been the Davis mantra was because boring just kept on yielding steady returns on an investment.

Shelby's grandson—like so many others—forgot the family mantra and instead saw beauty in the excitement Greenberg created, even if he wasn't quite sure how it worked.

The Government Lends $180 Billion to AIG

"AIG's financial condition had been deteriorating for some time," explained the chairman of the Federal Reserve, "caused by actual and expected losses on subprime mortgage-backed securities and on credit default swaps that AIG's Financial Products unit, AIG-FP, had written on mortgage-related securities. As confidence in the firm declined, and with efforts to find a private-sector solution unsuccessful, AIG faced severe liquidity pressures that threatened to force it imminently into bankruptcy." So testified Ben Bernanke before the House Financial Services Committee on March 24, 2009, as to why the Fed and Treasury decided to lend $85 billion to AIG in September 2008.

But $85 billion was only the beginning. By the time Bernanke testified, the government lifeline to the beleaguered financial entity would total nearly $180 billion.

The reason was fear of bankruptcy. It wasn't the rah-rah growth of AIG, nor the losing gambles its rah-rah growth spurred that prompted government intervention; the Federal Reserve and the Treasury were not in the business of spanking wayward enterprises like a fed-up parent grounding a too-reckless teenager. Policy, not parenting, was at issue. But it is also true that the rah-rah growth and the bad gambles fed into the problem that eventually became a policy issue with national and global implications.

In building AIG into the world's largest financial services company, Greenberg and AIG management had allowed the risk and leverage in the noncore Financial Products subsidiary to dwarf the insurance division. And even within the insurance division, AIG strayed into underwriting nontraditional risk in scary ways; selling protection against the default of complicated financial instruments like credit default swaps—insurance policies to protect against the default in subprime mortgages—added yet another layer of opaqueness and risk.

Greenberg himself never disputed that AIG had become much more than an insurance company; his postmortem on the collapse targeted the dismantling of the risk controls he had in effect on his watch, not the fact that the business lines were much riskier than those of a normal insurance company like Allstate or State Farm or General Re, the massive reinsurer owned by Warren Buffett's Berkshire Hathaway.

And, like Bear Stearns and Lehman Brothers, AIG suffered from leveraged exposure to the housing cycle through subprime mortgages and investments in esoteric investments that simply failed.

But what finally made it imperative for the government to step in was the fear of an AIG bankruptcy, the consequences of which could have been disastrous. Numerous banks and mutual funds around the world had lent AIG billions of dollars. Money market funds, a more than $3 trillion market thought to be the safest possible investment because their holdings were in the supposedly most creditworthy bonds, held significant AIG paper. If those banks, mutual funds, and money market funds were forced to write down the value of those loans, it would have frozen the credit markets and shattered confidence with even more cataclysmic and far-reaching effects than the Lehman Brothers failure. Moreover, even though AIG's traditional underwriting subsidiaries were set up independently from the main company—as required by regulations in most cases—the ability to pay off claims would have been called into doubt.

In essence, the government felt it had no choice. It stepped in—to the tune of $180 billion.

What Went Wrong?

The mistake was to invest in a black box—an insurance company so big and complex that it was impossible to understand or analyze. Davis had no visibility; AIG was an opaque entity offering all the lucidity of a bowl of pea soup. And while ultimately he would admit the mistake, his words gave no indication that he truly understood its nature.

In his winter 2009 letter to investors, Chris Davis concedes that the AIG investment was the firm's "largest mistake over the last five years." The loss, he says, took some 6 percent off the firm's total returns, "almost three times as much," Davis calculates, "as any other mistake." He attributes the mistake to a flawed analysis. But Davis says his analysis was flawed because of what he describes as "incorrectly assessing three factors." What he incorrectly assessed, says Davis, were "the financial sophistication of management, the leverage of derivatives and the danger of collateral requirements tied to mark-to-market accounting."

It's hard to argue with any of these factors. Certainly Martin Sullivan, the insurance veteran who succeeded Greenberg, was inadequate to the task of saving a giant company that was now only partly about insurance. Certainly derivatives leveraged to mortgage-backed securities were a disaster once the subprime mortgage crisis began its inexorable roll. And once the roll began, having to post collateral on the losses in resources marked to market certainly made the losses worse. But these were AIG's mistakes, not Davis's. The assertions in his letter to investors are true, but his reasoning is circular. His mistake wasn't that AIG made mistakes; his mistake was investing in AIG in the first place.

The heart of the matter is deeper than Davis's analysis is willing to go. **For his more fundamental flaw was not that AIG dabbled in dangerous instruments; it was that AIG had become a business that *at its core* dabbled in dangerous instruments while continuing to masquerade as a simple business. That is, it had become a business that Chris Davis did not understand, its offending attributes obscured from view.** He bought into the reputation, the historical performance, trusting perception instead of performing the analysis he was capable of. "Too big to fail," the government famously proclaimed. What that also meant was that AIG was too big and too complex and too spread out for anyone to see all the sides of it. Davis thought he was investing in an insurance company. He wasn't. And soon into the tenure of his investment—and certainly by 2007—Chris Davis should have seen that AIG had become a black box he couldn't see into.

Instead, either unaware of AIG's actual noninsurance exposure or unconcerned by it, Davis compounded his bad bet. He seized the "opportunity" presented by AIG's declining stock price to add to the number of shares owned by multiple Davis portfolios. He kept buying throughout 2007 and into the second quarter of 2008, almost three years after Greenberg had resigned over the allegations that he had improperly inflated company revenues. (As an aside, Hank was the second Greenberg forced to resign from an insurance company; his older son, Jeffrey, former CEO of Marsh & McLennan, was forced to resign for bid rigging that led to inflating company revenues. Marsh had to pay $850 million in fines for young Greenberg's infractions.[5])

It was Greenberg's expansive diversification strategy that had made it a black box. From that flowed everything else that brought the company down—everything Chris Davis cited in his letter to investors. To complain that Sullivan had, in Davis's words, "deep experience in the field of property and casualty insurance" but "virtually no expertise" in those new sectors into which AIG had carried its "operations and risks"—factor number one cited by Davis—spins the circle of Davis's reasoning: The source of the problem was the expansion into operations and risks so removed from insurance that a classic property and casualty guy couldn't cope with them.

That Hank Greenberg was a very successful CEO is not in dispute. Whatever you might think of his manner of managing, he took AIG from relative obscurity to a peak market capitalization of $170 billion during his 35-year tenure. He also increased the assets of the Starr Foundation, which he served as chairman, from $15 million to $2 billion. So his bona fides as a manager are substantial—and are not in question.

But for Davis to trivialize his own mistake and deflect blame onto Greenberg's successor is arguably disingenuous. Martin Sullivan's experience was that of an insurance executive. Naming him as CEO of AIG served to perpetuate the delusion that the company was an insurance business. It was also an obvious signal that Sullivan was woefully ill prepared to take over, since what he was inheriting was a diversified financial empire, not an insurance company. This was another reality Davis should have seen. Back in 1999, would you have bet on Brent Barry, Michael Jordan's de facto successor, to lead the Chicago Bulls to another six championship triumphs? Even to one more? No way. Barry was a yeomanlike professional ballplayer; Jordan was a cosmic phenomenon. Martin Sullivan was stepping into just as daunting a legacy and arguably was less prepared than Barry to assume the role he'd been given. Granted, it was not Davis's *fault* that Sullivan wasn't equipped to handle the responsibilities of his new position, but it was the money manager's misstep to turn a blind eye to it.

For as long as AIG's diversification worked, it fueled the unbelievable speed at which the company grew—a speed out of sync, by the way, with the manner in which an insurance company ought to grow. And perhaps, so long as everything was heading upward, Davis could tell himself that AIG was a highly successful insurance company. But when the businesses fueling the growth—derivatives, for example—stopped working, as such instruments always do, the loss was 100 percent, as it always is.

That old country proverb works perfectly here: If it smells like a duck, walks like a duck, and quacks like a duck, it's a duck. AIG smelled, walked, and quacked more like a hedge fund than an insurance company. In an interview with Morningstar's Justin Fuller in April 2008—when AIG was falling but had not yet collapsed—Davis and Ken Feinberg were both asked about the AIG investment. Although both men appeared uncomfortable answering, they stuck to their guns, citing the company's diversification as its great strength, even in what Davis called "a soft insurance cycle." Feinberg in particular waved the diversification banner, applauding the fact that the company wasn't just in classic property and casualty insurance but had branched out into "airplane leasing, asset management, and financial services." Of course, said Feinberg, as an investment target, financial services are "almost unknowable."[6]

That's the mistake right there: If you don't know what you're buying, don't buy it.

"Not His Grandfather's Insurance Company": Timeline

1972: Davis Funds first invests in AIG.
1991: Chris Davis takes over management of Davis Financial Fund.
2005: Davis significantly increases the investment in AIG.
2007–2008: AIG stock declines, Davis increases investment again.
April, 2008: Davis, in an interview, cites AIG's diversification as a strength.
2009: Davis concedes AIG investment was the firm's "largest mistake."

Trying to See Inside the Black Box

It wasn't as if research would not have revealed how much of a black box AIG had become. In a sense, the company's very opacity was there for all to see. The Financial Products group, for example, had come into existence in 1987; it was not a secret. Neither were the other "new sectors," as Davis had called them. A professional investor in particular didn't need a research analyst to shine a spotlight on AIG's diverse and un-insurance-like business model. As required by the Securities and Exchange Commission (SEC), the company left a large trail of breadcrumbs showing the way to the "other" businesses beyond insurance that AIG had entered, the proportions of the company the other businesses occupied, the dollar contributions those businesses provided—and their cost. Pick any 10-K report filed over the years—available to the public through the SEC's Web site or through the company itself—and you can see the operational complexities tumbling over one another and creating a seemingly impenetrable wall of financial complexities. You can see, in a sense, how much you can't really see.

Take 2006, a year after Davis significantly increased the investment in AIG, and check out the 10-K for that year. The first thing you might ask yourself as you peruse its pages is why an insurance company is suffering such a major loss in synfuels. Is synfuels a business an insurance company should be in?

You also might wonder about a chart comparing the results for financial services in the years 2004, 2005, and 2006—and specifically about the results for Capital Markets services—the work of the fabled Financial Products group, which traded those esoteric, arcane credit derivative swaps. Why, you might want to know, did revenues for Capital Markets activities go from $1.28 billion in 2004 up to $3.26 billion in 2005 and then suffer a loss of $186 million in 2006? You would note that operating income for Capital Markets in those years went from $662 million in 2004 to $2.66 billion in 2005 to a loss of $873 million in 2006!

You would read further that "the most significant component of Capital Markets operating expenses is compensation," and you would note that in 2006, the year of those extreme losses, compensation rose to $544 million. Why, you would be fully justified in asking, are they paying that kind of money for a loss? You likely also would consider that if AIG is paying $544 million to traders rather than to insurance people, it must think traders are the most important people in the company—a good hint that this really has stopped being your grandfather's insurance company.

You could peruse all these on-the-record items about synfuels and about the Capital Markets business, and you could consider what they tell you, and then you might logically think to yourself: *I don't understand why AIG is in these businesses.* And then you might say to yourself: *Why am I investing in this company—whose businesses I don't understand and whose mission is departing from the core competence I do understand?*

It wasn't bad management or leveraged derivatives or mark-to-market accounting that Davis "incorrectly assessed." It was all the signals coming out of what should have been ongoing scrutiny over the many years Davis Advisors held onto AIG stock. **They simply didn't know—or didn't understand—what they were investing in.**

They therefore should have cut the cord with AIG. If they didn't cut it when it became apparent that insurance was no longer the company's primary business, then they certainly should have done so when Greenberg was forced to resign. Instead, Davis and Feinberg went the other way, increasing their holdings in the financial conglomerate even as the market was telegraphing questions about the concern's solvency as only markets can do—by trouncing AIG's equity and bond securities.

It was a company they could not read, the kind of company Shelby M.C. Davis might have paid his son $50 to research as a learning experience but not something he would have invested in—at least not in this decade's AIG. Chris Davis, who grew up knowing about insurance and understanding how and why it paid to invest in the sector, should have seen that. When the habit of research confronts a black box, it isn't enough to call it "unknowable." It's much better just to stay away.

Lessons Learned

- *Review the annual report.* If you're thinking about investing in a company, check out its annual report. Specifically, look at the revenue and expense breakdown. This will provide greater insight into how a company makes or loses money than the business description written by marketing people.
- *Compare performance.* Measure the company's performance against other companies in the same industry. Slight outperformance may be a result of great management or a better product. Significant deviation from average industry performance may be a warning sign that the management is taking too much risk or that the company is not focusing on the business it appears to be in.
- *Beware outsized returns.* They almost always indicate greater risk. Be sure that you are willing to accept and can afford to tolerate the additional risk. Otherwise, keep it simple and conservative.

- *Check any management changes.* Pay attention to any change in senior management before investing in a company's stock, including the management of important divisions. Manager biographies usually are provided on the company Web site. The more complicated the business model, the more important it is for the key executive(s) to have a history of success in a similar business.

- *Examine a fund's past holdings.* Before investing in a mutual fund, examine the historic holdings—not just the current holdings—to ensure that the investment manager is not delving into sectors or companies that require expertise that he or she has never evidenced an affinity for.

- *Check for leveraged instruments in a fund.* AIG got into trouble for many reasons, but one was that it owned leveraged financial instruments. You also must be cautious of the existence of such leveraged instruments as exchange-traded funds (ETFs), both as an individual investor and as an investor in mutual funds that might include ETFs in their portfolios. Some ETFs essentially employ leverage and are designed to double or triple the performance of the underlying benchmark index, including the S&P 500, but they represent a directional bet on the market and are not the product of research on a company. Yet research is what you pay a mutual fund manager for. If you want to bet on the direction of the market rather than the stock-picking ability of a portfolio manager, invest in an index fund. The fees are significantly lower.

- *Check for fund staff changes.* As with investing in a single stock, pay attention to changes in investment staff of mutual funds, particularly the departure of a key portfolio manager. The mutual fund company "owns" the track record of the fund, and it survives the turnover of the portfolio manager. As such, the "new" portfolio team will be allowed to market the track record as if it created the performance that supports the documented return. For example, Chris Davis manages the Davis New York Venture Fund, which was founded in 1969, 20 years before he joined the firm. While Davis has continued the legacy of stellar performance, the same has not been true of other funds. Robert Stansky never met the performance expectations set for the massive Fidelity Magellan Fund by his predecessors, including Peter Lynch, who became the pop-star evangelist of mutual funds during the time he managed Magellan. One portfolio manager is not just like another.

Madoff Investors

HOOK, LINE, AND SUNK

Norma Hill, who lost $2.4 million and her expectations of a secure old age in the biggest Ponzi scheme in history, met Bernard Madoff once. It was 1988, she was 43 years old, and she had just been widowed. Only two weeks before his sudden and utterly unexpected death, her husband, Jack Hill, had invested somewhere around a quarter of a million dollars in Madoff's fund. The money was Hill's profit-sharing payout from the advertising company he had served for years, and he invested it with Madoff because several members of his family had their money in Madoff's fund and had recommended him. Then Hill, an athletic and active man, suffered a massive heart attack while riding his bicycle, leaving behind Norma and their five children.

Just a few weeks after Jack's death, another family member escorted Norma to the so-called Lipstick Building on New York's East Side—the shining, tubular skyscraper designed by Philip Johnson and John Burgee that housed the headquarters of Bernard L. Madoff Investment Securities.

"He was very nice," Hill said 21 years later of her meeting with Bernie Madoff. We were seated in Hill's comfortable home, at her dining table; it was the day before what would have been Jack's birthday, and her memories of her late husband and of that time were vivid. Madoff struck her as a vigorous, cheerful man—very pleasant. "He came out of his office to greet me. I remember that he put an arm around my shoulder and said how sorry he was for

215

my loss. He told me I shouldn't have anything to worry about, that from here on in, everything was going to be just fine. 'You don't have to sell the house,' he said. 'The kids can go to college. Don't worry.' Then I remember he added: 'But if you feel insecure about any of this, by all means, put it in CDs.'"

Hill, an attractive and luminously gracious woman in her early sixties, smiles wryly at the recollection, but it is probably safe to say that she wishes she had listened to Madoff's last remark and not to his reassurances.

"Never Really Gave It Any Thought"

At the time, however, the prospect she confronted seemed daunting: Two of the children were in college, one developmentally challenged son was already in the institutional residence in which he still lives, and there were two other children who would be going to college soon enough. Her aims were to support the children through college, pay off the mortgage on her house, and, if she could, have enough to ensure her own independence and something to leave as an endowment for her institutionalized son in gratitude for the care he was given.

By her own admission, she was not then and is not now an expert in finance. That's precisely why she wanted to invest with someone who was. When you're sick, you go to a doctor. When your car breaks down, you see a mechanic. When you want your savings to grow, you go to an investment advisor. Norma Hill went to the investment advisor whose name was on the lips of everyone she knew and trusted. She was looking for the expertise she lacked, and who could be more expert than this nice man whose resume sparkled with credentials and accolades—a former head of the Nasdaq, a university trustee, board member of a business school? She gave her money and her trust to Madoff, and after that, she says, "I never really gave it any thought."

She went to work, paid off the mortgage, took distributions from the investment to help put the kids through college, and replenished the investment with savings whenever she could. The money grew. Monthly statements arrived along with a stash of trading tickets recording the buying and selling of such blue-chip names as Merck and General Electric.

At the same time, her career advanced. With the children gone, Hill sold the big family-size house and, seeking "a smaller way of life," bought her comfortable house half the size in a cozy, quiet cul-de-sac within easy reach of the village and the two of her children who stayed in the New York area. Today, she is careful to assert—and does so proudly—that the house was bought with the money she and her late husband earned through work and saved through thrift. The Madoff funds were for her future. And indeed, whenever she told anyone that her money was invested with Madoff, they would tell her how lucky she was. "He's the gold standard of Wall Street," people would say. "He's brilliant. He'll always take care of you."

Over the years, that certainly seemed to be the case. Hill had the sense that Madoff investors like herself were all part of a family and that the reason the avuncular Madoff charged no fees was that the family was entitled to "special treatment." When, in 2004, the business she worked for was sold, Norma Hill took early retirement and the buy-out package and, of course, invested it with Bernie Madoff.

Today, she faces another daunting prospect: She will have to find another way to live, and she assumes she will have to start by selling her house. "I have to make a decision as to how I'm going to move forward," she says. But right now, as she conceded in our interview just a few months after losing everything, "I think I'm in mental paralysis." And, she adds, "I feel kind of worn out."

It's understandable. Hill has "come back" from adversity before—from perhaps more than her share of losses and sorrows—and it is hard to contemplate having to do so again. She will not be destitute: She has loving children ready to care for her and to take her in, but she is a woman to whom independence is precious, and she wants neither to intrude nor to compromise her own freedom.

It is the upending of expectations that weighs so heavily—almost visibly—on Norma Hill. Gone is the comfort of knowing she would have all she'd need for retirement and a secure old age—goals for which she worked hard all her life and, God knows, goals she deserves to have attained. Gone is the "extra" money she put aside in separate Madoff accounts to help her grandchildren with their education. Gone is the assurance that she could stay in her home and continue the life she built. It's a life of volunteering—education programs for inmates at the nearby women's prison; of time with her children and grandchildren and regular visits to her institutionalized son. Yet as she sits with her dog on her lap—a rescue dog, blind from old age—she still can speak of her loss more in resignation than bitterness.

Hill casts no blame on those who referred her husband to Madoff: as she points out, they lost money too. But she is also convinced that others besides Bernie Madoff himself bear responsibility. She is suspicious of all the Madoff family—and most especially of Madoff's wife, Ruth, questioning how a wife, especially one who worked as a bookkeeper, could *not* know of so vast and complex a scam.

Hill also has questions about David Friehling, son-in-law and partner of Jerome Horowitz in the tiny firm of Friehling & Horowitz that was engaged as Madoff's auditors and accountants. Indeed, six years before our interview, Hill had been persuaded to switch from the accounting firm she had used for years to Friehling & Horowitz. It just seemed easier. The Madoff office inundated her with monthly statements and trade confirmations—as it turned out, of course, for trades that were never executed. The result nonetheless was that every year, at tax time, she would spend hours going over the paperwork and reconciling the trades in preparation for her annual tax meeting with her accountant. It was Hill's sister-in-law, also a Madoff investor, who suggested it might be easier to work with Friehling, who, as Madoff's accountant since 1991, had a direct feed of data from Madoff headquarters. There would thus be no need for Norma Hill to spend those long hours reconciling the trading activity; Friehling simply could print out the needed reports directly from the linked system.

Hill had come to know Friehling and his family; she even attended the bat mitzvah of a Friehling daughter. But it was always a professional rather than a personal relationship—based on Friehling's fiduciary responsibility to his clients—and if truth be told, she found him a somewhat arrogant young man, full of swagger. Still, Hill took no particular pleasure from Friehling's arrest on fraud charges in March 2009, nor from the subsequent not-guilty plea seen as just a prelude to a deal in which Friehling would trade cooperation for leniency. Was he complicit or incompetent? Hill isn't sure. After all, as she notes, her prior accountant served a number of Madoff investors yet had never hoisted the flag of caution either. She also points out that Friehling's partner, Jerome Horowitz, was himself a Madoff victim; he lost his entire life savings in the scam and died, penniless, from cancer on the very day that Madoff pleaded guilty. Yet what irks Hill to this day is that, as the markets collapsed in 2008 and into 2009, she called Friehling, concerned about her investment—about her future. "Don't worry,"

Friehling told her, "Bernie knows what he's doing; your money's in good shape." Incompetence or complicity? A frightened man blustering to keep his spirits up, or an outright lie? The government claims the latter. Hill leaves it at that.

Norma Hill saw Bernie Madoff in person once more, although they didn't speak. It was March 12, 2009. She traveled to New York City, downtown to U.S. District Court, and watched as he entered his guilty plea and was immediately thereafter remanded into custody to await sentencing. He appeared shrunken to her, not the robust fellow who had assured her so many years before that she had no money worries. As he read aloud his statement—"in this monotone voice, showing no emotion at all"—all she could think of was the excess with which he had lived, the *things* for which he had "destroyed people's lives." Somewhere she had read about a set of sterling silver flatware the Madoffs had bought for $65,000, and it seemed to her to epitomize something worse than greed. And although Norma Hill is a woman to whom forgiveness and reconciliation are extremely important, at that moment she did not think she could ever forgive this man for having done what he did to so many lives like hers—just so that he could live more grandly than the kings of history ever did.

A Survivor, Not a Victim

Burt Ross takes a similar view—and is blunt in defining Madoff's behavior as evil. "What could be more evil than selling your soul for all these *things*?" he demands rhetorically. What could be worse than "hurting all these people so you can have dinner in some fancy restaurant," or own three homes, or buy another yacht?

Ross is one of the more vocal of the Madoff survivors—"Don't call us 'victims,'" he begs. He has been interviewed by news organizations from around the world. He has blogged on *The Daily Beast*, been profiled in the *Wall Street Journal*, been quoted in the New York *Daily News*, the *Palm Beach Press*, the *Dallas Morning News*. Part of this facility as a spokesman comes naturally. As a onetime mayor of Fort Lee, New Jersey, Ross is accustomed to being a public presence. What's more, his mayoralty was somewhat special. A gun-toting Mafioso offered Ross a $500,000 bribe. He not only turned it down, he reported it to the authorities and eventually testified in court. That put his life at risk, but it helped prosecutors win several convictions. Singed by another criminal 35 years later, Ross admits that going public about Madoff is cathartic and may even have given him "some highs" along the way. Having lost $5 million in the scandal, the bulk of 45 years' worth of savings, Ross deserves a few highs.

In fact, Ross and his wife were what you might call double losers. In 2003, they put money into J. Ezra Merkin's Ascot Funds, which, though they did not know it, was a feeder fund for Madoff. (In 2009, Merkin was charged with deliberately keeping that fact a secret from his investors in return for lavish fees from Madoff.) A couple of years later, says Ross, "calls were made" on his behalf to Madoff himself, who was eventually tracked down in Europe where he finally gave "permission" to accept Burt Ross as a Madoff investor. "It was harder to get into Bernie's fund than to get into Harvard," Ross told the *Wall Street Journal.*

Ross made it into both. From Harvard, he received an education and a degree. From the Madoff funds, Ross never took a distribution at all, although he extracted a small amount from his Ascot Funds. "By some miracle"—in his words—he did not invest everything with Bernie Madoff, but he did invest the majority of his net worth there—a mistake he readily acknowledges. He also acknowledges that he never questioned the steady success of the investments, but claims that "neither do 98 percent of people." The monthly statements showed a diversified portfolio of blue-chip stocks, and the balance was always higher than the previous month. "I understood nothing," Ross confesses. "I looked at the returns, said 'Hallelujah' and was a happy guy. I didn't try to understand it."

Like Norma Hill, Ross wonders how much he could have understood. This very savvy man—trained as a lawyer, a onetime Wall Street broker, a politician and government official, and a highly successful real estate principal—knew he didn't fully "get" the intricacies of the financial instruments that were being created and traded in markets around the globe in the early years of the twenty-first century. It's why he sought out expert professionals and put his money—and his trust—in their hands. "If you invest in what you're told is the biggest bank in the world, you're not going to sit there and try to figure out how they do their banking business," says Ross. "You go to an investment house for that. You cannot figure out every stock you invest in."

On the other hand, he says, "I have a brain. I am not an idiot." He knew it was unwise to put the majority of his savings in one place, he contravened that wisdom, and of course he is now paying for it in spades. Indeed, the experience made Ross wary of all his other investments, and he soon set about redeeming them. "If you don't understand an investment," he now says, "avoid it."

He sees himself as a creditor and expects that he might realize 20 cents on the dollar, if there is any payback forthcoming once the appointed trustee liquidates Madoff's investment firm and the courts have spoken. He is stunned by the "sense of entitlement" of some of his fellow creditors, who "want their money back—the profits and the interest. What planet are they on?" Ross asks. He isn't seeking a bailout; nor does he think those people who took distributions from their Madoff investments should be asked to return that money. What he does want, however, is relief for having paid a fortune in taxes on gains and income that never existed—the phantom "returns" on his investment that he declared to the Internal Revenue Service year after year—and he finds the waffling, indecision, and lack of communication on the tax issue at both state and federal government levels to be "unforgivable and unacceptable."

Unlike Norma Hill, the Rosses did not lose everything. They are not without resources. "Most people in this country would still think of me as extremely rich," Ross says. His expression turns to one of concern as he tells how he bleeds inwardly for the elderly, frail Madoff investors left without a home or access to medical care. "That is horrific," he says, and he is clearly thankful that he is not similarly afflicted.

But it isn't just financial resources that enable Ross to see himself as "a survivor, not a victim." It's a level of resilience that he says is simply part of his DNA. "I never defined myself materially. This is not so traumatic an adjustment for me because I don't define myself by what I own."

Perhaps that is why Ross is able to see the Madoff swindle as "the materialistic excess of our age run amok." Of Madoff and his wife, whom Ross sees as morally complicit whatever the courts may decide, Ross says that "everything about them has to do with money. Everything I hold dear—every value—they have sold to the devil for money." Ross reminds a listener that Dante reserves the lowest circle of hell, the frozen lake of his *Inferno*, for those who betrayed the bonds of love and trust: Cain who killed his brother; Brutus who assassinated his benefactor, Julius Caesar; Judas who sold out Jesus for 30 pieces of silver. "That's where Madoff belongs," says Ross—"with them. He betrayed people who treated him like a son."

And even at the end—revealed, reviled, his name a byword for deception—Madoff seemed to Ross not just without remorse for his crimes but without a clue as to the damage he had done. Ross was astonished at the tin ear displayed by the Madoffs and their legal representatives in the hearing at which Madoff pleaded guilty, a hearing Ross also attended. "When the lawyer spoke of Ruth Madoff's 'small house in France,' you could feel the hatred of the investors sitting there. It was palpable. You just don't say that: 'small house in France.' You just don't say that"—not in front of people who have lost their savings and their security to pay for that house in France, and the one in Florida, and the Park Avenue penthouse, and the yachts, and the rest of the excess.

Fraud Following Fraud . . .

A week after the Bernie Madoff story broke, another extraordinary fraud perpetrated by New York lawyer Marc S. Dreier almost threatened to knock it off the front pages. Dreier's fraud had a slightly smaller price tag than Madoff's. He did not rob charities, widows, and the elderly, as did Madoff. But what caught the headlines were the sheer brazenness of Dreier's actions and hushed hints about the odd, almost surreal impersonations carried out by Dreier and some of his accomplices.

"Colorful" doesn't begin to describe Marc Dreier. The son of a Polish immigrant who owned a chain of movie theaters, Dreier grew up on New York's Long Island—perhaps, given his father's profession, with a penchant for theatricality. A Yale graduate who earned a law degree from Harvard, Dreier worked for some of New York's most prestigious firms before starting his own law firm, Dreier LLP, headquartered on Manhattan's Park Avenue, in 1996. The high-profile firm eventually included 250 well-trained, well-compensated lawyers in offices in five cities. One of the perks of working for Dreier was the tight control he kept over the law firm's finances and administration, freeing the lawyers for the work they presumably loved to do: practice law.

Everything about Dreier was "Park Avenue." There was the triplex in Manhattan, the three homes in the Hamptons, the two condos in the West Indies, the house in Santa Monica, California. He could choose from among a fleet of Mercedes Benzes, BMWs, and a late-model Aston Martin to travel among his homes. Or he might sail in his 123-foot yacht, the Heesen-built *Lady Seascape*, one of only 10 such motor yachts on the planet. The crew of 10 kept the *Seascape* at the ready in Manhattan or St. Maarten; in both places, it was the scene of lavish late-night parties—certainly after Dreier's divorce in 2000.

Decorating this lifestyle, if that is what it was intended to do, was a stunning collection of masterpieces by the likes of painters David Hockney, Roy Lichtenstein, Picasso, and Matisse, and, by Andy Warhol, the "Jackie O" images.

And then it turned out that for at least four years, from 2004 through 2008, Dreier had been acting a grand charade in which he sold bogus debt obligations to some 40 investment funds managed by some of the nation's savviest investment managers. Simply put, Dreier peddled completely fictitious debt to hedge funds to the tune of some $380 million. And he seems to have done it by brazening his impeccably dressed way past receptionists and gatekeepers into the inner sanctums of investors he knew from the high-voltage millionaires' charity circuit and gulling them into buying what he claimed were discounted investments that had been unloaded by distressed sellers. Sometimes, it is alleged, he actually acted the part of players in the scheme. In fact, the jig was up when Dreier impersonated the lawyer of a pension plan that supposedly backed the sale of $33 million in fraudulent promissory notes, the ruse taking place in the plan's offices with the investor in attendance. Problem was the real-life attorney showed up unexpectedly and asked questions. Shades of Dreier's peripherally show-biz background?

Among the investors duped by Dreier's role-playing were three multi-billion-dollar, well-regarded firms including Fortress Investment Group, Elliott Associates, and hedge funds later acquired by the Blackstone group. One investor who was approached but who declined the invitation to invest was Nick Maounis of the Verition Fund.

More mundanely than forging these deceptions, Dreier also seems to have made off with $35 million held in escrow by his firm. In any event, the escrow money was missing the day Dreier was arrested, the day his firm's 250 lawyers learned their malpractice insurance hadn't been paid, their health insurance was in default, and their paychecks would not be forthcoming.

Like Madoff, Dreier was allowed, after serving some time in jail, to remain "free" on bail—actually, under house arrest in his Manhattan apartment and forced to pay for his own security—before he pleaded guilty in May 2009. Nevertheless, for both of these men to whom fraud came so easily and whose actions caused so much suffering, the pre-trial time at home recalls a comment made by Madoff victim Norma Hill on the subject—namely, that "if a guy from the Bronx had jumped a turnstile in the New York City subway system, he'd be rotting on Riker's Island," New York's infamous, overcrowded detention center, while these two "white-collar" miscreants, by law, enjoyed all the comforts of the extremely comfortable homes bought with money they stole.

Dreier left the apartment for sentencing July 13, 2009. He was ordered to pay $387.7 million in restitution and $746 million in forfeiture, and he was sentenced to 20 years in prison. The sentence would give the 59-year-old Dreier a single year of freedom should he live his actuarially expected span of 80 years.

The hearing was, says Ross, a "very emotional experience." To see the man clipped into handcuffs gave Burt Ross a sense that "there is such a thing as justice." It changed nothing; as another investor said, "It didn't put a penny back in my pocket." But it seemed to remind Ross that there was a structure to the universe and that "we're not run by mob rule."

It was also the first time Ross had ever seen Madoff in person, although he had once spoken with him by phone. "He had been doing so well for me," Ross recalls, "that I wanted to thank him by giving him my two front-row Knicks season tickets that the business owns—right behind the bench." So Ross telephoned. "I was flattered that he took my call—a busy man, after all. He seemed a perfect gentleman, very low-key." Madoff thanked Ross for the offer but said that he himself owned season tickets, so wouldn't Ross please give his to someone else. "I didn't know at the time," Ross muses dryly, "that he was using my money to buy his season tickets."

Seeing Madoff in court "altered something," says Ross. "It was chilling. He walks in wearing his million-dollar suit with not a hair out of place, and he looks like a businessman going to a meeting, not a defendant who's about to plead guilty. That's frightening." Because in the end, says Ross, the story isn't really about the excesses of our age, or even about betraying trust. It is about Madoff, "the all-time con artist. His Ponzi scheme stands on its own. There's nobody in the history of the world who is in this guy's league. Just look at the scale of it. He's a genius. An evil genius. The story is goddam Bernie Madoff. That's the story."

Loss: A Timeline

1988: Jack Hill invests $250,000 with Bernie Madoff; after Jack's death, Norma is introduced to Madoff, who comforts and reassures her.

1991: Certain she has found the gold standard of investment managers, for convenience, Hill replaces her personal accountant with Madoff's accountant, David Friehling.

2003: Burt Ross invests in Ezra Merkin's Ascot Funds.

2004: Having received steady returns on her investments with Madoff for some 16 years and having taken distributions for her children's education, Norma Hill elects to take an early retirement buy-out from her employer and invests it with Madoff.

2005: Ross gains "acceptance" into the club of Madoff investors and invests the majority of his net worth with Madoff.

2008: As the market declines sharply, Norma Hill appeals to Friehling, who assures her that "Bernie knows what he's doing."

March 12, 2009: Hill and Ross are both in court when Madoff pleads guilty and reads a statement "with no emotion at all," says Hill; Ross finds the courtroom event "chilling."

2009: Hill has lost $2.4 million, her entire savings for a secure retirement; Ross has lost $5 million, the bulk of 45 years' worth of savings.

The Anti-Ponzi: A Little Due Diligence Goes a Long Way

In a speech at the University of Minnesota in August 2008, billionaire appliance wholesaler Tom Petters listed four core values that he said characterized the numerous companies in his portfolio: caring, innovation, humility, and integrity.

Two months later, in October 2008, four was the number of charges on which Tom Petters was arrested and held by the Federal Bureau of Investigation (FBI): mail fraud, wire fraud, money laundering, and obstruction of justice—a far cry from caring, humility, and integrity, though perhaps not lacking in innovation.

Petters's alleged scam, news of which was almost eclipsed by the global financial crisis and utterly dimmed by the Madoff headlines two months later, was a different kind of Ponzi scheme, yet it cost its "investors" $3.5 billion, according to the charges, and had been going on since 1994. The way it worked was that Petters and a business broker would borrow money from investors in order to buy merchandise—primarily from two major suppliers. The merchandise would secure the loans, which would pay back double-digit interest to investors.

But there was no merchandise. There were no suppliers—just fake company names and real office addresses from which employees sent the money back to Petters, taking a small commission for their trouble. To support the elaborate scheme, Petters and his associates created fake purchase orders, bills of sale, statements, confirmations, reports, and other forms of documentation purportedly showing goods bought from minor retailers and sold, at a profit, to such major retailers as Wal-Mart. It was all a fiction. The money—"tens of billions of dollars," said the FBI charge—simply went through the phony suppliers' bank accounts to accounts in the name of Tom Petters and his companies.

Petters used the money to live a life of exceptionally conspicuous consumption. He owned five homes, a convoy of luxury cars, a fleet of expensive boats. He bought business after business—Polaroid, Sun Country Airlines, and more—and held assets in real estate, restaurants, and high-tech start-ups. He was a generous philanthropist, particularly where educational institutions were involved.

Unlike the Madoff case, there was much in Petters's background to give an investor pause. At the same time, there is a kind of sadness in some of the vicissitudes of his background that help one understand Tom Petters. In this, too, he differs from Bernie Madoff, a man whose motivations remain opaque, a man who demonstrates no affect whatsoever.

Petters, by contrast, offers a colorful personality, if not a particularly noble one. He was something of a born salesman who started selling stereo equipment to college kids while he himself was still in high school. His parents put the kibosh on that impulse and shut down the business. But Petters revived it when he became a college student, quickly dropping out to work for an electronics retailer. He borrowed money from his brother and a friend to start a wholesale brokerage business for surplus goods, and there found his own personal métier: By all accounts, the natural-born salesman was never so happy as when he was juggling the buying and selling of odd-lot shipments of whatever commodity was available that week.

It perhaps compensated for his personal life, which seemed unhappy. Petters was divorced. He underwent rehab for cocaine addiction. He had trouble keeping business partners, who routinely sued him for breach of contract. Then in 2004, Petters's 21-year-old son was murdered while visiting Italy on a college study trip. Petters responded by pledging $10 million to build a leadership center in his son's honor at his alma mater.

Three years later, Petters's net worth was estimated at $1.3 billion, and he could assert to that university audience in Minnesota that "to build connections or relationships, you can't survive without trust. You can't do anything." If such a declaration from an alleged Ponzi scheme mastermind is ironic, in Petters's case it is an irony tinged with melancholy. Somehow, it is possible to feel for the man.

Petters's game was up when a longtime employee more or less couldn't take it anymore, "lost confidence" in Petters's ability to pay back investors, and spilled the beans to the U.S. attorney. Also in contrast to the Madoff scandal, Petters was held in a county jail in Minnesota and not allowed to go home to his lavish Wayzata mansion, the midwestern counterpart to Madoff's Park Avenue penthouse.

Caught in the undertow of the debacle were a number of foundations; the president of one said his foundation had lost its ability to "donate to charities." Also part of the general Petters implosion were five funds of Lancelot Investment Management LLC, an Illinois-based hedge fund which had invested nearly all fund assets—some $1.8 billion—in Petters's business entities. Lancelot filed for bankruptcy almost immediately, becoming the largest creditor in the FBI case against Petters. It also filed its own racketeering suit against Petters, his associates, and his businesses. But Lancelot itself was sued by its investors for lending money to Petters in the first place, the plaintiffs claiming that "the security supposedly held by the Lancelot funds is fictitious or fraudulent," as the lawsuit filing expressed it. Ritchie Capital, a formerly "smart" hedge fund, was apparently attracted to interest rates paid by Petters that exceeded 360 percent. Maybe with banks paying only 2 percent to 3 percent, fund founder Thane Ritchie could have guessed something was wrong and saved the $275 million that is likely gone forever. Maybe Palm Beach Finance Partners wouldn't have lost more than $1 billion if they had done a bit of spadework.

As Petters's own defense lawyer put it, "What were these people thinking? . . . Aren't they required to do due diligence?"

Yes, they are. There are no shortcuts in investing, even—perhaps especially—in smart investing.

The Madoff case offered warning signs along the way. The warning signs in the Petters scheme were in the personality of Tom Petters himself—and they were there for all to see. A little due diligence would have gone a long way to preventing a big mistake.

What Went Wrong?

As of this writing, the details of Bernard Madoff's Ponzi scheme still are being unraveled, even as the man himself does his time—the outsized 150-year sentence meant in its profound weight somehow to answer for what the sentencing judge called "a staggering human toll." We don't yet know for certain who all the players were and how it all worked. And certainly we do not know now—and may never entirely know—the motivation or psychosis or whatever it was that drove Madoff to do what he did. But our concern here is not with Madoff himself, on whom millions of other words have already been written, with millions more to come. Rather, our concern is with the billion-dollar mistake made by the Madoff investors. For what the Madoff fraud does show, in sharp relief, is a good deal about the **psychology** of investing.

The unhappy truth is that there were warning signs. Plenty of them. And they weren't really hidden away. For it is a fact that where money is concerned, very few frauds are undiscoverable. The Madoff fraud is a case in point.

The old saying that "If it's too good to be true, then it probably isn't true" is at work in spades in this context. At the very least, something as good as being a Madoff investor deserved extra-special due diligence. That extra due diligence might have revealed what is typically the case and was certainly the case here: that something that good just is not true.

The very fact that this too-good-to-be-true deal was offered at a discount—no fees!—should have been a red flag to every investor. It should at the very least have prompted the investor to ask why. Why was Madoff being paid in commissions only—unlike the managers of most funds? There is always a reason behind fee structure; the "reasoning" behind this one, of course, became clear only after the fact.

Compounding this too-good-to-be-true fee structure for Madoff was the too-rich-to-be-ignored fee structure for the professionals who placed money with Madoff on behalf of others. Among these professionals were Ezra Merkin and his Ascot Funds as well as the Fairfield Greenwich Group, an asset management firm with $15 billion entrusted to it by others. Merkin and Fairfield realized hundreds of millions of dollars in fees for investing their clients' money with Madoff. Why? What exactly were they being paid such excessive fees *for*? It was yet another warning sign.

Even the steady low returns that the fund realized should have raised an alarm. Investing is naturally volatile; market behavior defies logic; returns are rarely steady and low. Steady-and-low looks a bit like trying to stay under the radar; it's like the poker player holding four aces and placing modest bets, hoping to lull the other players into a false sense of security about the cards they hold. Madoff, holding his cards close to his chest, had a performance record worthy of doubt.

The fact that people fought to become Madoff investors con-stitutes another warning sign. The very exclusivity of the Madoff club speaks more to marketing acumen and perception than to due diligence. "There was a status thing about investing with Bernie Madoff," in the words of *Wall Street Journal* reporter Heidi N. Moore; it put one in the company of "Palm Beach poobahs."[1] Somehow, investing with Madoff became the equivalent of dining in the res-taurant where no one can get a reservation. It was the Nehru jacket of the 1960s—everyone had to own one even though they looked good only on the Beatles and Sammy Davis Jr. Yet not every hard-to-get-into restaurant has good food, and eventually, the ugliness of the Nehru jacket wore down its popularity. It's hard not to be reminded of the immortal line of Groucho Marx: "I don't care to belong to any club that would have me as a member." Had inves-tors listened to Groucho, they would have asked why investing with Madoff was so exclusive, why the membership was so selective.

From Madoff's point of view, there was a simple answer: Membership by referral confers instant acceptance, automatic trust. It was worthwhile for Burt Ross to pull every string he could find to get into the Madoff club because look at who the other members were. How could you not feel you had solid gold if Mets owner Fred Wilpon and Hollywood genius Steven Spielberg and Nobel laureate Elie Wiesel were in on it? From one great name to another, the trust was passed on down the line till nobody could remember—and no one asked—where the line had begun. It was a brilliant coda on a very simple theme: Madoff needed money to perpetuate both his fraud and his lavish lifestyle. The high-toned celebrities who invested with him served as a come-on—a money magnet. Once you have duped Wilpon and Spielberg and Wiesel, it's easier to attract people like Burt Ross. And with more and more people like Ross clamoring to get into your club, you just keep taking in more and more money. This was another dynamic that should have raised a red flag.

Of course, it is easy to pose these questions and raise these alarms in retrospect, hindsight being 20/20—crystal-clear vision. But the fact is that these alarms *were* raised. There were individuals and institutions that did not invest with Madoff because they could not find the transparency they needed to make an informed judgment. Others didn't invest with him because they suspected him of fraud. Some were made uneasy by those steady low returns. Others saw there was not enough trading volume in some of the options being traded to execute the large-cap stock derivative strategy Madoff claimed to be executing.

And these individuals and institutions saw this despite what the evidence now shows to be true: that Madoff tried hard to obscure or disguise what was really going on. He sought a clientele from among people not particularly astute in the ways of finance and hired staff not particularly experienced in the securities trading business. It appears that his aim was to compartmentalize his enterprise and to keep each compartment from having a clear idea of what was going on in every other compartment. In short, he deliberately set out to obfuscate, and clearly, he succeeded.

However, there were some nonbelievers, individuals able to see behind the wizard's curtain. Harry Markopolos was one. The Securities and Exchange Commission's failure to act on the persistent reports he provided them is inexcusable. Markopolos called it; he said Madoff was running a Ponzi scheme. And the people who should have listened and done something instead listened and did nothing.

But while Markopolos was a professional, imbued with an educated eye, he wasn't the only one. The failure of the alarms raised in two articles in *Barron's* in 2001 to reach a wider audience is unfathomable. The articles were in plain language, and their meaning was clear and distinct. And the failure of those who suspected fraud—like Credit Suisse, for example—to broadcast their suspicions more widely and more vocally seems beyond the pale—especially to Norma Hill, who believes that any organization that serves the public has a responsibility to report such suspicions to the public. Where one Harry Markopolos and two *Barron's* articles might not be heard, a chorus of financial institutions and professional investors might have added enough fortissimo to echo even in the mainstream press.

Nevertheless, the warnings were there—too recondite perhaps for the great majority of retail investors—but there nevertheless.

The conclusion is inescapable that the real reason most people did not see or hear the warnings is that they did not want to see or hear them. They simply turned away and tuned out, or were intimidated by the complexity of the strategy. Either way, they fell for Madoff's charm, for the exclusivity of the club, or maybe for the contrived returns. They fell for it hook, line, and sinker.

It made for a con man's paradise.

Attention Must Be Paid

And as Burt Ross has said, this was a con man in a league of his own. He was appealing to people's greed all right, but not necessarily to their greed for money. It was greed for something else—for comfort, belonging, peace of mind. Deliberate or instinctive, planned or opportunistic, Madoff hit the hot buttons of these human needs with perfect timing and absolute precision. He would take care of you. We are all family. In many cases, we're all part of the same tribe: We share values, a history, an ethnic and religious background. There's nothing frightening here, nothing esoteric. The investments are in large-cap American companies, the names are blue chip and familiar, the returns are steady—no steep drops, no knockout punches. There's nothing to rock the boat or upset the apple cart. You don't have to pay attention because, as Madoff himself told Norma Hill, "from here on in, everything is going to be just fine."

And if that's what you expect from investing, I've got a bridge I'd like to sell you.

The fantasy Madoff was selling appealed to sophisticated financiers as well as to rank amateurs precisely because it wasn't about money. Madoff was buying yachts and palaces, but he was selling a modest vision of snug coziness. A warm fireside on a cold night. Safe shelter. Neither Hill nor Ross was seeking above-average returns on their money; they sought steady returns wrapped in a risk-averse strategy. And that's what Madoff appeared to deliver.

But it was, of course, a shell game. In Madoff's deft sleight-of-hand, you never saw reality. While he himself was leading a strange life as a solo high-flyer, he was offering his customers the warm communal embrace of membership in a special club. While he walked a high-wire tightrope to hold together the biggest scam in history, he was promising his investors peace of mind. He succeeded for as long as he did for that very reason—*because* he promised peace of mind. Madoff reached out—brilliantly—to touch the human heart of thousands of investors even as he emptied their wallets.

There is no peace of mind in investing. Unless, as Madoff hinted to Norma Hill, you want the security of government-insured certificates of deposit, you have to pay attention. That's the bottom line about investing that a swindler's psychology made everyone forget.

Norma Hill "never gave it any thought" because she knew she was no expert. Burt Ross didn't pay attention because Madoff had come recommended by friends Ross trusted; he trusted on the basis of others' trust. Both Hill and Ross were flattered to be part of a select, elite club. And both were shown in black and white that they were making money. So they turned aside and allowed themselves to be reassured.

But here's the question: Did they fail to pay attention because they trusted? Or did they trust because they did not want to do the work of paying attention?

Before Mr. Madoff stole his investors' money, he messed with their emotions. That's where the initial swindle took place. After that—alas!—it was easy.

Lessons Learned

- *Don't put all your eggs in one basket.* Diversify across investment advisors as well as across asset classes. Fraud, when committed by bright individuals, is difficult to detect; diversification is thus the most reliable defense, even if it provides only partial protection.
- *Referrals aren't gospel.* Don't treat them as such. The fact that someone you trust has invested successfully with a particular fund, advisor, or firm is no substitute for your own due diligence. The someone you trust may have a different tolerance for risk—or may know nothing about investing despite apparent investment "success"—a subjective term. Do all the diligence that is due—never less, more if possible.
- *Sophisticated investing is for sophisticated investors.* The less sophisticated an investor you are, the less you should invest in sophisticated strategies. Madoff made his strategy seem simple, but it wasn't; it was deliberately made difficult to understand. Only by knowing what questions to ask could an investor have penetrated the screen Madoff put up. Unless you're savvy enough to know what questions to ask and what the answers mean, stay away from the likes of a Madoff; stick with the likes of Fidelity Funds and its basic investment strategies.

- *Kick the tires.* Be sure to check on the administrative and support staff of a fund in which you're investing. Who is doing the research? How many people are responsible for managing how much money? Is the staff big enough? Good enough? Take a tour of the facilities as you would when shopping for a house; have a conversation with one or two of the employees to get a sense of the kind of place it is. Ask who provides the independent legal, auditing, accounting, and other key functions for the investment management company. Make sure the scale and reputation of support functions are equal to the task. Horowitz & Friehling, with a small office in New City, New York, could not be assumed to be a legitimate check and balance on a business the size of Madoff's investment fund.

- *Build firewalls.* Set up safeguards and firewalls between your diversified investments. Hire outside accountants knowledgeable about investments in general. Avoid dealing with service vendors locked into cozy relationships with investing principals—Madoff and Merkin, for example.

- *Wolf in sheep's clothing?* Remember that the calmer the sheep, the easier it is to sustain the fraud. Had Madoff promised returns that were twice the market performance, it is likely that more questions would have been posed. But because he set much more modest expectations, he was able to continue the fraud for much longer.

- *Be skeptical.* Do not allow yourself to be reasoned into unreasonable conclusions. No investment strategy consistently outperforms the market or is immune from major market moves. When your investment manager's results show otherwise, it's not an occasion for rejoicing or for sighing with relief; it's a signal to probe more deeply.

- *A sure thing?* Remember that there is no such animal.

- *Pay attention.* Above all, remember that the work of paying attention is every investor's essential task.

Me Too

MISTAKES I'VE MADE AND LESSONS I'VE LEARNED

I've never made a billion-dollar mistake—never had the opportunity—but I certainly have made many mistakes in my investing career. I've chased momentum, skimped on due diligence, and traded too often, leaving myself only the fading balance in my account and nowhere to turn for repentance.

I've exited positions out of emotion, only to turn around and let emotion drive me to buy the same stocks back again—as in *I'll show that stock. I'm going to buy it back and this time I'll win; I'll make money. That'll show them!* There is no "showing them" because no one cares. Stocks are inanimate objects that have no feelings and no memory. Move on. Every investment decision is a fresh decision.

I developed a couple of techniques for reminding myself of these mistakes so that I really could approach each investment decision afresh. The techniques are based on some fairly old technologies—paper and pen—but they work.

When I managed a portfolio at the hedge fund I cofounded, I kept a list of my investing mistakes in a 5- by 7-inch notebook. I also wrote there words of investing wisdom I unabashedly stole from reading what others had to say. The notebook had a neon-green cover and lived right on the top of my desk. I wanted it to be visible—like a string around the finger. Just seeing it out of the corner of my eye signaled me to refresh the discipline I was trying to enforce on myself, and every now and again, I would open it and read—just as a reminder.

If I ever repeated a mistake—and I have done so—I wrote the mistake down on a yellow Post-it and affixed it to the sides of my computer monitor. It really helped to see my errors brightly framing my trading activity. More than once, the scribbling on a Post-it stopped me in my tracks: *Oh no, don't do that one again!*

That's really how I got the idea for this book, for I truly believe that I have profited more from my mistakes than my successes. Of course, the mistakes were expensive, which may be one reason I appreciated them so much. Still, the lessons learned—like the lessons in each of the chapters of this book—have proven rewarding.

I wish the same for you. Let the stories in this book help you recognize your own investing mistakes, and may the lessons you learn both from your own blunders and from these billion dollar mistakes make you a better, more successful investor.

Notes

Chapter 1

1. Dial Torgerson, *Kerkorian: An American Success Story* (New York: Dial Press, 1974). There are numerous books about Kerkorian's business dealings, especially where Las Vegas is concerned. Try John L. Smith's *Sharks in the Desert* (Fort Lee, NJ: Barricade Books, 2005), and/or Christina Binkley's *Winner Takes All: Steve Wynn, Kirk Kerkorian, Gary Loveman, and the Race to Own Las Vegas* (New York: Hyperion, 2008).
2. K. J. Evans, "The Quiet Lion," *Las Vegas Review-Journal*, September 12, 1999, www.1st100.com/part3/kerkorian.html.
3. Douglas Gomery, "Transformation of the Hollywood System," http://leyendocine.blogspot.com/2007/05/transformation-of-hollywood-system.html.

Chapter 2

1. Washington Mutual Inc., SEC Form 10-Q, June 30, 2008, Commission File #1-14667.
2. Henny Sender, "Breakfast with the FT: David Bonderman," *Financial Times*, June 21, 2008, www.ft.com/cms/s/0/569a70ae-3e64-11dd-b16d-0000779fd2ac .html.
3. Nicholas Varchaver, "One False Move," *Fortune*, April 4, 2005,
4. Ellise Pierce, "Mondo Bondo," *Texas Monthly* (February 1996), www .texasmonthly.com/1996-02-01/reporter2.php.
5. Geraldine Fabrikant, "WaMu Tarnishes Star Equity Firm," *New York Times*, September 26, 2008, www.nytimes.com/2008/12/28/business/28wamu .html?_r=2&pagewanted=1.
6. Blog posted by Monica Guzman, March 11, 2008: http://blog.seattlepi.com/ thebigblog/archives/134038.asp.
7. Monica Guzman, Seattlepi.com, March 11, 2008, www.sfgate.com/cgi-bin/ article.cgi?file=/c/a/2007/08/12/BU72RBP6U.DTL.
8. John E. Morris, "Bonderman's Blues," *The Deal Magazine*, October 3, 2008, www.thedeal.com/newsweekly/insights/bonderman's-blues.php.
9. Sean Tully, "What Went Wrong at Wamu," *Fortune*, August 9, 2004, http:// money.cnn.com/magazines/fortune/fortune_archive/2004/08/09/377915/ index.htm.

Chapter 3

1. Private communication (e-mail) from Jeffrey L. Mobley, CFA, Senior Vice President—Investor Relations and Research, Chesapeake Energy Corporation, April 7, 2009.
2. Ben Casselman, "Margin Calls Hitting More Executive Suites," *Wall Street Journal*, October 13, 2008.
3. Fool.com: Liquid Lounge, Post of the Day, December 8, 2006.
4. Chesapeake Energy Corp. SEC File 1-13726, Accession Number 1193125-8 -94644, April 29, 2008, www.secinfo.com/d14D5a.t2sdr.htm.
5. Figures from Tom Reese and Paul Rubillo, "Chesapeake CEO Makes Big Bet,"Dividend.com 09.09.08, www.forbes.com/2008/09/09/potash -chesapeake-walter-pf-ii-in_pr_0909dividend_inl.html.
6. Casselman, "Margin Calls Hitting More Executive Suites."
7. Paul Monies, "Chief Executive Tells Why He Buys," NewsOK.com, June 6, 2006.

Chapter 4

1. www.thedeal.com/dealscape/2008/01/more_activists_were_circling_p.php.
2. Pershing Square Capital Management third-quarter 2008 Letter to Investors, http://stableboyselections.com/2008/11/15/pershing-square-q3-2008-investor -letter.
3. Presentation, Pershing Square Capital Management LP Annual Investor Dinner, January 22, 2009.
4. Pershing Square Capital Management third-quarter 2008 Letter to Investors.
5. Anderson, Mae. "Ackman Proposes Target Spin Off Property Company," *USA Today*, Associated Press, October 29, 2008.

Chapter 5

1. The U.S. Senate would later cite former Enron trader John Arnold, founder of Centaurus Advisors LLC, as having manipulated the energy market at this time.
2. *1 Amaranth LLC and Amaranth Advisors L.L.C. v. J.P. Morgan Chase & Co., J.P. Morgan Chase Bank N.A. and J.P. Morgan Futures Inc.*, New York State Supreme Court index #603756, www.portfolio.com/images/site/editorial/pdf/ Amaranth-Complaint.pdf. November 13, 2007.
3. Quoted in Thomas Landon Jr., "Billions in Losses Dim a Star Manager's Glow," *New York Times*, September 20, 2006. www.nytimes.com/2006/ 09/20/ business/20manager.html?_r=1&scp=2&sq=Thomas%20Landon%20jr%20bill ions%20in%20losses&st=cse

Chapter 6

1. Lawrence A. Armour, "A Top Pro Looks Ahead," *Fortune*, October 28, 1996.
2. Lois Peltz, *The New Investment Superstars* (Hoboken, NJ: John Wiley & Sons, 2001).

3. Peter Elkind, "The Incredible Half-Billion-Dollar Azerbaijani Oil Swindle Wherein We Learn Why Smart Players like Leon Cooperman, George Mitchell, and AIG Would Entrust Buckets of Their Money to Victor Kozeny, a.k.a. the Pirate of Prague. (Hint: Can you say 'greed'?)," *Fortune*, March 6, 2000.
4. Ibid.

Chapter 7

1. Presentation by Richard Pzena in Joel Greenblatt's Special Situations Value Investing Class at Columbia University Business School, Sept. 20, 2006.
2. Quoted in Joshua Lipton, "Doubling Down in Financials," Forbes.com, April 23, 2008.
3. Quoted in *Outstanding Investor Digest*, February 29, 2008.
4. Quoted in Lipton, "Doubling Down in Financials."

Chapter 8

1. James Mackintosh, "Wheels Come Off as Crunch Hits Peloton," *Financial Times*, March 1, 2008, www.ft.com/cms/s/0/364b8e40-e735-11dc-b5c3-0000779fd2ac.html.
2. "A Hedge Fund Crashes," Economist.com, February 29, 2008, www.economist.com/finance/displaystory.cfm?story_id=10789098&CFID=39118197&CFTOKEN=63919493.
3. Iain Day and Kate Walsh, "Pile-up as Peloton Runs out of Road," *Times* (London), March 29, 2009, http://business.timesonline.co.uk/tol/business/industry_sectors/banking_and_finance/article3465296.ece.

Chapter 9

1. Ben Beaumont-Thomas, "Adolf Merckle—The Bailout with a Human Face," post to badidea.co.uk, November 18, 2008, www.badidea.co.uk/2008/11/adolf-merckle-the-bailout-with-a-human-face.
2. Mike Esterl and Edward Taylor, "As Giant Rivals Stall, Porsche Engineers a Financial Windfall," *Wall Street Journal*, November 8, 2008. Gordon Rayner, "Porsche and VW Share Row: How Germany Got Revenge on the Hedge Fund 'Locusts,'" *The Telegraph*, October 29, 2008.
3. "Hedge Fund Manager Rakes in $3.7B," CNNMoney.com, April 16, 2008.
4. Louise Armitstead, "Hedge Funds Lose Billions as VW Share Price Dives," *The Telegraph*, October 29, 2008. www.telegraph.co.uk/finance/newsbysector/transport/3281888/Hedge-funds-lose-billions-as-VW-share-price-dives.html
5. Larry Robbins, letter to Partners dated March 19, 2009 on performance for Glenview Capital Partners (Cayman), Ltd. for the period ended December 31, 2008.
6. Rayner, "Porsche and VW Share Row."
7. Robbins letter.

Chapter 10

1. Scott Kays, *Five Key Lessons from Top Money Managers* (Hoboken, NJ: John Wiley & Sons, 2005).
2. Maurice R. Greenberg, Statement before the U.S. House of Representatives Committee on Oversight and Government Reform, October 7, 2008.
3. *Good Morning America*, ABC News, September 17, 2008.
4. Joseph B. Treaster, "Heir Apparent Leaves Post at Big Insurer," *New York Times*, September 20, 2000. www.nytimes.com/2000/09/20/business/heir-apparent-leaves -post-at-big-insurer.html?scp=5&sq=Treaster Heir apparent&st=cse
5. Joseph B. Treaster, "Insurance Broker Settles Spitzer Suit for $850 Million,"*New York Times*, February 1, 2005. www.nytimes.com/2005/02/01/business/ 01marsh.html?scp=1&sq=Treaster%20insurance%20broker%20settles&st=cse
6. "Morningstar: Justin Fuller's Ultimate Stock Picker," MSN Video, April 1, 2008.

Chapter 11

1. Adam Najberg and Julie Iannuzzi, *Inside the Madoff Scandal, Chapter One*, WSJ Digital Network, March 12, 2009. Dow Jones & Company, Inc.

Glossary

ABS (asset-backed securities): A pool of assets that behaves like a security and may be bought and sold in the same manner. An ABS consists of such contractual obligations as mortgages and auto loans. The value of the ABS pool will rise or fall in correlation with the underlying credit quality of the assets in the pool. Owners of the ABS receive periodic payments similar to dividends.

active investing: Buying and selling shares and moving in and out of the market based on ongoing analysis of fundamentals and of the business cycle—usually in an attempt to outperform market movements. (See "passive investing.")

activist investing: Investing by a nonmanagement shareholder who promotes change within the company designed to increase the value of the overall enterprise.

alpha: Incremental return on a security, fund, or portfolio; excess return relative to a benchmark index. For example, if the Standard & Poor's 500 index gains 10 percent on the year, and your portfolio generates a return of 12 percent, the alpha is 2 percent, or 200 basis points.

AUM (assets under management): The amount of money a fund or bank is managing; a measurement of size for comparison to competitors.

back office: The processing operations that support the trading of securities—that is, record keeping, confirmation, settlement, and regulatory compliance.

balance sheet: Statement of an organization's or individual's financial position expressed as assets, liabilities, and ownership equity.

book: A record of all the positions a trader holds, whether the position is an amount of securities owned (a long position) or borrowed (a short position).

241

book value: The value of a company measured to the extent its assets, after any write-downs, exceed its liabilities.

bricks-and-mortar: Physical locations—as of retail stores, bank branches, and the like—not Internet sites.

cash flow: Money flowing into an organization's or individual's cash account through revenue, financing, or investment less money flowing out through expenditure, thus continually changing the amount of cash on hand.

capital markets: The conduit for supply and demand of debt and equity capital, where stocks, bonds, and money market instruments are traded.

capital ratio: A bank's capital divided by risky assets, used as a determination of a bank's soundness—for example, the higher the capital ratio, the greater the perceived protection against operating losses.

clearing a trade: The process whereby trades are matched between parties. The details of the trade are matched, and the clearinghouse ensures that the buyer receives the security and the seller receives the cash.

collateral: An asset pledged for the repayment of a loan or margin. When a prime broker or bank lends an investment manager money to leverage a position in stocks, commodities, and the like, the broker or bank requires collateral in the form of cash or other marketable securities in return. Collateral requirements, also called margin requirements, may be increased as position size changes, as the value of the collateral declines, or if the bank or broker believes it is necessary in its sole discretion under the terms of the agreement with the fund.

counterparty: The other party in a financial transaction including trades, margin loans, and so on. The lender from whom you borrow, the buyer to whom you sell an asset, and the like.

cyclical stocks/cyclical companies: Stocks whose share price correlates to fluctuations in the overall economy; companies whose growth is correlated directly to the economy.

discounting: 1.   A method for measuring what a future payment is worth today.

2.   Period in advance of a turnaround in the markets or in a financial instrument, such as a stock, when all the bad news already is accounted for in the valuation/price.

due diligence: Investigation or audit of a possible investment in order to confirm its facts and assess its soundness.

duopoly: An industry controlled by only two companies.

enterprise value: The market capitalization of a company plus all debt on its balance sheet.

equity: Stock in a company. The amount of value that an individual owns in an asset—for example, the equity in a house is the value of the house less the mortgage.

ETF (exchange-traded fund):   A security constructed of multiple securities and intended to mimic the price movement of a sector or index. The XLF is the ETF for the financial sector and comprises a number of bank and brokerage stocks. The SSO is an ETF intended to replicate twice the price movement of the Standard & Poor's 500.

fixed income: An investment that yields a regular, fixed return, such as an interest payment.

Graham/Dodd: Benjamin Graham (1894–1979), called the father of value investing, was an economist, professional investor, and teacher at Columbia Business School. Graham agreed to teach his investment approach, which he called value investing, if someone would take notes. David LeFevre Dodd (1895–1988), then an instructor at Columbia, agreed to do so and helped Graham refine and articulate his teaching in their classic book, *Security Analysis*, originally published in 1934. That book, along with Graham's *The Intelligent Investor* (1949), represent the classic definition of value investing. As a result, the two men's names have become conjoined as a single noun, Graham/Dodd, standing for the principles they elucidated, or as an adjective, Graham-and-Dodd, describing those principles.

growth investing: Investing in companies you believe will achieve growth in excess of the anticipated rate of growth in the market or economy. These investments often are priced at a premium to other investments in the same asset class.

hedge fund: A pooled and private investment partnership, minimally regulated and therefore free to pursue aggressive investment strategies to seek maximum absolute returns. Hedge fund managers routinely are paid a management fee and collect a percentage of the profits (typically, 20 percent to 25 percent). Sometimes described as mutual funds for the superrich, hedge funds often speculate in unconventional and illiquid investments. Hedge funds operated with the intention of mitigating risk by taking long and short positions are sometimes riskier than funds taking long-only positions.

in the money: For a call option, when the stock price exceeds the strike price. For a put option, when the strike price exceeds the stock price.

investment attributes: The particular benefits of owning a particular investment.

investment banking: The function within a brokerage firm or bank that raises capital for companies by underwriting the issuance of their securities and by advising them on the placement of stock. Investment bankers also may advise companies on mergers and acquisitions as well as on other strategic matters.

investment discipline: The tenets of the investment style that govern all investment decisions.

investment style: The preference for a particular strategy or philosophy for putting money to work, the method one uses to invest—for example, value, growth, or momentum investing.

leverage: The use of debt, options, futures, and other financial instruments to finance assets or maximize return on an investment—that is, using financial resources you do not actually own to supplement funds you do own so as to enhance the potential positive return or minimize the potential negative outcome of an investment. To be levered is to have used leverage, and this can be measured as the level of debt relative to the amount of equity in an investment. For example, an individual buying a $5,000 asset with $1,000 of his or her own cash and $4,000 in borrowed money is said to be five times levered; or the leverage is 5:1.

long/short: To be long, to go long, to have a long position means you own the financial instrument and will profit if its price increases. (In the case of a derivative, you own the derivative and will profit if the price of the underlying instrument increases.) By contrast, to be short, to go short, to have a short position means that you have sold a borrowed financial instrument with the intention of buying it back at a lower price and returning it to the lender later, the difference being the profit.

macroeconomy: The behavior of the overall economy of a country, region, or of the world, including income, output, consumption, employment, inflation, savings, investment, trade, and finance. By contrast, microeconomics focuses on the behavior of an individual firm or consumer in a specific market.

margin, to be on margin, margin call: Investing with borrowed money that the lender can call in at any time—a margin call—to cover his or her counterparty credit risk. Investing on margin can greatly amplify the gains of an investment, but it also can amplify the loss.

mark-to-market accounting: A method of accounting in which a value is assigned to a financial instrument based on the current market price. If you mark to market a futures contract the value of which will not be known until its expiration nine months hence, this accounting methodology assigns that contract the value it would have in today's open market.

market capitalization: A company's outstanding shares multiplied by its share price.

momentum investing: Investing in securities trending upward or selling those trending downward to try to capture gains from the momentum of the trend. The momentum investor takes a long position in an upward-trending security and short sells a down stock on the theory that the momentum will continue.

monetize: To sell an asset and realize the proceeds. When Target sold a portion of its credit card receivables to J.P. Morgan in return for cash, it partially monetized the asset.

net cash: The amount of cash remaining on a company's balance sheet after deducting all debt obligations.

operating margins: The profit that remains after deducting all costs for operating a business.

option: A contract to buy (call) or sell (put) a particular financial asset (the underlying asset) at an agreed price (the strike price) and to exercise that call or put during an agreed period of time or on a specific date. If the buyer of the option chooses to exercise the option, the seller is obligated to sell or buy the underlying asset, but a buyer may allow the option to expire without exercising it. That makes options extremely versatile, and it is one reason they can be used both to speculate and to hedge risk.

out of the money: For a call option, when the stock price is below the strike. For a put option, when the stock price is higher than the strike price.

passive investing: Managing a portfolio by focusing on limiting the number of buy or sell transactions, often by investing in a fund that mimics the performance of a particular market index. Passive investing minimizes transaction costs and capital gains tax liability. A passive investor owns an interest in a business, such as stock in a corporation, and does not attempt to influence management as would an activist investor. (See "passive investing.")

premium: In reference to options, the cost of the right to own the option; also, the amount by which the cost exceeds the strike price.

prime broker: For certain clients like hedge funds, the prime broker division of brokerage firms or investment banks provides special services. Typical among these are securities lending, leveraged trade executions, cash management, global custody, high-tech reporting, and more.

private equity: Equity securities in companies that are not publicly traded on an exchange. Institutional and retail investors and funds invest directly into an operating company or may acquire the company.

quantitative modeling: By assigning numerical values to a range of variables, quantitative analysts try to model reality mathematically—typically, to measure performance, to value a financial instrument, or to predict changes in price.

risk management: The discipline of identifying, quantifying, accepting, or trying to mitigate the risk in deciding on an investment.

ROC (return on capital):   The amount of earnings on your capital. In a retail situation, the sales generated from invested capital.

ROC (rate of change):   The ratio between a change in one variable and a corresponding change in another; the difference between the two points is called the delta.

ROI (return on investment):   The profit or loss of an investment—typically measured as the gain or loss divided by its cost, and expressed as a percentage or ratio. It's the money you made or lost compared to the money you invested.

REIT (real estate investment trust):   A security traded on exchanges that invests in a range of real estate opportunities. Sometimes referred to as mutual funds for real estate, REITs offer retail investors a way of participating in the real estate market. The rents or sale proceeds are paid out to shareholders.

short squeeze: When a large percentage of a stock's outstanding float is held short and demand for the stock exceeds the supply, the stock price will rise. Short sellers will be squeezed as too many buyers chase too few available shares.

spread: The difference between the price asked and the price bid for a security or an asset.

time value: The additional cost paid for an option because of a longer duration before expiration. For example, you would pay a higher premium—a time value premium—for an option due to expire in December 2011 than for one that expires in June 2011.

trade/trading: Of course, to "trade" means to exchange one thing for another, but the term has come to stand for the concept of numbers of parties negotiating an exchange of securities, goods, and services through a mechanism known as a market, then transacting the exchange.

valuation: Determining the economic value of an asset or liability—for example, by examining the underlying company's management, its capital structure, assets, and forecasted future earnings. Also, determination of the value the market places on a stock or bond.

value investing: Investing in stocks perceived to be undervalued by the market and therefore to trade for less than their intrinsic value. Value investors typically look for stocks with lower-than-average price-to-book or price-to-earnings ratios and/or high dividend yields, and they see opportunity for profit in buying these underpriced stocks. Value investing is classic Graham/Dodd investing.

volatility: The manifestation of the uncertainty about or risk inherent in the changes in a security's value. High volatility means that the price of the security can change dramatically and quickly—either up or down. Low volatility means that the security's value changes steadily over time rather than fluctuating wildly.

write-down: Reduction in the book value of an asset that is overvalued compared to the market value.

About the Author

Stephen L. Weiss's circuitous route to Wall Street took him from financial planning to tax law to the entertainment industry where he represented some very well-known personalities, providing both career and investment advice. But the investment business was his first love, and he finally answered its call—first in institutional equity sales, where he dealt with some of the most accomplished professional investors at both mutual funds and hedge funds, then in senior management positions at Salomon Brothers, SAC Capital, and Lehman Brothers (he played no role in its demise). He currently is a Senior Managing Director and Partner at Leerink Swann, LLC, an investment bank in New York City. Mr. Weiss lives in Short Hills, New Jersey with his wife, two daughters, and two dogs. *The Billion Dollar Mistake* is his first published book.

Index

Accountants, 233
Accounting shorts, 176
Ackman, William A. (Bill)
  and activist investing, 69–74, 77, 79,
    80, 85, 87
  background, 72–75
  Barnes & Noble, 75–79, 85
  Borders Group Inc., 75–80, 84, 85,
    87, 88
  due diligence, 69, 74, 76
  Gotham Partners, 72, 73
  investment discipline, 69–71, 73–76,
    84, 85, 87, 88
  lessons learned, 88
  leverage, use of, 73, 74, 76, 84–87
  option purchases, 81–88
  Pershing Square Capital
    Management, 72–83, 85
  Target, 78, 80–86
Activist investing, 69–74, 77, 79, 80,
  85, 87
AIG. See American International
  Group (AIG)
Aliyev, Heydar, 121, 125
Amaranth Advisors LLC, 89, 92–107
Amazon.com, 79
American Clean Skies Foundation, 54,
  58, 62
American International Group (AIG),
  196, 199, 201–213
American Savings & Loan, 38–40, 43,
  44, 46
Amoco, 130–132
Angelo, Gordon & Co., 91
Angelo, John, 90, 91
Annual report, 212

Appaloosa, 93
Arora, Harry, 95
Ascot Funds, 220, 225, 228
Asset-backed securities (ABSs), 42,
  156–168
Auction bidding, 130–132
Automobile industry, 17–24
Azerbaijan, 117, 119–127

Bahamas, 114, 115, 117, 124
Banks, 134–136. See also Financial stocks
Barnes & Noble, 75–79, 85
Barnes, Florence (Pancho), 14
Bass, Robert M., 33, 35–37, 39
Bear Stearns, 43, 177, 207
Berkowitz, David P., 73
Bernanke, Ben, 206
Bernard L. Madoff Investment
  Securities, 215. See also Madoff,
  Bernard L.
Bernstein. See Sanford C. Bernstein &
  Co. (Bernstein)
Berra, Yogi, 144
Billionaire investors, characteristics
  of, 6–9
Black, Steven D., 102
Blackstone, 223
Blankfein, Lloyd, 152
Bloomberg, 189
Bloomberg, Michael, 154
Boesky, Ivan, 8
Bonderman, David
  and American Savings & Loan,
    38–40, 43, 44, 46
  background, 32–35
  due diligence, 44, 45, 47, 48

Bonderman (*continued*)
  independent analysis, need for,
    47–49
  investing background, 35–40
  investments, 31, 32
  and Killinger, Kerry, 39–48
  lessons learned, 49
  TPG, 31, 32, 34–37, 39, 40, 43–46,
    48, 49
  and Washington Mutual (WaMu),
    39–48
Borders Group Inc., 75–80, 84, 85, 87, 88
Bourke, Frederic (Rick), 117, 121, 124
Brokers
  churning, 108
  motives of, 29, 102, 104, 105, 108
  track record and credentials, 108
Buffett, Warren, 4, 5, 206

C. V. Starr and Company, 203, 204
"Can't miss" opportunities, 3
Capital ratios, 135
Catalyst shorts, 176, 192
Cerberus Capital Management,
    19, 21, 185
Charles Schwab & Co. Inc., 201
Chesapeake Energy, 53–67
China, 128, 202
Chrysler, 18–28
Churning, 108
Citadel Investment Group, 93, 101, 102
Citicorp, 135–137
Citigroup, 44, 136, 137, 140, 141, 143,
    145, 147, 148
Cohen, Gary, 100
Cohen, Steve, 8, 9, 178, 185
Collateralized debt obligations
    (CDOs), 204
Collins, Jim, 94
Commodities trading, 93, 107, 108
Common money mistakes, 2, 3
Complacency, 12
Continental Airlines, 39
Convertible arbitrage, 90, 91
Cooperman, Leon (Lee), 7, 8
  background, 110–112
  due diligence, 110, 119, 125–127

and Kozeny, Viktor, 112–126
  lessons learned, 127, 128
  and Lewis, Clayton, 117–126
  Omega Advisors, 110, 111, 117–126
Coulter, James, 37–39, 43, 46
Countrywide Financial, 177
Credit derivative swaps, 204–206, 211
Credit Suisse, 230
Crocs, 190–192
Crowded short, 175, 191
Cruz, Zoe, 152
Cyprus, 116
Czechoslovakia, 113–117, 124, 127

D. E. Shaw, 93
Daimler-Benz, 18–20
Daimler-Chrysler, 19, 26, 27, 185
Daventree, Ltd., 116
Davis, Christopher C. (Chris)
  and AIG, 196, 199, 201–212
  background, 195–198
  community involvement, 200
  Davis Advisors, 195, 198, 201, 212
  Davis Funds, 198, 200, 202
  Davis New York Venture Fund, 197,
    200, 201, 213
  Financial Fund, 198, 201, 210
  insurance business overview, 198, 199
  investment style, 200
  lessons learned, 212, 213
  Selected American Shares Fund, 198,
    200, 201
  stewardship, 200, 201
  value investing, 200
Davis, Shelby Cullom, 195, 196, 198, 205
Davis, Shelby M. C., 197, 198, 201, 212
Deutsche Bank (DB), 96, 103
Dimon, Jamie, 102
Dingman, Michael, 115, 116
Diversification
  and buying on margin, 60, 61, 67
  and exchange-traded funds
    (ETFs), 187
  in investment advisors, 232
  investment styles, 169
  investments at AIG, 208–210
  and risk, 61, 106, 128

Dot-com bubble, 184, 192
Dreier, Marc S., 222–224
Drexel Burnham Lambert, 130
Due diligence
  and activist investing, 69, 74, 76
  administrative and support staff, 233
  Bonderman, David, 44, 45, 47, 48
  Cooperman, Leon, 110, 119, 125–127
  importance of, 232
  independent research, 28, 29
  Kerkorian, Kirk, 20, 21, 28, 29
  and Madoff Ponzi scheme, 228, 229
  parties involved in investment, 127
  on professional advisors to
    investment management
    company, 233
  Pzena, Richard, 131, 142, 144
  and short selling, 189–191
  and Tom Petters Ponzi scheme,
    225, 227

Ebbers, Bernie, 5
Economic downturns, 11, 12, 17, 27,
  42, 63, 148. *See also* Pzena, Richard
  (Rich); Recessions
Einhorn, David, 178, 185
Einhorn, Steve, 111
Elliott Associates, 223
Emerging markets, 109–111, 115–120,
  124–128
Emerson, Ralph Waldo, 146
Emotional investment, 131, 137, 143,
  144, 146–148, 235
Energy derivatives, 92, 95–106
Enron, 92, 95
Exchange-traded funds (ETFs),
  186–188, 213

FactSet Research Systems, 72
Fairfield Greenwich Group, 228
Fannie Mae, 141, 142, 144, 147
Federal Home Mortgage Corporation
  (Freddie Mac), 141, 142,
  144, 147
Federal National Mortgage Association
  (Fannie Mae), 141, 142, 144, 147
Feinberg, Kenneth, 198, 210

Feinberg, Steve, 21, 185
Fidelity Magellan Fund, 213
Financial derivatives, 199, 204, 205
Financial stocks
  investing in, 133–137, 140–147, 202
  temporary ban on short selling of,
    176, 177
Firewalls, 233
Fisher, George, 22
Fleck, Aaron, 117, 121
Flight to quality, 157
Float, 175
Ford Motor Company, 20–25, 27,
  28, 115
Foreign Corrupt Practices Act, 120, 124
Foreign exchange (FX), 152–154
Form 13-D, 71, 80
Form 13-G, 71
Form 10-K, 211
Fortress Investment Group, 223
Fraud. *See also* Kozeny, Viktor; Lewis,
    Clayton
  avoiding, 232, 233
  Dreier, Marc S., 222–224
  lessons learned, 232, 233
  Madoff Ponzi scheme, 3, 215–222,
    224–233
  Tom Petters Ponzi scheme, 225, 227
  warning signs, 227–231
Freddie Mac, 141, 142, 144, 147
Friedman, Richard, 117
Friehling, David, 218, 219, 225
Fuller, Justin, 210
Fund managers
  experience, 148
  investment style, 150, 151, 169
  and style drift, 169. *See also* Style drift
  track record and credentials,
    108, 150

Gains, playing with "house money," 49
General Motors (GM), 19–23, 26, 28
Ghosn, Carlos, 22
Glenview Capital, 178, 180, 184
Goldman Sachs, 40, 81, 100, 102,
  110–112, 118, 142, 152–155, 158,
  159, 168

Gordon, Michael, 91
Gotham Partners, 72, 73
Government bailouts, 43, 144, 196, 199,
    204, 206, 207. *See also* American
    International Group (AIG)
Government-sponsored enterprises
    (GSEs), 141
Graham-and-Dodd investing,
    130–132, 134
Grant, Geoff
    background, 149, 151–154
    and Beller, Ron, 154–160, 163,
        165–168
    investment style, 150, 151
    lessons learned, 169
    margin calls, 160, 162–164
    Peloton Partners LLP, 154–169
    style drift, 151, 158–160, 164–169
Greenberg, Jeffrey, 208
Greenberg, Maurice (Hank), 202–206,
    208, 209, 212
Greenblatt, Joel, 130
Greenlight Capital, 178
Growth investing, 150

Haerter, Holger, 185
Hardy, Jean Maree, 13
Harvard Funds, 113–116
Havel, Vaclav, 113
Hedge funds. *See also* Fund managers
    Angelo, Gordon & Co., 91
    Citadel Investment Group, 93, 101
    JWM, 108
    Liquid Macro, 168, 169
    Long Term Capital Management,
        108, 111
    Och-Ziff Capital Management, 100
    Peloton Partners LLP, 101, 154, 155.
        See also Peloton Partners LLP
    Pershing Square Capital
        Management, 72–83, 85
    short selling, 177–179. *See also* Short
        selling
    Solengo Capital Advisors, 104
    Verition Fund Management LLC,
        106, 107, 223
Hedging

commodity risk, 108
and exchange-traded funds (ETFs),
    188. *See also* Exchange-traded
    funds (ETFs)
and short selling, 173
Henley Group, 115
Hill, Jack, 215, 225
Hill, Norma, 215–220, 223, 225,
    231, 232
Hindsight, 29
Historical performance, 129, 137,
    139, 148
Horowitz & Friehling, 218, 233
Horowitz, Jerome, 218
"House money," 17, 49
Howard, Peter, 158, 162, 165–168
Hunter, Brian, 96–106, 108

Iacocca, Lee, 18
Icahn, Carl, 5
Impulse buying, 49
Inconsistencies as red flags, 29. *See also*
    Warning signs
Independent analysis, need for, 47–49
Insider activity, risk in following, 56, 58,
    60, 64, 65, 67
Insurance business, 198, 199
Investing mistakes. *See* Mistakes
Investment advice, questioning source
    of, 29
Investment discipline, 69–71, 73–76, 84,
    85, 87, 88, 200, 235, 236
Investment style, 150, 151, 169, 200.
    See also Style drift
Investor psychology
    buying when others are selling,
        131, 133
    emotional investing, 131, 137, 143,
        144, 146–148, 235
    impulse buying, 49
    liquidity panic, 144
    and momentum investing, 139
    power of, 147

J. P. Morgan, 43, 44, 101, 102
James, William, 146
Jones, George, 78, 79

Jones, Rob, 105
JPMorgan Chase, 82, 83
JWM, 108

Keating, Frank, 53
Kerkorian, Ahron, 11, 12, 27
Kerkorian, Kirk
    automobile industry investments,
        17–28
    background, 11–14
    and changes in macroeconomy,
        17, 28
    due diligence, 20, 21, 28, 29
    gambling, 14, 15
    Hollywood investments, 15, 16
    investing mistakes, 24–28
    Las Vegas investments, 15–17
    lessons learned, 28, 29
    passion and investment strategy,
        14–18, 24, 25, 27, 28
    patience for market conditions, 16,
        17, 28
    personality, 14, 15
    Tracinda Corporation, 13, 19, 24, 25
    value investing, 15–17
Kerkorian, Lily, 11
Kerkorian, Linda, 13
Kerkorian, Tracy, 13
Kerr, Robert S., 53
Kerr-McGee, 53
Killinger, Kerry, 39–48
Kingdon Capital, 5
Kozeny, Viktor, 112–126
Kravis, Henry, 38

L. F. Rothschild, 90, 91
LaGuardia, Fiorello H., 9
Lancelot Investment Management
    LLC, 227
Lay, Ken, 5
Leclair, Don, 25
LeClair, Donat, 23
Lehman Brothers, 5, 40, 44, 118, 161,
    178, 185, 207
Lessons learned
    Ackman, William A., 88
    Bonderman, David, 49

Cooperman, Leon (Lee), 127, 128
Davis, Christopher C., 212, 213
    fraudulent investment schemes,
        232, 233
    Grant, Geoff, 169
    Kerkorian, Kirk, 28, 29
    Maounis, Nick, 107, 108
    McClendon, Aubrey, 67
    Pzena, Richard, 147, 148
    short selling, 191–193
Leverage, use of
    Ackman, William A., 73, 74, 76,
        84–87
    AIG, 206–208
    checking for leveraged instruments
        in a fund, 213
    and commodity markets, 107, 108
    exchange-traded funds (ETFs), 188
    Grant, Geoff, 156, 158, 161
    Lehman Brothers, 161
    macro trading, 156
    Maounis, Nick, 98, 101, 106–108
    McClendon, Aubrey, 51–53, 55, 56,
        59–63, 66, 67
    Peloton Partners, 161
    and value investing, 147
Leveraged buyouts (LBOs), 35–38
Lewis, Clayton, 117–126
Liddy, Edward, 204
Liquid Macro, 168, 169
Lloyd's of London, 199
Long Term Capital Management,
    108, 111
Losses
    and fraud, 126
    and investment risk, 109
    never risk what you cannot afford to
        lose, 53, 67, 128
    short selling, lessening chances of
        loss, 193
Lynch, Peter, 213

Macklowe, Harry, 9
Macro trading, 152, 154–158, 164–169
Macroeconomy, 12, 17, 28, 29, 48, 155
Madoff, Bernard L., 3, 215–222,
    224–233

Madoff, Ruth, 218, 221, 222
Management, changes in, 213
Maounis, Nick
  Amaranth Advisors LLC, 89, 92–107
  Angelo, Gordon & Co., 91
  background, 89–92
  and Dreier, Marc S., 223
  energy derivatives, 92, 95–106
  lessons learned, 107, 108
  margin accounts and margin calls,
    97, 102
  mistakes, learning from, 89, 108
  Paloma Partners, 91–93, 105
  risk management, 90, 94–100, 102,
    105–108
  Verition Fund Management LLC,
    106, 107, 223
Margin accounts and margin calls
  described, 52, 53
  "don't buy what you can't afford to
    own and can't afford to lose,"
    53, 67
  Grant, Geoff (Peloton), 160, 162–164
  Maounis, Nick, 97, 102
  McClendon, Aubrey (Chesapeake
    Energy), 53, 59–61, 63, 64
  and short selling, 174, 180, 182–184,
    188, 192
  use of, 67
Markopolos, Harry, 230
Mark-to-market accounting, 144,
    207, 212
Marsh & McLennan, 208
Marshall, Paul, 178
Marshall, Ron, 79
Marshall Wace, 178
Maxwell, Charles, 57
McClendon, Aubrey
  background, 51, 53–55
  and Chesapeake Energy, 53–67
  diversification, lack of, 60–63, 67
  and insider activity, 56, 58, 60, 64,
    65, 67
  lessons learned, 67
  leverage, use of, 51–53, 55, 56, 59–63,
    66, 67
  margin account, 52, 53, 59–61, 63,
    64, 67

  margin calls, 59, 60
  wine collection, 55, 66
McDonald's, 75, 78, 82, 87,
    189, 190
McGuire, Richard (Mick), 74–79
Merckle, Adolf, 171–174, 177, 178, 182,
    183, 192, 193
Meriwether, John, 108
Merkin, J. Ezra, 220, 225, 228, 233
Merrill Lynch, 101
Metrics for identifying short
    candidates, 175
Metzger, Leon M., 105
MGM, 15–17, 24, 31
Milken, Michael, 130
Minaret Group, 120, 122
Mistakes
  common money mistakes, 2, 3
  investing mistakes, 24–28
  learning from, 89, 108, 235, 236
  and risk, 10
  scale of investing mistakes, 9, 10
Mitchell, George, 117, 121
Momentum investing, 131, 134,
    138–139, 144, 146
Morefar Back O'Beyond golf
    course, 203
Morgan Stanley, 149, 151, 152
Morgenthau, Robert, 123
Morningstar, 169, 210
Mortgages
  commercial real estate, 135
  and leverage, 52
  residential mortgage collapse, 141
  subprime, 38, 40, 41, 52, 53, 143, 157,
    164, 199, 204, 206–208
Moses, Jennifer, 154
MSN Money, 189
Mulally, Alan, 23–25
Multistrategy investment model,
    91, 92, 105
Mutual funds. *See also* Fund managers
  emerging markets, 128
  Harvard Funds, 113–116. *See also*
    Kozeny, Viktor
  Morningstar ratings, 169
  past holdings, examining, 213
  portfolio managers, 4, 213

Never risk what you cannot afford to
   lose, 53, 67, 128
Newberg, Bruce, 130
Nickles, Don, 53
Niederhoffer, Victor, 108
Nissan, 22
Normalized earnings, 136–139,
   143–146, 148

Och, Dan, 100
Och-Ziff Capital Management, 100
Odey Asset Management, 178
Odey, Crispin, 177, 178
Oklahoma Thunder, 53, 58
Omega Advisors, 5, 110, 111, 117–126
Oppenheimer & Co., 5
Option purchases, 81–88

Paloma Partners, 91–93, 105
Passion, and investment strategy, 14–18,
   24, 25, 27, 28
Past performance, 29
Patience for market conditions, 16, 17,
   28, 134, 145, 146, 148
Paulson, Henry (Hank), 142
Peak Ridge, 104
Peloton Partners LLP, 101
Performance
   comparison, 212
   historical performance, 129, 137,
      139, 148
   past performance, analyzing, 29
   review of company performance, 49
Pershing Square Capital Management,
   72–83, 85
Petters, Tom, 225–227
P.F. Chang's China Bistro, 190
Pickens, T. Boone, 5, 54
Pirate of Prague, 112, 113. *See also*
   Kozeny, Viktor
Ponzi schemes
   Bernard Madoff, 3, 215–222, 224–233
   Tom Petters, 225, 227
Porsche, 127, 178–182, 184, 185, 192
Portfolio allocation, 95, 128. *See also*
   Diversification
Portfolio managers, 4, 213
Price, William, 39

Private equity firms, 36, 37, 39, 40.
   See also Texas Pacific Group (TPG)
ProShares, 188
Psychology. *See* Investor psychology
Public relations, 2
Put options, 186–187
Pzena Investment Management, 129,
   137–140, 143, 145
Pzena, Richard (Rich), 7
   background, 129–134
   due diligence, 131, 142, 144
   financial stocks, investing in,
      133–137, 140–147
   lessons learned, 147, 148
   momentum investing, 131, 134, 138,
      139, 144, 146
   patience for market conditions, 134,
      145, 146, 148
   Pzena Investment Management, 129,
      137–140, 143, 145
   value investing, 130–141,
      143–148, 150

Quantitative modeling, 155

Real estate investment trusts (REITs),
   75, 82
Recessions, 138, 139, 144
Recommendations, investment
   opportunities, 2, 3, 29
Red flags. *See* Warning signs
Reed, John, 136
Referrals, 218, 229, 232
Regulation AB (asset-backed
   securities), 160, 161
Regulations. *See also* Securities and
   Exchange Commission (SEC)
   emerging markets, 127
   foreign countries, 114–116,
      125, 127
   insurance companies, 199
   research on, 127, 128
Relatives
   investment opportunities,
      recommendations by, 2, 3
   relationships with, 3
Reliance Insurance, 199
Renault, 22

Research, 189, 191. *See also*
Due diligence
Risk
and avoiding mistakes, 10
and emerging markets, 109, 128
and excessive returns, 169, 212
and flight to quality, 157
and investment style, 150
management, 90, 94–100, 102, 105–108
"never risk what you cannot afford to
lose," 53, 67, 128
and portfolio allocation, 88
short selling, 173, 181–184, 186, 187,
191, 193
tail risk, 105, 107
and use of mutual funds, 128
Risk management, 90, 94–100, 102,
105–108
Ritchie Capital, 227
Ritchie, Thane, 227
RMBG, 33, 35, 37–39
Robbins, Larry, 178, 180, 184
Roosevelt, Eleanor, 10
Ross, Burt, 219–222, 224, 225,
229, 231, 232
Rule 10-b-5, 65
Ruth, Babe, 35, 37

SAC Capital, 5, 9, 178
Salomon Brothers, 5, 8
Sanford C. Bernstein & Co.
(Bernstein), 132, 139
Santayana, George, 1
al-Saud, al-Waleed bin Talal bin Abdul
Aziz, 136
Savings and loans (S&Ls), 38
Schmidt, Francis, 4
Sears, 75
Securities and Exchange Commission
(SEC)
failure to investigate Bernard
Madoff, 230
Form 13-D, 71, 80
Form 13-G, 71
Form 10-K, 211
investigation of Amaranth, 101
Regulation AB (asset-backed
securities), 160, 161

Rule 10-b-5, insider trading, 65
temporary ban on short selling of
financial stocks, 176, 177
Web site, 127
SharkWatch, 72
Short interest ratio, 192
Short selling
accounting shorts, 176
catalyst shorts, 176, 192
Crocs, 190–192
crowded short, 175, 191
described, 173, 174
and dot-com bubble, 184, 192
due diligence, 189–191
float, 175
lessons learned, 191–193
loss, lessening chances of, 193
and margin accounts, 174, 180, 182,
183, 188, 192
and Merckle, Adolf, 171–174, 177,
178, 182, 183, 192, 193
methods of for average investor,
186, 187
metrics for identifying short
candidates, 175
P.F. Chang's China Bistro, 190
risk, 173, 181–184, 186, 187, 191, 193
role of, 176
sell signals, 175
short interest ratio, 192
short squeeze, 175, 180, 192
single stocks, 189, 190
stop-loss, 193
thematic shorts, 176
through buying put options, 186, 187
through exchange-traded funds
(ETFs), 186–188
timing, 184, 190, 191
types of shorts, 176
valuation short, 175
Volkswagen, 127, 172–174, 177–184,
186, 192
Short squeeze, 175, 180, 192
Skepticism, 233
Skilling, Jeff, 5
Sklo Union Teplice, 116
Smart money, following, 49
SOCAR, 117, 121–125

Solengo Capital Advisors, 104
Sophisticated investors, 232
Soros Management, 5
Speculation, 88
Spielberg, Steven, 229
Spitzer, Eliot, 73, 204
Stansky, Robert, 213
Starr, Cornelius Vander, 203
Starr Foundation, 209
Steel, Robert, 142
Stevens, Wallace, 195
Stock prices, declining, 49
Stop-loss, 193
Style drift, 105, 151, 158–160, 164–169
Subprime mortgages, 38, 40, 41, 52, 53,
    143, 157, 164, 199, 204, 206–208
Success and winner's effect, 28
Sullivan, Martin, 204, 208, 209
Sussman, Donald, 91
Sutton, Willie, 90

Target, 78, 80–86
Texas Pacific Group (TPG), 31, 32,
    34–37, 39, 40, 43–46, 48, 49
Thematic shorts, 176
Tiger Management, 5
Tim Hortons Inc., 74
Time, Inc., 115
Timing and short selling, 184, 190, 191
TPG. See Texas Pacific Group (TPG)
Tracinda Corporation, 13, 19, 24, 25
Trading versus investing, 2
Trump, Donald, 31, 37
Turner, Ted, 16

Ulrich, Bob, 81

Valuation short, 175
Value at risk (VAR), 96, 105

Value investing, 111, 130–141, 143–148,
    150, 200
  Graham-and-Dodd investing,
    130–132, 134
Value investors, 8, 12, 131, 134, 145,
    146, 150. *See also* Pzena, Richard
    (Rich)
Velvet Revolution, 113
Verition Fund Management LLC, 106,
    107, 223
Vincent, Eric, 121, 122
Volkswagen (VW), 127, 172–174,
    177–184, 186, 192

Wace, Ian, 178
Wagoner, Rick, 22
al-Waleed, bin Talal bin Abdul Aziz
    al-Saud, 136
Ward, Tom, 55, 58
Warning signs, 29, 227–231
Washington Mutual (WaMu), 39–48
Watson, David, 158
Weiss, Stephen L.
  background and experience, 1–6
  mistakes made and lessons learned,
    235, 236
Wendy's, 74, 75, 78, 82
Wiedeking, Wendelin, 184
Wiesel, Elie, 229
Wilpon, Fred, 229
Winner's effect, 28
Winters, William T., 102
Wolfe, Thomas, 47

Yahoo!, 189
York, Jerome (Jerry), 19, 21–22,
    25–27

Zetsche, Dieter, 185